THE STORY OF THE
GUARDS ARMOURED DIVISION

DEDICATED TO ALL THOSE WHO SERVED
IN THE GUARDS ARMOURED DIVISION
AND TO THOSE WHO ASSISTED
IN ITS FORMATION AND TRAINING

THE STORY OF THE GUARDS ARMOURED DIVISION

CAPTAIN THE EARL OF ROSSE & COLONEL E. R. HILL DSO

FOREWORD BY FIELD MARSHAL THE LORD GUTHRIE OF CRAIGIEBANK GCB LVO OBE DL

Pen & Sword

MILITARY

First published in Great Britain in 1956 by Geoffrey Bles Ltd

Reprinted in this format in 2017 and again in 2021 by
Pen & Sword Military
An imprint of
Pen & Sword Books Ltd
Yorkshire – Philadelphia

ISBN 978 1 39901 347 5

A CIP catalogue record for this book is available from the British Library

Printed in the UK by CPI Group (UK) Ltd, Croydon, CR0 4YY

Pen & Sword Books Limited incorporates the imprints of Atlas, Archaeology, Aviation, Discovery, Family History, Fiction, History, Maritime, Military, Military Classics, Politics, Select, Transport, True Crime, Air World, Frontline Publishing, Leo Cooper, Remember When, Seaforth Publishing, The Praetorian Press, Wharncliffe Local History, Wharncliffe Transport, Wharncliffe True Crime and White Owl.

For a complete list of Pen & Sword titles please contact

PEN & SWORD BOOKS LIMITED
47 Church Street, Barnsley, South Yorkshire, S70 2AS, England
E-mail: enquiries@pen-and-sword.co.uk
Website: www.pen-and-sword.co.uk

Or
PEN AND SWORD BOOKS
1950 Lawrence Rd, Havertown, PA 19083, USA
E-mail: Uspen-and-sword@casematepublishers.com
Website: www.penandswordbooks.com

Foreword to New Edition

By Field Marshal the Lord Guthrie of Craigiebank GCB LVO OBE DL
Colonel, The Life Guards

More than seventy years have passed since Major General Sir Allan Adair's Guards Armoured Division fought with such élan and distinction through France, the Low Countries and into the heartland of Hitler's Germany.

In that time the world has moved on in quite extraordinary ways. Virtually all physical traces of that appalling conflict have been erased or repaired, less what have been preserved intentionally.

The intervening years have not been peaceful. Regiments of the Household Division have been in the forefront of many campaigns and actions and proudly reinforced the fighting reputation of their predecessors.

There was, however, something quite unique about the Guards Armoured Division. How fortunate it is that its exploits were recorded so competently early in the post-war years by two serving officers who saw action.

Re-reading this book brought home to me yet again how much there is to be learnt from the past. Despite the many changes, the value of regimental loyalty, comradeship, discipline and mutual trust between all ranks are as fundamental today as they were when the Guards Armoured Division was in action.

I am delighted to endorse the re-publication of this timeless book and recommend it unreservedly.

Horse Guards
March 2017

Foreword

BY MAJOR-GENERAL SIR ALLAN ADAIR, BART., C.B., D.S.O., M.C.

I MUST FIRST pay tribute to the remarkable way in which officers and men of the Brigade of Guards adapted themselves to the unfamiliar role of an Armoured Division. This was no easy task, but their fine discipline, cheerfulness and enthusiasm swept aside every difficulty.

But, above all, it was the co-operation and efficiency of all arms and services that transformed the Division into a powerful fighting force.

With such a happy, adventurous and brave team, the Guards Armoured Division went into the forefront of the battle in North-West Europe, achieved an advance unexcelled in the campaign and finally bade "Farewell to Armour" with its task triumphantly accomplished.

I am proud to have had the honour to command such a magnificent formation.

Preface

THE WAR HISTORY of a division runs the risk of falling between two stools. The intimacy which comes naturally in a Regimental or Battalion History is denied it, while at the same time a Division is little concerned with the higher realms of politics and strategy. To strike a happy mean is no easy task, yet an attempt to include both some personal touches and also elements of the broader aspects of the campaign must be made; for a catalogue of purely military events would be tedious to all but experts, and it is to the relations and friends of those who fought in the Guards Armoured Division that this book is primarily addressed.

The original intention was for the History to be written by a serving officer who would be released from all other duties in order to complete it as soon as possible after the end of hostilities. Captain A. D. Pryce-Jones, while still on the Staff of Divisional Headquarters, set to work to collect the necessary material and to piece it together, but it proved unexpectedly difficult to obtain and, despite much tedious preliminary work, for which I am greatly indebted to him, it was still quite fragmentary and altogether lacking in several important respects when he left the army to take up a full-time civilian appointment. No further progress was made for some time and finally, after several fruitless attempts to find a suitably qualified serving officer, Major-General J. C. O. Marriott (now Sir John Marriott), who was then commanding the Guards Division, asked me if I would undertake it. I had to ask to be allowed to take my own time, but subject to that I agreed, albeit with considerable diffidence, since it patently could not be allowed to go by default.

Mistakes are probably unavoidable in such a work, but every care has been taken to ensure that the story is as accurate as possible. Almost all passages dealing with the division's activities are taken directly from accounts written down at the actual time;

not only did most units keep War Diaries, but certain individual officers kept records in notebooks from time to time. In the end, a large amount of material was consequently made available, and the difficulty has rather lain in the need to sift it and to keep a balance between the various units and aspects. At the same time, both the quantity and the quality has been distinctly uneven; in some cases complete to the most minute detail and in others almost entirely lacking in spite of every effort to bring it to light. If certain important matters have been left out, it is for that reason.

My task of checking and reconciling the various accounts has been made easier by the fact that, as Intelligence Officer of the 32nd Guards Brigade, I made a point of distributing every other day throughout the campaign a summary of the activities of the previous forty-eight hours. I had preserved a complete series of these summaries, but unfortunately nothing similar has survived for the 5th Guards Armoured Brigade. While the 32nd Guards Brigade summaries sought to cover the whole division, my knowledge of my own brigade's doings was obviously much more complete. If this fact is reflected in the ensuing narrative it is not due to any lack of effort to deal equally fully with both brigades.

It is regrettable also that no official accounts from Divisional Headquarters remain. As against this, Major the Hon. F. F. G. Hennessy, who as G.S.O. II almost always accompanied Major-General Adair as his personal staff officer, wrote three excellent narratives covering all the earlier months up to Nijmegen. These were distributed throughout the division at the time and have been most valuable. I am very grateful to him for having allowed me to make use of them and occasionally to quote from them.

The mention of individuals other than senior officers cannot help being invidious to some degree. I have tried to include something about most exploits for which awards were made, but undoubtedly there were others of which no record has reached me. I have tried to avoid the use of technical terms that might be obscure to many readers of the book and have only employed a very few, of which "flak" and "Piat" are examples; in these cases elaboration would be cumbersome and I think that they will be generally understood.

The original draft was read by most senior officers who fought in the division in order to lessen the chances of major errors being made and of matters of real importance being omitted. It took a considerable time to incorporate the many additions and corrections suggested by these officers, and this further delayed publication, but the greater degree of accuracy that has been achieved fully compensates for this, since otherwise the book's value as a historical document would have been seriously reduced. I gladly acknowledge the debt I owe to all those who kindly gave me help in this way. Many must have taken a great deal of trouble and devoted much time to the work. For this my grateful thanks are due to Brigadiers H. C. Phipps, C. P. Jones, N. W. Gwatkin, B. J. Daunt, J. O. E. Vandeleur, J. N. R. Moore and R. F. S. Gooch, to Colonels H. Abel Smith, D. H. FitzGerald, J. C. Windsor-Lewis, D. M. L. Gordon-Watson, B. Wilson, J. S. Atkins, and J. N. Thomas, and to Majors the Hon. Michael Fitzalan-Howard and T. F. Blackwell.

This stage was reached as long ago as January, 1951, and I then hoped that the book would be printed and published within a year of that date. But further quite unexpected difficulties and delays arose and it is only after the passage of almost a further five years that it has at last proved possible to offer it to the public.

Both Major-General Marriott and later Major-General J. A. Gascoigne, when commanding the Brigade of Guards, and Major-General G. F. Johnson, their present successor in that appointment, have given me constant support and help. General Marriott kindly arranged for the typing and issue of all copies of the original draft, and members of the Staff of Headquarters London District have always been made available to give advice. A singularly happy stroke of fortune brought Major the Hon. Michael Fitzalan-Howard to London as Brigade Major, Brigade of Guards, in 1949 and the very active co-operation that he gave, naturally inclined to sympathy with the project as he was by the long period that he spent with the Division, was especially valuable to me. His successors, Major A. M. H. Gregory-Hood and Major V. F. Erskine Crum, have also been most helpful.

It has not been easy to find suitable photographs, particularly ones which have not previously been used in other books. I am especially grateful to Major G. B. Mackean, of the 5th Bn. Coldstream Guards, for allowing me to use for the first time five excellent pictures taken by him. I should also like to express my thanks to the Imperial War Museum and to Messrs. Gale & Polden Ltd., publishers of *Welsh Guards at War* by Major L. F. Ellis, for kindly giving permission to reproduce the other photographs as individually acknowledged.

I was seriously concerned from the start about the problem of dealing adequately with the subject of Administration; I never had any personal experience of this branch and therefore felt quite unqualified to write about it. It is an aspect that is too often almost cursorily treated in war histories, and yet the results of battles depend on the efficiency with which it is carried out; indeed, in modern warfare it has become more important than ever before. Lieutenant-Colonel (now Brigadier) W. M. Sale was responsible, more than any other individual, for the admirable organisation of the Division's administrative machine in the Field; readers of the ensuing History are fortunate in that he kindly agreed to check the original draft, in addition to contributing a special Appendix.

I owe most of all to Colonel E. R. Hill. He had made especially valuable comments and additions to the original draft and most kindly agreed subsequently to help me in moulding the narrative into its final shape. I had always realised that, as a purely war-time soldier, I should need the assistance of a regular officer more thoroughly versed in military art if the picture of our local activities were to be fitted appropriately into the wider framework of the whole campaign. Colonel Hill was admirably qualified to do this; not only has he made the necessary additions and corrections, but he has also helped in the selection of photographs and has arranged for the provision of the Orders of Battle and of the maps.

April 1956 R.

Contents

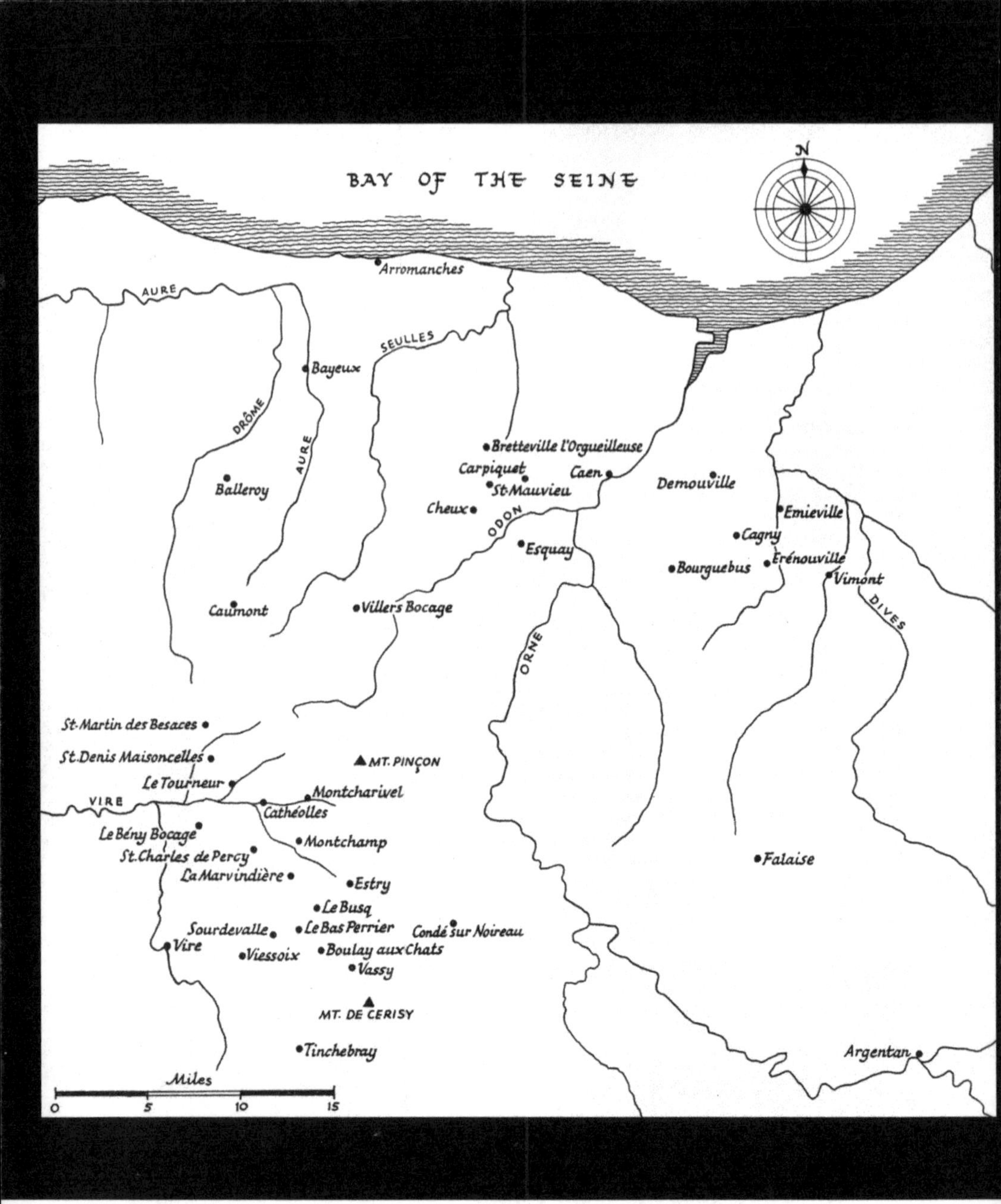
BAY OF THE SEINE
N
Arromanches
AURE
SEULLES
Bayeux
DRÔME
AURE
Balleroy
Caumont
Bretteville l'Orgueilleuse
Carpiquet
St-Mauvieu
Caen
Cheux
ODON
Esquay
Villers Bocage
Demouville
Emieville
Cagny
Bourguebus
Erénouville
Vimont
DIVES
ORNE
St-Martin des Besaces
St.Denis Maisoncelles
MT. PINÇON
Le Tourneur
VIRE
Montcharivel
Cathéolles
Le Bény Bocage
Montchamp
St.Charles de Percy
La Marvindière
Estry
Le Busq
Sourdevalle
Le Bas Perrier
Condé sur Noireau
Vire
Viessoix
Boulay aux Chats
Vassy
MT. DE CERISY
Tinchebray
Falaise
Argentan
Miles
0
5
10
15

NORMANDY

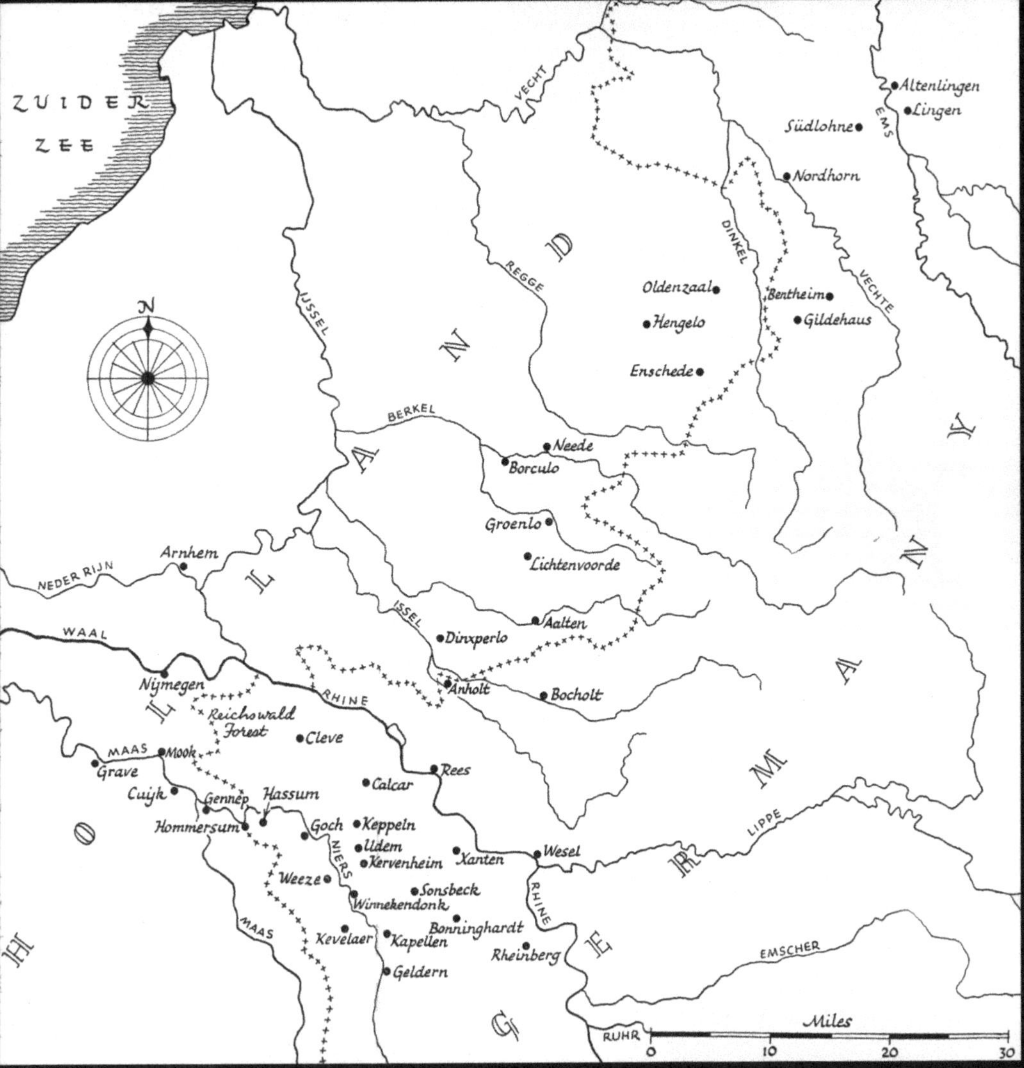

THE RHINELAND

Chapter One

BEFORE D-DAY

DURING THE late Spring of 1941 the Commander-in-Chief Home Forces, General Sir Alan Brooke, came to the conclusion that he should be ready to meet a full-scale German invasion by a force which would include a serious proportion of armoured divisions and a considerable number of airborne troops.

To meet such a threat he had at his disposal only a very limited number of armoured formations and he decided that he must, as a first step and with the greatest possible speed, convert two infantry divisions to armour. Although the Brigade of Guards was traditionally infantry, and believed by many to be the best in the world, there were certain advantages in forming a Guards Armoured Division. The Regiments of Foot Guards had the officers and men of the right type available, they could be converted probably more quickly than other units, and a large number of officers in the Brigade, holding the general view that armour rather than infantry was becoming the predominant arm, were keen to embark on the venture. The Regimental Lieutenant-Colonels all welcomed the idea, and the Major-General Commanding the Brigade of Guards, Lieutenant-General Sir Bertram Sergison-Brooke, after consultation with His Majesty the King, expressed himself as being strongly in favour of the proposal.

After various deliberations between the Major-General and the War Office approval was given for the Guards Armoured Division to be formed, and at the end of May 1941 certain senior officers in the Brigade were summoned to a conference at Headquarters, London District, at Leconfield House. The Major-General told them of the proposal and of the reasons for it, while his G.S.O. I (Training) explained the policy for the initial training and handed out a detailed programme of mechanical, gunnery and wireless courses. None of the assembled officers knew anything about tanks and they left the room feeling slightly dazed. A week later the first course started; the staff of the Royal Armoured Corps responsible for our training were extremely kind and helpful and everything ran so smoothly that by September a large number of officers and men had passed through Bovington or Lulworth.

Divisional Headquarters had meanwhile been formed at Leconfield House on June 19th under Major-General Sir Oliver Leese, who had been appointed commander. It moved in early July to Crow Clump, a large house on St. George's Hill near Weybridge, where it became a hive of activity with a whole series of lectures and discussions, which gave the senior officers who attended a good idea of what was going to be required. This continued until September 15th, when the division as a whole started to assemble in the area round Salisbury Plain—Divisional Headquarters was at Redlynch House and in Wincanton, the 5th Guards Armoured Brigade was grouped around Warminster and Shaftesbury, the 6th Guards Armoured Brigade was at Codford, the Guards Support Group was around Castle Cary, Frome and Midsomer Norton and the 2nd Household Cavalry Regiment was at Bulford.

The composition of the division in 1942 is given in Appendix 1 at the end of the book, together with similar details at various subsequent moments in its career. Before the arrival of the 32nd Guards Brigade there was a tremendous preponderance of armour; as against six armoured battalions there were no more than three of infantry, two motor and one lorry borne. All practical experience in armoured warfare had hitherto been gained in the desert, and only a prophet could have foreseen at that time the essential need that there would be for plenty of infantry in an armoured division fighting under European conditions. The Guards Support Group, which from the first was a curiously cumbrous entity, was strengthened in the late Autumn by the addition of the 94th Light Anti-Aircraft Regiment which, as a recently converted battalion of the King's Own Yorkshire Light Infantry, had the difficult task of training immediately for a completely new and unfamiliar role. Early in 1942 a second Field Regiment arrived; this was the West Somerset Yeomanry.

It may be opportune to digress at this moment in order to discover why it was decided to adopt as the divisional sign the famous "Eye" that had been used by the Guards Division in the 1914–1918 War. At first the divisional commander, anxious to find one that would suggest something of the particular fighting characteristics of the modern armoured division, had invited all senior officers to obtain suggestions from their units. A large selection of ideas was soon collected but, although many artists and draughtsmen tried their skill, no sign was produced which was sufficiently simple or original and at the same time typical of the spirit of the division. Sir Oliver had originally felt some diffidence about going back to the "Eye" of the previous war as he felt that some officers and men who had served then might not care for their sign to be resurrected by a new division; but when no obviously suitable sign was forthcoming he decided to consult a number of distinguished officers of the last war and he found that they appeared pleased at the idea of the "Eye" being used again. He was confident that all who had not fought in the last war would welcome a sign associated with the glorious traditions of the Guards Division, and he therefore decided to adopt the "Eye" with slight modifications. The services of the distinguished artist Rex Whistler, who was serving as a Lieutenant in the Welsh Guards, were called upon; he painted different eyes on each of a dozen vehicles, which then paraded for the winner to be chosen by a group of specially selected officers. The choice was quickly made and before long every vehicle in the division was provided with its "Eye".

Most units had moved in wet weather into unfinished camps with no hard standings and instead only indescribable mud. However, armoured battalions soon had model rooms, tank miniature ranges, wireless and gunnery centres and, as the flow of non-commissioned officers began to arrive from the training schools, classes were started with the aim of training all of the rank of full corporal and above in the main subjects of gunnery, wireless, and driving and maintenance. In those days it quickly became apparent that equipment, or rather the lack of it, was going to be the main problem; it is doubtful if any one of the armoured battalions had more than six tanks before the end of the year. What was worse, these few were truly decrepit looking monsters that were all too obvious discards from the Royal Tank Regiment. However, through the very frequency with which they broke down, invaluable practice was gained by the crews in repairing the machines under field conditions. Before the end of the year each armoured battalion was in possession of a limited number of skeleton gun-turrets which gave the rolling and pitching movement of a tank, and new wireless sets started to make their appearance. Those responsible for the driving and maintenance side of the training were not slow to collect an amazing assortment of every kind of piece of engine and mechanical equipment, and soon troop training had started, during which it was quickly discovered that a map of Salisbury Plain was of little assistance to any but the most expert of map readers. Conversation everywhere was of tanks, troop formations and wireless procedure, and new words and phrases were being learned each day. Tremendous enthusiasm was shown by everyone, all sorts of means being devised in order to get over the shortage of tanks; sometimes they were represented by carriers, sometimes by trucks, and at times even by men on foot communicating to each other by means of flag signals. When a troop leader was lucky enough to lay hands on three tanks simultaneously the excitement was felt by everybody in the troop; though it frequently turned out a mixed blessing, as one was almost bound to break down and this probably entailed a night out on Salisbury Plain.

Early in 1942, as each battalion gradually came up to strength in tanks, exercises began to take place on a squadron, and soon on a battalion basis; as the divisional commander never tired of pointing out, the lack of this or that piece of vital equipment was unlikely to prevent the Germans from invading, should they so decide. In March the first visits were paid to the tank ranges at Linney Head, a remote spot on the coast of South Wales. Up to this moment nobody had yet fired the two-pounder and Besa guns from tanks on the move and in fact it was a great test for all; especially for the troop leaders who suddenly had it brought home to them how incredible a number of things they had to do at the same time. There is no doubt that these battle practices—each armoured battalion visited Linney Head several times before the invasion of Normandy—were of inestimable value in that they provided excellent and almost realistic training for what was eventually to come.

There was meanwhile plenty to be done by the non-armoured portions of the division. Such varied things as orders of march, map reference codes and methods of undercarriage lighting had all to be considered, and the "soft" vehicles indulged in innumerable and seemingly interminable movement exercises during the winter. They took place by day and by night under all possible conditions and, exasperating though they were to the participants at the time, they undoubtedly provided valuable training and experience; good road discipline is a matter of vast importance in an armoured division, for it is no easy problem to converge three thousand vehicles and get them moving along smoothly, and the narrow Somerset roads were to prove a useful introduction to the similar ones of Normandy.

The gunners were kept busy at numerous practice shoots on the artillery ranges on Salisbury Plain under the expert and brilliant tuition of Brigadier L. C. Manners-Smith, in addition to undergoing their fair share of the movement exercises. The 21st Anti-Tank Regiment also went on two occasions to Dunkery Beacon on Exmoor, where a range for shooting at moving tanks had been constructed. As live ammunition was not used and excellent billets were available in an attractive village at the foot of the Beacon, there was considerable competition among the armoured battalions for the honour of providing the targets.

For the staff officers down to battalion level there were also Signal Exercises. These were designed largely to enable them to become proficient in wireless procedure, but they also provided useful tactical lessons, among them the remarkable powers of endurance that the strictly limited amount of infantry then allotted to the division would have to show under active service conditions. For some time past observers from the Middle East had been reporting the need for more infantry in the armoured divisions even in the desert, where it could be more easily dispensed with than in Europe; a new policy was decided upon and general agreement on taking the necessary action in our case was therefore quickly reached.

On May 30th 1942 the 32nd Guards Brigade, which had been engaged up till then in the defence of the Northern perimeter of London, joined the division and took over the infantry role. Lieutenant-Colonel G. H. G. L. Verney, Commanding Officer of the 2nd Bn. Irish Guards, was nominated Brigade Commander. The 32nd Guards Brigade brought with it two battalions, the 5th Bn. Coldstream Guards and the 4th Bn. Scots Guards, commanded respectively by Lieutenant-Colonel Lord Stratheden and Lieutenant-Colonel A. V. C. Douglas, and took over the 1st Bn. Welsh Guards in place of its third battalion, which it relinquished. The Guards Support Group as such was disbanded and became a normal Headquarters Royal Artillery; since by now it comprised four artillery regiments, the inclusion of the infantry battalion had in latter days rendered it distinctly unwieldy.

In April Brigade Exercises had started and in July, soon after the arrival of the 32nd Guards Brigade, the first Divisional Exercise with troops—"Cheddar"—took place, followed rapidly by "Lilo" and "Pegasus". After that came "Sarum", which lasted four days and was the longest ordeal that the division had yet to face. As a military operation it lacked conviction, but it was the first time that maintenance under field conditions for more than twenty-four hours had been attempted. Units started to realise that there are tasks other than those they had already studied but which nevertheless are equally essential even to armoured soldiers—how to live, feed, sleep and make oneself as little uncomfortable as possible whilst in the field. "Sarum" was followed in August by "Ebor" and "Redlynch", each lasting two days, and then a period of maintenance and reorganisation set in.

During the whole of the latter period in the Salisbury Plain area the division had an operational role, known as Operation "Sun Chariot". In retrospect it is interesting to observe that this operation would have become a reality had the Germans landed; for it is now known that Weymouth and the South Dorset coast was to be one of their main points of attack, and the role of the Guards Armoured Division was to counter-attack immediately in that precise area.

On September 10th Major-General Sir Oliver Leese was suddenly ordered to relinquish command of the division in order to take over a corps in the Middle East; he was urgently required and left within twenty-four hours. He had laid the foundations very surely and above all had instilled that drive and enthusiasm which are the vital attributes of an armoured division. He had made an entity of it in a remarkably short space of time by sheer force of personality and was responsible for the gunners, sappers and members of the Services feeling every bit as proud of belonging to it as were the guardsmen themselves, no mean achievement in the circumstances. No point was ever too small for his attention and woe betide any officer or man who counted on being too unimportant for the notice of the divisional commander. None who were present will ever forget the brilliant way in which he would hold a conference of all officers after an exercise. Without a single note he would unerringly discuss every phase of the past "battle", remembering every detail and referring to units and sub-units and even to individuals by name—occasionally to the consternation and embarrassment of certain of the audience. We hated to see our well-loved commander go but realised that he was rightly destined for higher spheres. For his part, he no doubt felt that he could now safely confide his creation to other carefully chosen hands.

Brigadier A. H. S. Adair was nominated to take over command of the division. Brigadier Verney was transferred to the 6th Guards Armoured Brigade to replace him owing to his experience of armour, while Brigadier J. C. O. Marriott, who had recently returned from the Middle East, took over the 32nd Guards

Brigade. Having commanded an infantry brigade in Abyssinia and the 201st Guards Brigade throughout the desert campaign culminating in the battle of the Knightsbridge Box, he was particularly well qualified to train infantry for the job of fighting in close co-operation with armour under modern conditions of warfare.

Rumours now began to be heard of a further reorganisation of the division and, at his first conference in October, Major-General Adair announced what form this was to take. The 6th Guards Armoured Brigade was to leave and to be converted to Churchill tanks and to call itself the 6th Guards Tank Brigade; it was not until after the end of the war in Germany that it was finally to come back to us again. Another change was that the 2nd Household Cavalry Regiment was to leave the division in order to become Corps troops. In its place the 2nd Bn. Welsh Guards was to be converted to an armoured reconnaissance regiment. The original choice for the role, since no place existed for a motor battalion in a tank brigade, was the 4th Bn. Coldstream Guards. But the need for a very high standard of wireless training was recognised as essential and this battalion was, by its establishment, very short of the required number of operators trained in the use of wireless; the 2nd Bn. Welsh Guards, on the other hand, owing to its armoured training, could already show over one hundred and thirty trained and trade-tested operators, and this factor tipped the scale. Had anyone fully appreciated that almost two years were still to elapse before either battalion was called to battle, the decision might well have been different, although in any case it was probably as well not to include three Coldstream battalions in the division.

Before the end of 1942 the armoured battalions were equipped with six-pounder Crusader tanks. This did not entail the mastering of much new equipment and the conversion was a comparatively simple affair, although there was just enough in it to keep everyone interested during the dreary winter months. Christmas came and went, and at the arrival of 1943 the talk within the division was once more of invasion, but this time rather about the possibility of a British invasion than of a German one, though the latter remained as a remote contingency which must still be guarded against.

In February 1943 came exercise "Spartan", well-named in that it was designed to test the stamina as well as the skill of the larger part of the troops then stationed in England. It was the biggest exercise ever to take place in the country and lasted a fortnight, during which time the weather was extremely kind, considering what an English February can produce if it tries. Much valuable experience was gained, especially by the staffs of the Higher Formations, who had hitherto had little opportunity for putting their theoretical ideas into practice with troops on the ground. On the whole it was less instructive to the troops themselves, but at least all who took part were hardened and matured by the enormous distances covered, with long night drives, breakdowns, and all the trials and difficulties that a fortnight's living in the open entails; also by the hurried and inevitable changes of plan typical of what always does occur in action. The division ended with a good tank gallop through some of the best of the hunting country near Towcester, which gave it great satisfaction even if it did not please the umpires.

At the end of Exercise "Spartan", we moved direct to the other side of England, Norfolk. Some people were lucky, such as the 1st Bn. Welsh Guards, whose new home was King's Lynn, and who had the honour of providing a special guard for the King when in residence at Sandringham, also the 4th Bn. Scots Guards and the 5th Bn. Coldstream, who were stationed on the sea at Hunstanton; but the area will be remembered chiefly for its depressing hutted camps in woods of endless stunted pine trees and for the appalling roads which linked them together. The towns and villages are lovely, with almost invariably exquisite churches, but most of us saw all too little of them and the general landscape is undoubtedly more appealing to pheasants and partridges, which were incidentally tantalisingly out of season, than it is to the average human being. There was a first-class anti-tank range at Hunstanton on the beach and a horribly realistic assault course hidden rather incongruously behind the superb eighteenth-century holm-oaks at Holkham, while the Stanford battle area provided excellent opportunity for field firing, though it was not big enough for large-scale exercises. During the four months spent here the main event was the issue of Sherman tanks to the 5th Guards Brigade and of Centaurs (later to be replaced by Cromwells) to the 2nd Bn. Welsh Guards. This made it pretty clear that no invasion of Europe was likely in 1943, to the intense disappointment of the vast majority, who felt themselves keyed up and ready after such long and intensive training.

During this period too the division was for the first time attached to a Higher Formation. Up till now we had been Army troops but in future we were permanently to form part of VIII Corps until the invasion. A series of Corps Signal Exercises for the benefit of the various staffs began, similar in purpose to those which had taken place within the division during the first winter of its existence.

Towards the end of June 1943 the division moved once more, this time to Yorkshire, where the Wolds were the scene of our last and most important period of training. Here at length we had the space that we required for realistic battle practices and, tragic as the sight of the ruined crops and hedgerows must have been to the local landowners and farmers, the value of the lessons provided for us was immeasurable. There were scores of these Exercises of every scale from the squadron-company level upwards, culminating in VIII Corps Exercise "Eagle" which lasted for ten days during February weather such as only the Wolds know how to produce. The discomfort to all participants was very great but, while less ambitious in conception than "Spartan", it was infinitely more true to life; as such it was highly instructive to all ranks down to the individual guardsmen.

Our training during this time included every conceivable task with which it was thought we might be faced on active service. Our sappers built every kind of bridge and raft so that we could practise crossing river-obstacles; we also practised passing through gaps in minefields, night moves, quick artillery co-operation, vehicle recovery, petrol and ammunition supply and evacuation of casualties; we practised embarking on small craft, scrambling up on to steamers, and driving waterproofed vehicles ashore at Scarborough and elsewhere. Shooting at Kircudbright, in South-west Scotland, similar to that at Linney Head, but on a larger scale, gave armoured battalions an opportunity to get some practice in indirect fire with the seventy-five-millimetre gun. More significant perhaps of things to come than anything was a short period of training in the co-operation of tanks and infantry towards the end of the winter.

Both Brigades experienced changes of command while in Yorkshire. Brigadier W. A. F. L. Fox-Pitt left to command an area in South-Eastern Command and Brigadier J. C. O. Marriott for a post at the War Office. After a short period under Brigadier C. M. D. Venables-Llewellyn, Lieutenant-Colonel N. W. Gwatkin, who had commanded the 4th (Tank) Bn. Coldstream Guards, was nominated commander of the 5th Guards Brigade. The 32nd Guards Brigade was taken over by Brigadier G. F. Johnson, who had also served with the division in the early days as commanding officer of the 3rd Scots Guards and later as second-in-command of the Guards Support Group; he had left to succeed Brigadier Marriott in command of the 201st Guards Brigade in the Middle East, only to be taken prisoner at Tobruk within a few days; he had just recently escaped from prison subsequent to the invasion of Italy. This time the succession between these two officers took place in more auspicious circumstances.

An important addition was made too to the 32nd Guards Brigade. For some considerable time it had been thought that the infantry of an armoured division could well do with heavier support than it could provide out of its own resources. A first attempt had been made in Wiltshire to form a support company from the Welsh Guards and a subsequent one in Norfolk from the Grenadiers. Both had had to be given up owing to demands for reinforcements from other battalions for the Middle East. The man-power resources of the Brigade of Guards were already stretched to their utmost and the Northumberland Fusiliers were brought by the War Office to the rescue. A battalion was divided into three companies, of which the other two were allotted in a similar role to the 7th and 11th Armoured Divisions. They were all armed with heavy machine-guns and mortars and were destined to prove quite invaluable. Our company was commanded by Major R. M. Pratt and installed itself at Birdsall, next door to the 32nd Guards Brigade Headquarters at Langton.

By the New Year the prospects of invasion of the Continent were fast becoming a reality. In January 1944 the divisional commander was given an outline of the plan for the landings and subsequent operations by Lieutenant-General Sir Richard O'Connor, the Corps Commander. Shortly afterwards a small room at Divisional Headquarters at Brompton Hall was surrounded by barbed wire and in it were placed four officers and two clerks who, under the direction of Lieutenant-Colonel W. M. Sale, proceeded to work out the most complicated tables of vehicles, men, guns and equipment, and to determine how they were to be loaded on to ships. Rumours were rife, while security became the watchword and the horrors of unit censorship, an embarrassment to the men and a fatigue for the officers, became a reality.

A flood of distinguished persons visited us during these last months. Some outsiders would come along and suggest that our whole training was too reminiscent of the barrack-square, and that the discipline of the Brigade of Guards and the dash required of armour would not combine in battle; but those above us expressed full confidence and we could only await results. General Marshall, the American Chairman of the Combined Chiefs of Staff, paid us a visit, as did the Commander-in-Chief, General Sir Bernard Montgomery, who inspected every man in the division on Driffield Airfield. The Prime Minister, Mr. Winston Churchill, came and amongst other things watched a day's training on the Wolds. Finally, the greatest enthusiasm of all was aroused when on March 25th the King and Queen and Princess Elizabeth spent a whole day touring the division.

For final concentration we moved South in April in the greatest secrecy, with only a few people knowing the final destination.

This proved to be the Brighton–Eastbourne area, and there the final stages of preparation took place. The austere Regency houses of Brighton have seen many strange happenings in their time, but never before can serried rows of tanks have been backed up against their railings. It was a busy sight; tracks had to be changed, extra armour plating had to be riveted on, waterproofing had to be completed and every tank tested by passing through the local swimming-pool. Lectures were held on marshalling areas, enemy documents, twenty-four-hour packs, escaping, cooking, sea-sickness and a host of other subjects. Endless farewell parties took place; but nothing happened, and we sat around and waited.

Divisional Headquarters was at Heathfield and there, in a top-floor room, wired in and guarded day and night, was unfolded the plan for D-Day. The division was not required to start landing before D plus 18, as part of the build-up force under VIII Corps.

The Supreme Commander, General Dwight D. Eisenhower, made a deep impression when he came and spoke to us at this time. May came and went, and brigades and unit commanders were briefed, but no information concerning D-Day was forthcoming; still nothing happened, and still we waited.

June 6th dawned. The sea looked rough and threatening and it seemed a bold decision that the Operation should go through as planned. We had a superb view of the immense fleets of ships and aircraft crossing to France and we waited breathlessly for news of the first landings. Once this had come through and it had become evident that sizable bridgeheads had been established, our whole thoughts were fixed on the question of when we should get across ourselves.

For most of us some considerable time was yet due to elapse before this moment arrived. Even the advance party, after moving to Purfleet on June 12th, was held up there for several days and finally was unable to land on arrival near Courcelles till June 22nd. This latter delay was the result of the severe storm which seriously interrupted the whole programme of landings and which was responsible also for holding up the bulk of the division as they were about to sail. Although the moves of the main body to the marshalling areas took place between June 16th and 18th, the actual crossings did not start till several days later. Most of the 32nd Guards Brigade sailed from various docks in London on the 22nd and 23rd, while the 5th Guards Brigade, which had assembled at the Solent, did not get off till the 28th and 29th. All men in the division obtained during this period some personal experience of the flying bombs, which made their initial appearance very shortly after the first landings. In retrospect it is interesting to reflect that they could have interfered very seriously with our plans for invasion. Fortunately the attacks lacked any concerted plan, nor were the bombs directed with precision, and the division did not suffer a single casualty from them. Nevertheless, the knowledge of the danger to which so many of our families were subjected by these new attacks inspired us with an even keener resolve to drive the Germans from the shores of France with all possible speed.

By the end of June the whole division had crossed to Normandy.

Chapter Two

NORMANDY—THE BATTLE FOR CAEN

THE FIRST view of the coast of Normandy inspired emotion and awe. Emotion obviously, because we had all anticipated this moment so often and so long, and awe from the realisation that we were but one small part of the largest combined operation that had ever taken place in history. The sight of the artificial harbour and the vast quantity of ships of all types extending along the coast in each direction as far as the eye could see, all covered by a balloon barrage, brought home to each soldier fully, in a way that is not always easy for him to comprehend, the meaning and benefits of the sea and air power about which he so often reads.

As has been mentioned before, the Guards Armoured Division under Major-General Allan Adair was now, with the 11th Armoured and the 15th Infantry Divisions, part of VIII Corps under Lieutenant-General Sir Richard O'Connor. This in turn together with I, XII and XXX Corps formed part of the Second British Army under the command of Lieutenant-General Sir Miles Dempsey, which again, together with the First Canadian and the First U.S. Army made up the 21st Army Group under General Sir Bernard Montgomery. On D-Day the Americans had assaulted on the right and the British on the left and by the time the leading elements of the Guards Armoured Division were arriving in Normandy the bridgehead had been extended to a general depth of some eighteen miles from the coast. The Americans captured Cherbourg on June 27th but Caen on the extreme left still remained in German hands.

Apart from the coastline itself, we found surprisingly little trace of war as we drove inland towards Bayeux. The weather was glorious, the roses in full bloom, and it was very pleasant to find an atmosphere so different from what had been expected; but the bridgehead was still very shallow and Bayeux was crowded

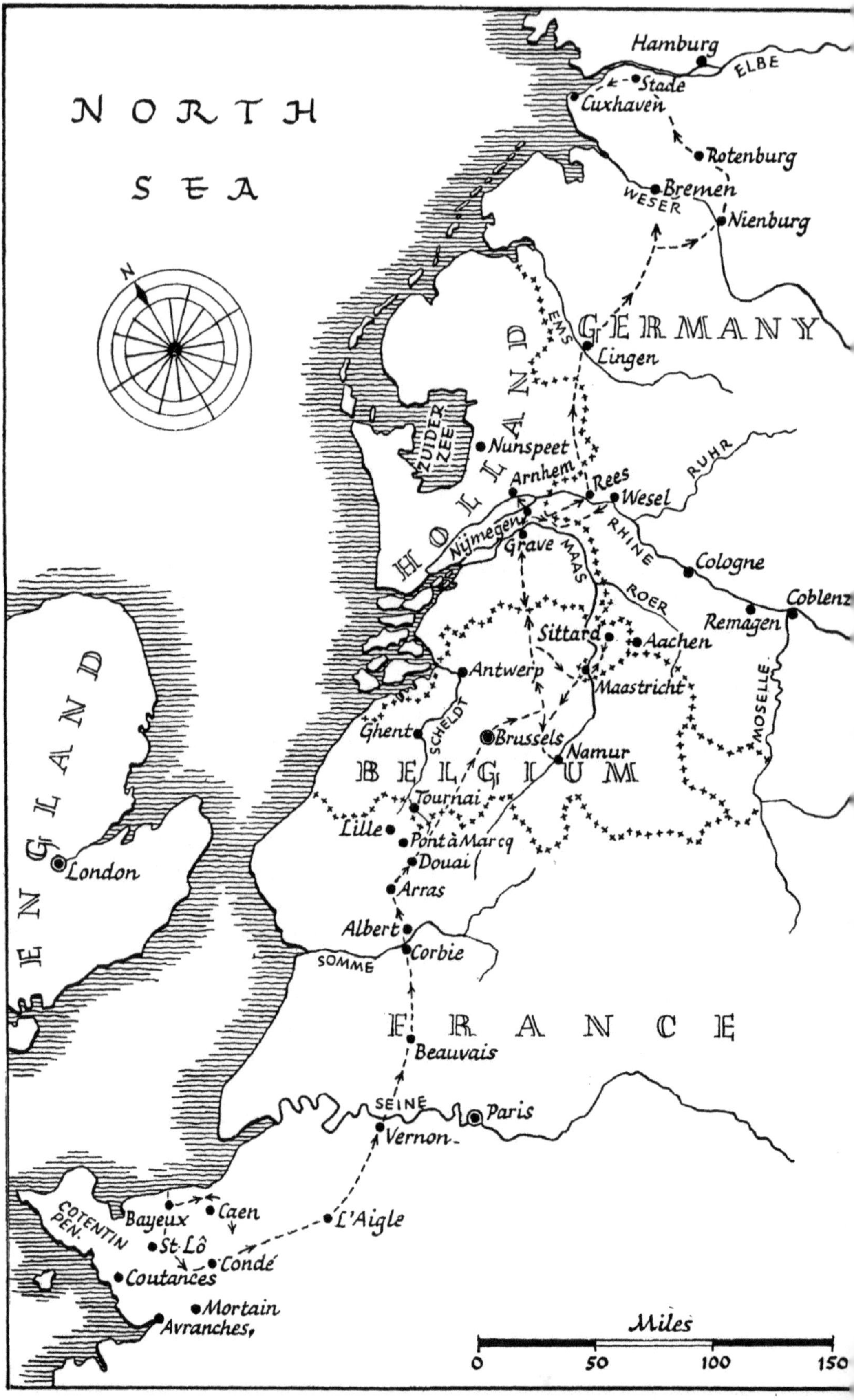
NORTH SEA
N
Hamburg
ELBE
Stade
Cuxhaven
Rotenburg
Bremen
WESER
Nienburg
GERMANY
EMS
Lingen
HOLLAND
ZUIDER ZEE
Nunspeet
Arnhem
Rees
Wesel
RUHR
Nijmegen
Grave
MAAS
RHINE
Cologne
ROER
Coblenz
Remagen
Sittard
Aachen
Antwerp
Maastricht
MOSELLE
ENGLAND
Ghent
SCHELDT
Brussels
Namur
BELGIUM
Tournai
Lille
Pont à Marcq
London
Douai
Arras
Albert
Corbie
SOMME
FRANCE
Beauvais
SEINE
Paris
Vernon
COTENTIN PEN.
Bayeux
Caen
L'Aigle
St. Lô
Condé
Coutances
Mortain
Avranches
Miles
0
50
100
150

out with streams of military transport and refugees. By the evening of June 26th, the 32nd Guards Brigade, the only portion of the division yet to have arrived, was concentrated in a restful, if tightly packed, area interspersed with orchards immediately South-West of Bayeux.

The precedence given to the 32nd Guards Brigade over the crossing was not accidental. The first few days of fighting in the very close country of which most of Normandy consists had shown very clearly that a great deal more infantry than armour would be needed in the first stages of the battle. Those who had hoped for a peaceful few days pending the arrival of the other brigade received therefore a rude awakening when the 32nd Guards Brigade was put under direct command of VIII Corps on June 27th and ordered to move the following day to occupy a pivot position near Bretteville l'Orgueilleuse. The brigade was to come under command of the 43rd Division (in XII Corps) on arrival and was to include, in addition to its own normal complement, the West Somerset Yeomanry, the 21st Anti-Tank Regiment, less one battery, and the 615th Field Squadron. The idea was that, with all the anti-tank guns and other resources which an armoured division could provide, it would form a particularly strong base in case an attack, which other elements of VIII Corps were to make across the River Odon, went wrong in any respect; at the same time, without being engaged in the front line or suffering too many casualties, it was hoped that everybody would get experience which would be of value later.

The position was duly occupied the next day, and the full realisation of what war means was soon brought home to us. About half-way from Bayeux the aspect of the country changed quite suddenly and scenes of appalling devastation met us; most of the trees were smashed by shells and bombs, and little but bare walls remained of the buildings. The villages looked as if somebody had pulled them down with a gigantic rake, the roads and fields were pitted with craters, and, most unpleasant of all, the stench of dead animals pervaded the whole atmosphere. The sight and smell of dead cows and horses were to become almost normal and remain one of the worst aspects of the first stage of the campaign, because of the extraordinary numbers of live-stock in Normandy. But it was soon found that a bulldozer provided a ready means of disposing of them, and in future these invaluable vehicles were in constant request for the purpose whenever a protracted stay in any particular neighbourhood was expected.

The 5th Bn. Coldstream occupied the villages of St. Mauvieu and Marcelet, where they were in contact with German troops holding Carpiquet Airfield; the 3rd Bn. Irish Guards was centred on La Garde, two miles further West, and the 1st Bn. Welsh Guards about the same distance again beyond and round Cheux, which had been almost completely destroyed by a German counter-attack with tanks the day before. The brigade spent exactly a fortnight in this pivot position, and on the whole it was not a pleasant first experience. Shelling and mortaring were almost continuous in the forward areas during the first few days, with heavier resultant casualties than had been anticipated, and the fact that no direct retaliation was possible made them all the harder to bear. The Coldstream and Irish had the opportunity of gaining some valuable experience in patrolling on the outskirts of Carpiquet Airfield, but the Welsh could do but little even in this direction. They were also the most unlucky in casualties in that direct hits were suffered on Battalion Headquarters on the two successive evenings of June 29th and 30th. The first wounded the commanding officer and second-in-command, Lieutenant-Colonel G. W. Browning and Major M. E. C. Smart, together with two other officers and several men, while the second killed Lieutenant-Colonel J. E. Fass, who had subsequently taken over command. The battalion had thus lost its three senior officers before even going into action, and the Command passed to Lieutenant-Colonel C. H. R. Heber-Percy, M.C. The Coldstream also suffered a severe loss when Major M. P. G. Howard was mortally wounded by a stray shell on July 2nd.

During the first week the brigade formed the firm base for limited attacks across the Odon which were designed to attract the enemy reserves, particularly of armour, rather than to make important gains of ground. The German reactions were fairly spirited and in particular a tank attack on the evening of June 29th, at a moment when the relief of a battalion in the line was taking place, achieved considerable penetration towards Cheux from the South-West. Several Panthers got through almost as far as the village before they were destroyed and even the West Somerset Yeomanry, who were in support in the Brigade Headquarters area just South of Putot-en-Bessin, received the ominous order "Prepare for Tanks" at their gun-lines—the only occasion incidentally on which they ever did receive it. But nothing arrived that far, and the formidable array of anti-tank guns with which the whole position was studded had no opportunity of showing their mettle.

On July 4th a battalion of the Highland Light Infantry was put under command of the brigade to take over the positions in St. Mauvieu which had hitherto been held by the Coldstream; the whole battalion then moved up to Marcelet, which had always been held with a company, in order to form a firm base for an attack by the 3rd Canadian Division on the Carpiquet Airfield. This attack met very strong opposition and the airfield, with its heavily fortified buildings and the long fields of fire, proved such a stiff task that it had temporarily to be called off; but the second attempt on July 8th effected its capture. Material assistance was given to the Canadians on the latter occasion by the Northumberland Fusiliers with both mortars and machine-guns. Although they had been deployed for action since arrival in the area, and each machine-gun platoon allotted to the battalion with which it was to remain more or less permanently in future, this was the first occasion when they were seriously employed, and the results were very gratifying.

This second attack was in conjunction with the long-expected main attack on Caen by the whole of I Corps and most of us were able to witness the bombing of the German positions the previous evening; this was carried out by a gigantic fleet of aircraft and was an awe-inspiring sight. Within forty-eight hours of the initial assault all the objectives had been reached and the whole of

Caen, excepting only the suburbs South of the River Orne, was in our hands. VIII Corps no longer now had any real need of the 32nd Guards Brigade, but it was retained for two days longer as an additional safeguard until a new attack on Esquay and Maltot was launched; as the 43rd Division was taking a leading part, it was put under command of the 15th (Scottish) Division.

On July 11th, the 32nd Guards Brigade returned to the peaceful atmosphere of Bayeux. It had been a trying and expensive fortnight but, in addition to gaining valuable experience from living under fire, some personal knowledge of the Germans and their characteristics had been obtained. For the most part we had been up against the 12th S.S. Panzer Division (Hitlerjugend), and the acquaintance with them more than confirmed the stories we had been told of the degraded type of individual that was to be found in its ranks. One could admire their courage, but all else about them was repellent and horrifying and there could be little question but that these men—or, rather more often, boys—were fit for nothing but the slaughter for which they had so deliberately been schooled.

Interesting and useful as it had been in many ways for the infantry to work on its own for a period, the return to normal command and organisation was very welcome. The whole division was concentrated in a comparatively small space consisting of rich pasture fields and orchards just East of Bayeux. Apart from some maintenance, activities were largely confined to such pleasant pursuits as bathing and cinema-going, also to consuming large quantities of delicious cider and Camembert cheese, of which the supplies in Normandy seemed inexhaustible.

This was too agreeable an existence to last, and on July 14th a warning order was received that the division was to take part in a major attack East of Caen; rather unkindly, as we thought, it was to be called "Operation Goodwood". It was obviously vital to increase the size of the bridgehead and, with the object of pinning down the bulk of the enemy armour while the Americans attacked, VIII Corps was to break out on a one-divisional front, making for the high ground just South-East of Caen and then, if all went well, on towards Falaise. All three British armoured divisions were to be used, the 11th Armoured Division leading, the 7th Armoured Division following on the right, the Guards Armoured Division on the left. Two of the four bridges over the River Orne were allotted to us; after crossing them we then had to pass through a gap in our own minefield and make for Cagny, after which we were to exploit towards Vimont and protect the left flank.

On Sunday, July 16th, a perfect summer morning, all officers assembled at Divisional Headquarters to be addressed by General Adair on the impending battle. Besides talking about the Operation in detail he stressed that it was the first in which the division as a whole was to take part and spoke so much from his heart that all who heard him were deeply moved and impressed. They left inspired with the determination to prove worthy of their traditions and of the confidence placed in them by their commander.

At dusk the following evening we moved off for the approach march to the bridges, which was to be completed before dawn. The 5th Guards Armoured Brigade led the way, the tanks moving across the fields along bulldozed tracks marked with white tape, so as to avoid the final ruination of the few still serviceable roads. The heat was intense, the dust and the dirt indescribable and the night inky black; apart from the discomfort thus caused and in spite of excellent signposting by the Divisional Provost Company, the finding of the tracks was an almost impossible task. Somehow nevertheless the column was lined up in its correct order and position by daybreak and we halted for a couple of hours, during which we had a grandstand view of the colossal bombing operations by over two thousand aircraft which preceded the attack. They were on an even larger scale than those at Caen ten days previously and, after the heavy bombers had stopped, fighter bombers took their place, many of them taking off from an airstrip alongside part of the divisional column. After a few minutes the whole of what was to be our battle area was covered with a thick fog of dust thrown up by the terrific pounding of the villages and roads; tracer ammunition sped through the sky and occasionally an aircraft would fall like a swaying leaf, flaming to the ground. As the light increased the bombardment from the air died down and the massed artillery took over. At the appointed hour the wireless opened up and the column started very slowly to move forward.

On either side, as we descended the slope towards the Orne, could be seen the remains of countless gliders that had been used to transport some of the 6th Airborne Division on D-Day, and the scope of that operation was once more vividly driven home. Towards eight o'clock the bombardment came to an end, and the attack started; but by then we were again stationary and, as the 11th Armoured Division was directly in front of us on the same route, it was some time before the road cleared sufficiently for us to move on. There was an extensive minefield on this front and there had only been time to open two narrow lanes through it whose surfaces were atrocious and both of which were kept under almost continuous shell-fire. Passage through these lanes was consequently very laborious but, once the 11th Armoured Division had deployed and was engaged on the far side of the minefield, our armour made good progress and was shortly also at grips with the enemy.

The fighting throughout the day was extremely confused and it is not easy to give a coherent account of it. Each battalion of the armoured brigade had a motor company of the 1st Bn. Grenadier Guards under command, in accordance with the then commonly accepted organisation for battle; the 2nd Bn. Grenadier Guards led the way, followed by the 2nd Bn. Irish Guards and Brigade Headquarters, with the 1st Bn. Coldstream Guards bringing up the rear. The 11th Armoured Division had originally been given the task of seizing Cagny and then pushing on South-West to Bourguebus and the road to Falaise; but Cagny proved to be protected by a strong anti-tank screen and the leading armour proceeded to by-pass it to the right, becoming involved in a tank battle to the South-West. This news was sent back by Captain A. G. Heywood, who had gone forward with the rear armoured regiment of the 11th Armoured Division as liaison officer, and who added that the motor battalion which was in the rear of the division was moving across the fields to the North of the village in the wake of the tanks. As the Grenadiers debouched from the minefield they could see the last of the vehicles of this motor battalion disappearing, while on the horizon the yet unfamiliar black oily smoke was billowing up from two blazing Shermans. The country in view consisted of large corn and root fields, for the most part flat and divided by thick hedges and interspersed with belts of tall trees; soon, across one or two intervening hedges and orchards, the village of Cagny could be discerned.

No. 2 Squadron, which was in the lead, was about two thousand yards away from the village when it was met by heavy anti-tank gun-fire which knocked out two tanks; attempts to feel its way to either side met with no success and it quickly became evident that for the moment the advance was held up. At this point the commanding officer, Lieutenant-Colonel J. N. R. Moore, went up to see Major Sir Arthur Grant, the squadron leader, to confer on the situation; but he had only just returned to his own tank when Sir Arthur's tank was hit and he was killed, although the crew got out. Lieutenant-Colonel Moore now decided to send two troops of No. 1 Squadron under Captain J. A. P. Jones, M.C., round the left flank, which offered the only covered approach, to see if they could reach Cagny from that side. At the same time No. 3 Squadron, in view of a report that Tiger tanks were operating somewhere in the woods to the left and left rear, was ordered to take up a position guarding the exposed flank in the direction of Emieville. It continued in this role throughout the day and had some sharp engagements with enemy tanks, in one of which Lieutenant the Hon. J. P. Corbett's tank was hit and unfortunately none of the crew escaped. The force of No. 1 Squadron meanwhile was making progress and, although Captain Jones's tank was hit and the whole crew wounded or severely burned through manning their guns after the tank had been set on fire, the leading troop eventually reached the outskirts of the village. It was now about four o'clock in the afternoon, the operation to invest Cagny having begun at ten o'clock, and this achievement at last gave the accompanying infantry an opportunity. After a preliminary bombardment by the field battery of the Leicestershire Yeomanry under command, the King's Company, under Major N. E. W. Baker, was sent in to clear and occupy the village. This was quickly and successfully carried out against negligible opposition, as the Germans had by then mostly withdrawn, leaving behind them three eighty-eight-millimetre anti-tank guns and a mass of other equipment.

The tanks of the 2nd Bn. Irish Guards had moved up behind the Grenadiers but their progress was necessarily slow. When they reached the line of the main road and railway running East from Caen, just the far side of the minefield, they were faced with the depressing sight of no less than nine Grenadier tanks burning sombrely ahead of them, while to the left some tanks of the 11th Armoured Division, all of which they had hoped would be far in front, were carrying on a furious battle with German tanks and anti-tank guns hidden in the thick woods towards Banneville. The ground to the East rose slightly and, with the dense vegetation which clothed its crest, provided admirable defensive positions from which the left flank and rear of our attack could be continuously harassed. The morning passed for the Irish with a series of scattered engagements, not without losses, and in the early afternoon, when movement in front had practically come to a standstill, they were ordered to by-pass Cagny to the North and then to cut South on to the Cagny–Vimont Road, to be followed, if possible, by an advance on Vimont. But as they started to pass Cagny, they ran straight into trouble from the tanks and anti-tank guns sited in the woods to the East. The fighting which ensued was notable for a gallant action which won the Military Cross for Lieutenant J. R. Gorman, a troop leader in No. 2 Squadron, and the Military Medal for his driver, Lance-Corporal Barron. When the leading troop was held up by anti-tank gun-fire from the left, Lieutenant Gorman decided to make for the top of a small rise about four hundred yards ahead to see if he could help. As he reached it, at a point where a road intersected two tall hedgerows, he saw four German tanks, two of them Tigers, less than two hundred yards away. For some reason his traversing gun refused to operate, so he ordered the driver to charge and ram the nearest Tiger; Lance-Corporal Barron succeeded in doing this a split second before the Germans could traverse their guns sufficiently. Both crews baled out and, being unarmed, disappeared into different ditches. Lieutenant Gorman knew that only a Firefly—the name given to the one seventeen-pounder Sherman in each troop—could compete with the other Tiger; he ran back and found one whose commander had been killed and, after reassembling the crew, returned in it up the rise, swinging a bit further to the right. Taking up a position behind a hedge, he put further shots into the turret of the rammed Tiger, which set it on fire, and obtained two hits on the other. As the remaining tanks, of which one was a Panther, were now traversed towards him and there were badly wounded men to evacuate, he then broke off the engagement. The rammed Tiger was duly found the next day, though the damaged one had been towed away.

Eventually the Irish penetrated to the Cagny–Vimont Road after considerable losses but here they ran into further trouble from self-propelled guns and lost two more tanks quickly. The open country on either side of the road was bounded by thick woods which offered excellent defensive sites and progress towards Vimont until they were cleared was out of the question.

The 1st Bn. Coldstream Guards was left little room for manœuvre by the preceding battalions. It was subjected to severe shelling after coming through the minefield which caused the death, among others, of Major P. S. Buxton; he was the Commander of the 131st Battery of the Leicestershire Yeomanry, which worked normally with the Coldstream, and he was killed instantly by a shell just as he was getting out of his tank to go and confer with the commanding officer. No. 1 Squadron was then directed against the woods to the left which had caused so much trouble, where Lieutenant M. E. Lock achieved the distinction of knocking out a Panther with his first shot. Later on the battalion went round South of Cagny and some hide-and-seek ensued with German tanks that were hidden in the orchards South of the railway. It was a confused and not very healthy position, with neither side able to make a decisive effort.

The 2nd Bn. Welsh Guards had followed immediately behind the Armoured Brigade and, acting under divisional control, had been entrusted with the task of safeguarding both flanks. This was a very necessary one for which the superior mobility of their Cromwells fitted them, and they suffered considerable casualties in carrying it out. A loss that was mourned widely in other circles as well as within the division was that of Lieutenant R. J. Whistler, who was killed by a mortar bomb when he had got out of his tank to confer with one of his tank commanders. Apart from his great distinction as an artist, of which all were aware as his talents in this direction had always been liberally at the disposal of the division, and particularly of his battalion, for the asking, Rex Whistler had gained the affection and respect of his brother officers and of the men under his command to an unusual degree. The shining example that he set provides the answer to those self-important young men who considered their artistic or intellectual abilities too exceptional to be wasted in the realms of active service.

The 32nd Guards Brigade had meanwhile been moving up behind, but owing to the congestion caused by the narrow passage through the minefields progress was slow and went by fits and starts. The passage was a particularly unnerving episode for the infantry in their cumbrous and vulnerable troop-carrying vehicles, and a considerable number of casualties resulted, among the fatal ones being Major W. S. Stewart-Brown, D.S.O., second-in-command of the 5th Bn. Coldstream, and Captain I. D. R. Grant of the 3rd Bn. Irish. Evening was approaching by the time the infantry had finally come up with the armour. The 1st Bn. Welsh Guards was ordered to take over Cagny from the Grenadiers and the 5th Coldstream Guards to position itself just East of the village; the 3rd Bn. Irish Guards was told to move directly across country to occupy Frénouville, screened until dark by the tanks of the 2nd Bn. Irish Guards situated along the Vimont road. Nothing was known of the situation there and there was no time to reconnoitre the ground before nightfall. There was also no time to lose, so the advance started and it turned out a most exciting if disturbing night. All vehicles were to remain behind Cagny with the adjutant, who was to bring them up if and when Frénouville was reached by the fighting troops advancing on foot in deployed formation. No. 2 Company, under Major A. R. Eardley-Wilmot, led off at a lively pace followed by No. 1 Company under Captain P. A. McCall. After they had gone, and too late to retrieve more than the rear half of No. 1 Company, new orders came for the advance to take place through Cagny and along the main road from there. The remainder of the battalion therefore worked their way gingerly through the appalling ruins of Cagny, but before long were met by bullets whistling down the only road. It was fairly clear that Frénouville was held. The axis was changed on to a compass bearing parallel with the road but, after wending their way laboriously for perhaps a quarter of a mile through standing corn, a crack of machine-guns and the flash of small-arms fire loomed straight ahead. Verey lights and star-shells shot into the sky and every form of unpleasantness including mortar shells began to rain down on them; to make matters worse it seemed that our own troops were also now shooting in their direction. However, at last luck came their way and they happened on some men of their own armoured battalion, who gave them some sound advice about the situation. It was decided to dig in for the night after evolving some sort of defensive lay-out. When dawn broke the positions were seen to be scarcely conventional, but by the mercy of providence the leading elements were about three feet behind the top of a reverse slope, with patrols just over the crest in contact with the Germans all mixed up in the hedgerows. With the dawn appeared also Major Eardley-Wilmot; he had unerringly led the way by compass to the outskirts of Frénouville, where he found himself suddenly up against the German defenders. It was by then pitch dark and after a short but sharp engagement he gave orders to dig in. He could neither give nor receive news as his wireless set had been broken; a runner would never find his way back in the dark and yet it was essential to report back. In broad daylight it might well prove impossible to get back alive and he decided to make the attempt himself in the half-light of early morning. By dint of crawling along the ditches he succeeded and, after finding Lieutenant-Colonel J. O. E. Vandeleur and arranging with him for the laying of a smoke screen, he crawled forward again and extricated his men under its cover. For the exceptional leadership that he displayed he received an immediate award of the Military Cross.

On the next morning, in view of the exposed salient in which the three armoured divisions found themselves, and of reports of enemy reserves moving up, the corps commander ordered them to improve their positions by local advances and then to hold firm bases pending a further plan. Although this put an end for the moment to our advance on Vimont, it was nevertheless the job of the infantry to probe forward and obtain vantage points and accordingly the 1st Bn. Welsh Guards was ordered to attack Le Poirier that evening and the 5th Bn. Coldstream Guards Frénouville the following morning. Nos. 2 and 4 Companies led the Welsh attack, which was quickly successful, very little opposition being encountered, though four enemy tanks were destroyed. The Coldstream, after handing over the defence of their area to the 1st Bn. Grenadier Guards, which came under command of the 32nd Guards Brigade for the purpose, met with even less resistance as they advanced to occupy Frénouville after a barrage at first light and were soon in full possession. Both battalions dug in and remained holding these positions for three days. Some valuable patrolling was carried out during this period; a counter-attack was confidently expected but it never materialised, as it was broken up by heavy gun-fire on the enemy forming-up positions, details of which had been obtained from prisoners. The shelling and mortaring were, however, extremely severe. Lieutenant-Colonel Lord Stratheden, commanding officer of the 5th Bn. Coldstream, was wounded in both legs on July 21st and had to be evacuated; Major J. D. A. Syrett, a Welsh Guards company commander, was killed next day. Up till July 20th this nuisance was mainly confined to the more forward areas, but the Germans then brought some more guns up to the hilly ground East of Emieville, from which they could obtain a bird's eye view over all our positions and supply roads. Any considerable movement was likely to lead to trouble, and the General had a lucky escape when, just after mid-day on July 21st, a shell fell directly on the Divisional Command Post, which was sited next to the 32nd Guards Brigade Headquarters in a field just South-East of Demouville. If the Command White Scout Car had not been bulldozed about six feet into the ground the death-roll would have been very heavy. As it was, he himself was only very slightly wounded but one of his staff officers, Captain J. W. Burden, Scots Guards, was killed and another, Lieutenant Sir Anthony Meyer, Scots Guards, seriously wounded, together with four guardsmen killed and three wounded. Captain Burden was a United States citizen who had come over with the American Red Cross at the beginning of the War. Soon after his arrival in England he joined the Scots Guards and had served with the division since its formation; he had already done much useful liaison work with the American Army and his death so early in the campaign was a severe loss.

The Germans also profited from the fact that we were in a salient to adopt rather bolder air tactics than of late. They made a number of air reconnaissances and dropped a few bombs, though it was interesting to note that not less than a dozen aircraft together seemed to like to face the job. When a formation of them attempted to attack the 32nd Guards Brigade Headquarters area on the afternoon of July 19th the 324th Battery of the 94th Light Anti-Aircraft Regiment sent one crashing down in flames and the rest made off hurriedly, two of them smoking and losing height. During the next two days two more aircraft definitely fell to the regiment and three more were damaged, while Company-Sergeant-Major Ford, of the 1st Bn. Grenadier Guards, claimed the destruction of yet another with considerable justification. The importance of Bofors guns had not always been fully appreciated in the past, but undoubtedly the division would have suffered considerable casualties at this time if their crews had not been alert and well trained, as the Luftwaffe attacks were sharp and determined. As it was, they were all successfully beaten off before they could be pressed home, and we were duly grateful.

For the first three days of Operation "Goodwood" the weather was glorious, and indeed was the only solace for the unpleasantness of life in general. But at tea-time on July 20th a torrential thunderstorm broke with tropical violence, and within a few minutes all slit-trenches were a foot deep in water and any persons or things in them were soaked. For the best part of forty-eight hours the rain continued almost without cease and the whole area became a sea of mud, in which it was impossible to move without sinking up to one's knees. The condition of the ground became such that no major attack could possibly be undertaken for three or four days, and the army commander decided to relieve the armoured divisions and to replace them with infantry, taking VIII Corps altogether out of the line. The relief was originally planned to be put through complete on the evening of July 21st, but the roads in our sector were literally impassable to wheeled vehicles in many places and therefore only the armoured brigade moved out on that day. The 32nd Guards Brigade, supported by the 2nd Bn. Welsh Guards, remained on till the next night under command of I Corps, when it was finally relieved by the 154th Brigade of the 51st Highland Division.

The first battle fought by the division had not been entirely successful, and we could not in all fairness blame outside circumstances exclusively. The armoured brigade had outstripped the infantry brigade, which had no chance to close up and influence the battle at the vital moment. As a consequence this was the last, as well as the first, occasion on which we fought on the lines according to which we had been trained. In Western Europe we were seldom likely to find ideal country for tanks on their own, and somehow we had to evolve a system whereby the infantry was always right up with them.

And yet there was a good deal to show on the credit side.

Although the extent of the gain in ground was disappointing, severe losses in men and equipment, that he could ill afford, had been inflicted on the enemy. In addition to numerous anti-tank guns and mortars a very considerable number of his tanks had been destroyed and the 21st Anti-Tank Regiment had every reason to feel proud of its share and confident in its guns. Q "Sanna's Post" Battery under Captain E. D. G. Smith knocked out three Panthers on the occasion of the Welsh Guards attack on Le Poirier and Lieutenant A. C. T. Handford added to this score by accounting for a further Panther the next day. Y Battery also, on July 19th and when operating with the 2nd Bn. Welsh Guards, destroyed two Tigers, an action which won the Military Cross for Lieutenant F. A. Hook and the Military Medal for Sergeant F. Holford. As against the German losses in armour our own were admittedly more severe, but this is almost inevitable in an attacking force and we could better afford them; furthermore, whereas all his damaged tanks fell into our hands, we retained all our own and in fact more than half of them were serviceable again within forty-eight hours.

In addition to the casualties we had cause for gratification in two important identifications, that of the 1st S.S. Panzer Division in the attack on Le Poirier and that of the 12th S.S. at Frénouville. The first of these divisions had been brought from the other side of the River Orne, where it had been recently fighting, while the second was the only mobile reserve that the enemy was thought to possess; it had been taken out of the line after the Carpiquet battle, where we had first met it, and its recommittal so soon showed fairly clearly that nothing else was available. It has already been stated that one of the main objects of the operation had been to attract as many as possible of the Panzer divisions away from the West, and therefore these identifications were highly encouraging.

If it had been possible for us to know at the time what was going on behind the enemy lines the grounds for encouragement would have been positively staggering. If the battle had been bewildering and generally a bit unsatisfactory to ourselves it had been a nightmare to our opponents. By dint of admittedly clever tactics, by which they made their numbers seem greater than they actually were, together with a bit of good luck here and there, they had just succeeded in holding us. But their Commander-in-Chief, Field-Marshal von Kluge, was under no illusions after less than three weeks in Normandy. A letter which he wrote to Hitler on July 21st contained the following sentences: "I came here with the fixed determination of making effective your order to stand fast at any price. But now I have seen by experience that this price must be paid by the slow but sure annihilation of the force. In spite of intense efforts the moment has drawn near when the front, already so heavily strained, will break. And once the enemy is in open country an orderly Command will hardly be practicable in view of the insufficient mobility of our own troops." Von Kluge was to commit suicide within a month, but his Chief-of-Staff, General Blumentritt, confirmed later on when a prisoner that the Field-Marshal's earlier optimism finally vanished altogether as the direct result of the nearness to disaster experienced by the Germans in Operation "Goodwood".

Delighted though we all were to leave our sodden and crumbling slit-trenches, the so-called rest area in the industrial suburbs on the Southern fringe of Caen was no paradise. It had been one of the chief targets of the gigantic bombing operations that we had witnessed and subsequently had been the scene of very severe fighting before its final capture. Part of it had also been a German minefield and by no means all the mines had been removed. The whole place was pitted with gigantic craters and stank of corpses and burst drains; refuse and smashed furniture was scattered piecemeal on all sides. The most repellent of all was the factory district of Colombelles, which was a tangled mass of steel and concrete hurled about at crazy angles under which were buried innumerable bodies; but none of it was pleasant. Moreover, we were still within range of the enemy artillery and periodical shells came hurtling into our midst. These and anti-personnel bombs from occasional aircraft caused quite a number of casualties. The 2nd Bn. Grenadier Guards lost two officers killed on one occasion (including the Chaplain, the Reverend W. Berry) and two ammunition lorries together with their complete signal equipment on another; both drill sergeants of the 1st Bn. Welsh Guards were wounded. German aircraft also indulged in some night bombing directed on the bridges over the river immediately behind us, and one night it was very heavy and prolonged. But they never hit a bridge, and the only one that was put out of action was due to the ignorance of a British soldier who attempted to drive a captured Panther across, not realising that it weighed some ten tons more than the bridge was designed to carry. It fell straight through the middle.

The division spent a week under these unattractive conditions, but there was good reason for us having to put up with them. The 11th Armoured Division, which had suffered the heaviest losses both in tanks and men, had been sent back across the Orne to rest and refit; but it was considered necessary to retain ourselves and the 7th Armoured Division East of the river for two reasons. We might be needed in the event of any major counter-attack on our newly-won positions South of Caen and we might have to carry out an exploitation role in a further operation due to take place on July 25th. This was to be carried out by II Canadian Corps, under whose command we were now put and whose two infantry divisions were holding the line in this sector. The General held a conference on the afternoon of July 24th, when he gave out orders for Operation "Spring", as it was called. At half-past three the next morning the 2nd and 3rd Canadian Divisions were to break through the enemy line astride the Caen–Falaise road with the assistance of artificial moonlight. The 7th Armoured Division was to follow through and seize a commanding feature on the road further South. Then, if everything had so far gone according to plan, we were to take over from the 7th Armoured Division and exploit to the East, while they secured the important river-crossing at Bretteville-sur-Laize.

Such was the plan, but it never succeeded in developing as far as the point where we were to be used. The Canadians gained their first objectives without great difficulty, but were held up in the second phase. This was not altogether surprising, as air photographs had shown that they were now up against a main line of defence supported by a large number of guns and mortars. An attempt by the 7th Armoured Division to wheel round to the East was met by enemy tanks and shortly afterwards sharp counter-attacks began to develop, made by infantry supported both by tanks and self-propelled guns. Fierce fighting ensued for the remainder of the day and, though the original gains were firmly consolidated, no further progress was made and we were never called upon to move. At mid-day the next day we were put back to four hours' notice and placed once more in Corps reserve.

The failure of this attack, coming after the comparative lack of success of Operation "Goodwood", was a bit depressing at the time. But if the full balance sheet was studied even in the light of our knowledge then, the position as a whole was not really unsatisfactory. The Germans were fully aware that the corridor between the Rivers Orne and Dives provided the only good tank going on the front and they were determined to hold it at all costs. We were kept there fundamentally as a threat which they could not ignore and the whole allied plan lay in making them think that our main armoured attack was coming in on this sector. The Second Army had first attacked across the Odon to try to secure the right flank and now, after securing the communications through Caen, should be due to put in the main drive towards Falaise. That we were successful in deceiving him is shown by the fact that, of eight Panzer divisions and three Tiger tank battalions altogether available, six of the former and all three of the latter were by now facing the Second Army, the great majority East of the Orne at that. Only two Panzer divisions, both of which had been fully engaged for some time, were left to deal with the American onslaught when it was launched at mid-day on July 25th, a few hours after Operation "Spring".

On the afternoon of July 28th, as increasingly favourable accounts of the Americans' progress came in, the division was ordered to cross back over the Orne and rejoin VIII Corps. At first light on July 30th we moved and found ourselves in the very orchards and fields near Bayeux that we had left almost a fortnight before. Hopes of a day or two of peace and quiet ran high at first but were dashed to the ground when orders came through in the early afternoon to move again during the night. Much as we should have liked at least one night's complete rest we were on the whole content. We knew that we were to take part in the decisive break-through and already felt convinced that this was destined to end in the total defeat of the German forces in France.

Chapter Three

NORMANDY—THE CAUMONT OFFENSIVE

THE MAIN attack of the Second Army, to follow up and protect the left flank of that of the Americans instituted a week earlier between St. Lo and Coutances, went in on the morning of July 30th, as we started to cross back over the Orne. The major role was allotted to VIII Corps, which took over a few days previously the Caumont sector; this had up till now been held by the Americans, who had asked to be relieved of it in order to free more infantry for the assault on St. Lo. XXX Corps, on the left of VIII Corps, also attacked in conformity; V U.S. Corps, however, was unable to make a major effort on the right in view of the American expenditure of resources further West, though it undertook to move forward as soon as the position in front eased sufficiently.

The object was to support the American advance and to protect its vulnerable left flank as it started to fan out behind the German front in accordance with the strategy laid down by the Commander-in-Chief before the invasion. In the words of the corps commander at the time, "the enemy is doing everything in his power to restrict the area of penetration by the Americans, but to do this successfully he must hinge his forces on some important feature of the ground, holding fast to this position, and being prepared to give ground slowly on his left flank". This important feature was the broken wooded country South of Caumont, culminating in Mount Pinçon to the South-East and aptly known as "Norman Switzerland". It was ideal country for defence, while behind it lay a generally far easier stretch with excellent lateral roads to facilitate a counter-offensive against the American flank at its narrowest point at the base of the Cotentin peninsula. So far the attacks in the Caen area had successfully deluded the Germans, who had once more reacted as desired to the recent

Canadian effort, but it could not be long before they realised from which direction the real threat lay. It was vital for us to act before they did.

On July 30th VIII Corps attacked on a two-divisional front, with the 11th Armoured Division on the right and the 15th (Scottish) Division, together with the 6th Guards Tank Brigade, on the left; the latter was commanded by Brigadier G. H. G. L. Verney, as previously mentioned, and this was its first appearance in action. Heavy and concentrated bombing preceded the operation, despite unfavourable weather, as the Germans had had a full month of comparative peace in which to prepare this section of the line and were known to have dug in deeply and to have laid extensive minefields. This precaution was well advised, as in addition the defending troops proved to be of better quality than had been anticipated. They fought well, and penetration was at first slow, but by the afternoon the line had crumbled and our troops had advanced some three miles. The break-through had been a fine achievement and all troops concerned had greatly distinguished themselves, notably our fellow guardsmen on their initial experience of battle conditions.

Unfortunately XXX Corps was unable to make much progress during the first day, largely owing to the presence of a stream across a great part of its front whose steep banks proved impassable to tanks; this had the result of the 15th (Scottish) Division finding itself eventually in a very exposed position and of having to content itself during July 31st with consolidating the ground won and with beating off a series of determined counter-attacks. The 11th Armoured Division, however, was more happily placed and succeeded in capturing the village of St. Martin des Besaces from the West by the early afternoon; this was a place of the highest importance, since from it radiated the road system of the entire area. Meanwhile a troop of the 2nd Household Cavalry, which was operating as the Corps reconnaissance regiment ahead of the 11th Armoured Division, discovered a track leading through the dense Forêt de l'Evêque, which lay to the South-West of St. Martin, which was neither defended nor mined; it transpired later that the track lay along the boundary of the German 326th Infantry and 3rd Parachute Divisions and that each thought the other responsible. With customary dash the armoured cars pushed ri ht through the forest and to their astonishment found the bridge carrying the main road from St. Lo to Le Bény Bocage over the Souleuvre not only intact but unguarded. This river formed a major obstacle across the whole line of advance and its capture was as important as it was unexpected; two troops of tanks were at once sent up to ensure its retention until the main body could get up. The 11th Armoured Division was meanwhile told to reinforce success and to occupy the high ground on which Le Bény Bocage stands during the ensuing night, with a view to seizing the remaining bridges over the Souleuvre from the far side the next morning.

This spectacular advance drove the 3rd Parachute Division to withdraw on the front of V U.S. Corps, which consequently followed up and safeguarded the right flank, but the position on the left continued to be far less satisfactory. XXX Corps had now been able to make some advance, but not sufficient to prevent the 15th (Scottish) Division from having to wheel round to defend the now very vulnerable left flank of VIII Corps. The need to attain our main objectives was vital and as Guards Armoured Division was by this time available it was ordered to take up the advance alongside and on the left of 11th Armoured Division.

We had arrived during the early hours of the morning of July 31st to find ourselves in the pleasantest surroundings yet seen since arrival in France. The country North of Caumont had been evacuated quickly by the Germans soon after the initial landings and was quite untouched by the ravages of war, but the thunder of the guns reminded all effectively that the battle was still not far away. We were not indeed given the opportunity of enjoying the scenery for long. At luncheon time the General held a conference at which he announced that a new regrouping within the division was to take place immediately. Each brigade would in future consist of a more balanced team of tanks and infantry; the 5th Bn. Coldstream Guards was transferred to the 5th

Guards Brigade to form one battle-group with the 2nd Bn. Irish Guards, while the two Grenadier battalions formed the other; the 1st Bn. Coldstream Guards was in turn transferred to the 32nd Guards Brigade. The General had been contemplating some such change ever since experience at Cagny had shown that some means must be devised under European conditions of getting the infantry right forward with the tanks. In the thick bocage country which we were now facing it was going to be even more essential than it had been in the comparatively open fields around Caen and the 11th Armoured Division had already adopted a roughly similar arrangement. It was destined to work admirably and in fact the division fought increasingly along these lines during most of the remainder of the campaign.

The division was directed along the main road from Caumont to Vire. After passing through St. Martin des Besaces, this road dipped down to the valley of a tributary of the Souleuvre at the hamlet of Le Brun and rose again on the far side to traverse a ridge for about three miles before crossing the Souleuvre at a point where it ran through a defile to Cathéolles; two-thirds of the way across the ridge it dropped down into the valley of another small tributary at the village of Le Tourneur. After crossing the Souleuvre it ran up a steep and wooded gorge for over a mile before emerging into more open country at St. Charles de Percy, where it crossed another main road running East from Le Bény Bocage. The gorge could be made impassable by resolute defenders, since it was dominated by the Le Bény Bocage ridge on the West and by an even higher and thickly wooded feature on the East.

The 5th Guards Brigade was given the lead and ordered the 2nd Bn. Irish Guards and the 5th Bn. Coldstream Guards to occupy as much of the ridge beyond St. Martin as possible before nightfall with a view to crossing the Souleuvre next morning. But as soon as they had passed through the leading Scottish infantry and were approaching the bottom of the first valley, a sharp concentration came down upon them, making it very plain that the ridge was in German hands. Nothing daunted, the leading squadron, under Major J. W. R. Madden, forded the stream and rushed up the far slope. The Coldstream infantry followed and reached the crest as darkness fell; they were met by heavy machine-gun fire and Major M. E. Adeane, who was in command, ordered a halt for the night while an attack was prepared for the early morning. Casualties so far had not been heavy though the Irish Squadron had lost their second-in-command, Captain H. E. J. Dormer, and his tank. He had twice earlier in the war been dropped in France by parachute on special missions for which he had received the Distinguished Service Order and his death in such circumstances seemed almost paradoxical.

At dawn on August 1st the attack was resumed and a morning of very heavy fighting ensued before the Germans were dislodged from their positions on the twin summits of the ridge. The 15th (Scottish) Division had already identified the reconnaissance regiment of he 21st Panzer Division the previous evening as the first element of a mobile German formation to arrive from the Caen area, and it was quickly evident that both tanks and infantry from it had been thrown in immediately on arrival across our axis of advance. Although they had had little time in which to organise the defence the sunken lanes with thick banks and hedges so typical of the country enabled them, equipped as they were with both Panthers and Tigers, to take a fairly heavy toll of us both in tanks and in men before they were finally driven away at about mid-day. Major Adeane and one of his company commanders, Major K. Thornton, were both wounded by a mortar bomb and had to be evacuated, whereupon Lieutenant-Colonel C. K. Finlay of the 2nd Bn. Irish Guards took over command of the Group. Among the tanks destroyed was that of a troop leader, Lieutenant M. Maconchy, and both he and all his crew were killed.

VIII Corps intelligence staff had by now deduced that the main body of the 21st Panzer Division was blocking our path and that resistance must be expected to remain strong. The 5th Guards Brigade was therefore ordered to consolidate the ground already gained—the Grenadier Group was garrisoning St. Martin with one company reinforcing the Coldstream on the ridge—and the 32nd Guards Brigade was brought up to resume the advance.

Brigadier Johnson gave out his orders just behind St. Martin. He ordered the 1st Bn. Welsh Guards to extend the front to the right by occupying St. Denis Maisoncelles and to link up with the 11th Armoured Division across the valley beyond. The 3rd Bn. Irish Guards, with one squadron of Coldstream tanks and the support of the whole divisional artillery, was to drive the enemy off the further lip of the ridge above the Le Tourneur valley, which they were still holding; once it was established there, the King's Company of the Grenadiers and a troop of Irish tanks were to attempt to rush and seize the bridge in Le Tourneur, supported by the 615th Field Squadron. As if to emphasise the urgency of the situation, and the uncomfortable fact that the Germans still had observation over almost the whole area in which we were operating, a hail of shells fell all around as the final orders were being given. Among many casualties were Sergeant Clerke, the driver of Brigadier Johnson's scout-car, who was killed, and Lieutenant-Colonel W. L. Newell, D.S.O., commander of the West Somerset Yeomanry, who was seriously wounded.

The 3rd Bn. Irish Guards had full observation of the objective from the crest of the ridge and sufficient, if not ample, time in which to stage the attack and to get full information from their fellow guardsmen. Despite heavy fire in the early stages the operation was quickly successful and all the Germans either killed or driven out. The Grenadiers and the Irish tanks then went through, but the light was already failing and they found that Le Tourneur comprised a large number of houses which contained an even larger number of Germans. It was too considerable an undertaking for one company at such an hour, and the tanks could not operate in the dark. They were ordered back and Lieutenant-Colonel Vandeleur was told to send his two reserve companies through in the early hours of the morning. At two o'clock they set forth, one company on either side of the main road. All went smoothly and after some time Major Neale, commander of the 615th Field Squadron, decided to try to get through to the bridge. He could not get any infantry support to take him through the village as that had been by-passed by the two wings of the attack; it was in flames and the night was very black, but he decided to take a chance and went forward in his scout-car with Lieutenant A. G. C. Jones, who had been forward reconnaissance officer on that route throughout the previous day. As they reached a little square by the church Major Neale, who was looking out of the turret, saw a dark and sinister shape close by with a long ugly gun pointing up the road; it was a German Mark IV tank and, what was more, he could see through a chink in the armour that the light inside was switched on. Quickly he told the driver to turn down a side lane and stopped when out of view. He got out and went on foot to reconnoitre the bridge, which happily was quite intact. On returning to the scout-car he found that Lieutenant Jones had been thinking on the same lines about the tank as himself; he had armed some grenades to lob inside it to destroy it with its crew. They all three crept stealthily up but what was their surprise to discover that it was unoccupied, having presumably been abandoned during the heavy bombardment preceding the advance. It was later recovered and found to be in perfect working order, so it was presented to the 5th Guards Brigade Workshops, where it did yeoman service as a recovery vehicle. Long before daylight the 3rd Bn. Irish Guards was in full possession of Le Tourneur and of its bridge.

It had been a gruelling day and a relatively expensive one in casualties. At the same time it had been successful, both on our own sector and even more notably on our right flank. This we discovered when the Irish pushed down the Le Tourneur valley to the point where it meets that of the Souleuvre and crossed the bridge to find that the 11th Armoured Division had duly occupied Le Bény Bocage that afternoon without serious opposition. It had also been able to take possession of the bridge carrying the main road over the Souleuvre from the far side later in the evening and to occupy the cross-roads at St. Charles de Percy. All therefore seemed set for a continuation of the advance at increased speed the next day, August 2nd, and both divisions issued ambitious orders. Ours were to make for Vassy led by the Cromwells of the 2nd Bn. Welsh Guards for the first time in their original role of divisional reconnaissance; the 5th Guards Brigade was ordered to move on two centre-lines after crossing the Souleuvre; the Grenadier Group was to turn sharp left and follow the course of the valley to Montcharivel, crossing a shoulder of the Mont Pinçon massif before coming down on the South side; the Coldstream-Irish Group was to continue straight on to St. Charles de Percy, where it also turned left to Montchamp and Estry. The idea was excellent, but the Germans were equally doing some quick thinking and had by now become fully aware of where their danger lay. The commander of the 21st Panzer Division also correctly appreciated the importance of the bridge at Cathéolles and the suitability of the area for defence and in the event we seem only just to have forestalled him by a very short head.

Cathéolles was reached and the bridge crossed without incident in the early morning. No. 1 Squadron of the 2nd Bn. Welsh Guards under Major A. A. Bushell then proceeded along the road towards Montcharivel. On the right rose a steep slope covered for the most part with trees and on the left lay a narrow marshy valley with another hill on the far side. It was impossible for tanks to leave the road, which was narrow and winding and often quite blind. Despite some sniping and mortaring and one deliberate attack by infantry they had almost reached Montcharivel when the leading tank was hit and set on fire. The road was completely blocked and Major Bushell was ordered to withdraw and hand over to the Grenadiers.

Major W. L. Consett led No. 3 Squadron through St. Charles de Percy but found his path blocked at Courteil, which was strongly held. The country here was easier and he probed round to Maisoncelles, only to find that full of resolute Germans also. Undismayed he struck out still further to the South and succeeded in reaching the high ground South of La Marvindière, from where he sent patrols towards Estry which came up against strong opposition. The other two Squadrons eventually followed and also established themselves in this area.

The first essential for the Grenadiers was to seize the outlying spur on the right on which stood the village Drouet, since it lay between the two axes of advance and effectively commanded both. In order to clear their own way, however, they must also drive the Germans from the hill on the North side of the Souleuvre on which lay the village of Arclais. The left flank was in any case extremely vulnerable, as XXX Corps was still held up and the 15th (Scottish) Division had only been able in consequence to make a very limited advance. At the same time the King's Company and No. 2 Squadron were sent to drive away a force of tanks and infantry that were threatening the main road at close quarters. This they accomplished successfully, but the other assignments were very much more difficult. No. 4 Company's attack on the Arclais hill failed entirely; it was strongly held and too steep for the troop of tanks in support to negotiate. No. 2 Company did indeed succeed in occupying Drouet on the all-important spur, but the tanks of No. 3 Squadron, which was with them, could get no further, and attempts by the infantry to push on to the higher ground beyond were met with murderous fire. They were counter-attacked with tanks in the evening and withdrew from the village, digging in on the crest of the spur for the night all too conscious of their precarious position.

The Irish-Coldstream Group had great difficulty in getting through at all, owing to the unexpectedly early hold-up of the Grenadiers. They were forced to halt while a way through was cleared and, as a long stretch of road short of Cathéolles was in full view of the Germans on both the Drouet and Arclais hills, they were heavily shelled and mortared. The 5th Bn. Coldstream Guards lost their second commanding officer in two days when Lieutenant-Colonel B. E. Luard was wounded on this occasion. But eventually the tanks succeeded in forcing a way through with most of the Coldstream infantry riding on them. The Grenadier attacks by this time saved them from any unwelcome attention from the Germans as they wound their way through the defile to St. Charles de Percy but, like the Welsh Guards before them, they found all approaches to Courteil barred. Eventually they too struck Southwards across country and harboured when night came just short of La Marvindière; although they were within a few fields of the Welsh Guards neither knew it till the next day.

The 11th Armoured Division also came up against increased resistance that day and, though it succeeded in penetrating to the main road to Vassy at one point about four miles East of Vire, reported that opposition was becoming extremely strong in all directions. Further West XIX U.S. Corps, after advancing almost as far as Vire, found the 3rd Parachute Division dug in in strength on the outskirts.

The 5th Guards Brigade was fully committed in two widely divergent directions and the 32nd Guards Brigade was ordered that evening to force a way through the main road to Montchamp and Estry the next day. Brigadier Johnson deputed the 3rd Bn. Irish Guards to undertake this, supported by a squadron of Coldstream tanks, at the same time bringing the 1st Bn. Welsh Guards up at once to the area immediately South of Cathéolles bridge in order to provide a firm base. When they arrived there were still Germans within six hundred yards who put in a small counter-attack, but they withdrew during the night.

No transport was available to bring the Irish up and it took them almost the whole day to make their way on foot to St. Charles de Percy. The road was littered with dead horses and destroyed transport and shelling was almost continuous, so it was not a pleasant trip. No sooner arrived in the late afternoon than No. 1 Company under Major D. G. Kingsford moved off towards Courteil. In view of the experience gained at Cagny the advance was carried out cautiously from one limited objective to another, making each in turn a base for the next move. Major Kingsford ran into heavy fire and was held up short of the first objective and an attempt to feel his way round to the left was equally unsuccessful. Major T. R. D. Batt, the Coldstream squadron commander, then led up one of his troops on foot and together with Major Kingsford made a third attempt. This was not only successful in itself but enabled the second objective at the far end of Courteil to be captured without further difficulty. It was now quite dark and, as the country on either side consisted of the usual confusing small fields with thick hedgerows and deep ditches, Lieutenant-Colonel Vandeleur decided to wait till daylight before attempting to attack the considerably larger village of Maisoncelles.

The Grenadiers had meanwhile been subject to constant attention from the Germans all day, particularly those established on the Drouet Spur. Three deliberate counter-attacks were launched against them; the most determined was the last, at about eight o'clock in the evening, and it was undoubtedly intended not only to recapture the spur but also the Cathéolles bridge. At one moment the situation was critical and it was largely owing to the pluck and determination of the company commander, Major R. H. Bromley, who refused to leave even when wounded and rendered deaf by a shell, that the position was held.

It had become a matter of absolute urgency to capture the whole of the high ridge beyond Drouet. The Germans had indeed failed in their primary object of preventing us from crossing the Souleuvre through being forestalled at Le Bény Bocage. But possession of the slightly higher Easterly ridge gives observation over all the ground in every direction; quite a small force, if well equipped, could force a far superior body of troops to deploy and make a deliberate attack to capture it before any further advance could be possible, and this is what the Germans had decided to do. In view of their known disorganised state it had been worth while making the attempt to by-pass it, but the arrival of another reinforcement of first-class calibre that day in the shape of the 9th S.S. Panzer Division made a halt to capture it essential.

The ridge presented great difficulties to an attack, in that the slopes were too steep, and often also too densely wooded, to be practicable for tanks, as the Grenadiers had already discovered. It was essentially a job for infantry and in view of its size it would need quite a large number. XXX Corps had by this time moved up sufficiently for the 15th (Scottish) Division to be spared some of its task of flank protection, and General O'Connor, commanding VIII Corps, ordered a brigade to be provided. This was the 44th (Lowland) Brigade, and the 1st Bn. Welsh Guards was temporarily put under its command as a fourth battalion. After an artillery barrage of large proportions, the advance started at half-past six on the morning of August 4th, and proceeded well against only minor opposition, the Germans having withdrawn their main forces after imposing the desired delay. The Welsh were on the right flank and by mid-day had reached and cut the road from Montcharivel to Montchamp at Les Fieffes. On the way they took twenty prisoners.

The German withdrawal from the ridge was a welcome relief throughout the division, since the observation that it afforded had made life distinctly uncomfortable. This did not only apply to the forward units, as even Divisional Headquarters came in for a fair share of the punishment; although itself sited on a reverse slope West of Le Tourneur, the turning off the main road was in full view of the enemy, who did not fail to take advantage of the fact each time that a conference assembled or dispersed. The Reverend A. S. Pryor, a popular figure who had been Chaplain to the Leicestershire Yeomanry since the outbreak of war, was killed on one such occasion when a shell burst directly in front of his car. Major-General G. H. A. MacMillan, commander of the 15th (Scottish) Division, was wounded in the leg sufficiently badly to have to be sent back to England.

Brigadier Gwatkin also had a narrow escape from serious injury the same day. The defile through which the main road passed near the crossing of the Souleuvre has already been mentioned; so regularly did the enemy make use of his ability to observe it that it quickly became christened "Mortar Gulch". The 5th Guards Brigade had moved its Tactical Headquarters forward to St. Charles de Percy and Brigadier Gwatkin was summoned back to a conference at Divisional Headquarters. He set off perched on top of a scout-car, counting on the Germans paying no attention to one solitary vehicle, but a burst came down just after he reached the far side of the river. The scout-car drove on and he remained imperturbable on the top, but all was not as well as it seemed. He had received several pieces of shrapnel in his face and neck; the driver was severely wounded in the face and head and narrowly missed losing an eye. The greatest credit was due to this man, Lance-Corporal Burton, as he drove on as far as the 19th Field Ambulance, more than a mile up the road, as if nothing had happened. Only on arrival there were the facts realised and it became a matter for speculation how the scout-car had continued so far, since both offside tyres were flat and the brakes did not function at all, while the car itself looked like a pepper-pot.

While the 1st Bn. Welsh Guards was advancing along the ridge, the 3rd Bn. Irish Guards continued with the previous evening's plan and captured the main portion of Maisoncelles in the morning without great difficulty. But there were plenty of Germans with offensive intent around, as had been shown earlier when an attack which had somehow missed the forward companies came in directly on Battalion Headquarters near St. Charles de Percy. It was unco-ordinated and unsupported and was driven off at the cost of thirty dead and eleven prisoners but none the less it had been pressed home bravely enough. The explanation was soon forthcoming when it was found that the men belonged to the 9th S.S. Panzer Division and had been put into battle against us immediately on arrival and before any preparation was possible. This counter-attack, in combination with news that had filtered through of constant attacks on the other Irish-Coldstream Group at La Marvindière, made Lieutentant-Colonel Vandeleur decide to secure his right flank before swinging left to Montchamp. He therefore directed X Company Scots Guards to seize a cross-roads a short way out from Maisoncelles in the direction of La Marvindière. It got there all right, but just short of it had a brisk encounter during which the accompanying Coldstream tanks destroyed a Panther and an assault gun. The Germans meanwhile started to show their resentment in no uncertain terms with heavy shelling and mortaring and, as he had apparently touched on a sensitive spot, Lieutenant-Colonel Vandeleur proceeded to build up a thorough defence of the village, bringing up some of his own mortars and also a section of seventeen-pounder guns of the 21st Anti-Tank Regiment.

The battalions of the 44th Brigade had been equally successful to the North of the 1st Bn. Welsh Guards, so, as soon as our hold on the ridge was consolidated and since the 3rd Bn. Irish Guards was already fully occupied, orders came to Lieutenant-Colonel Heber-Percy to turn right and descend to the plain to capture Montchamp. As a precaution he first sent Nos. 3 and 4 Companies to occupy intermediate objectives, which they did without great difficulty, although they took a good number of prisoners. Then, soon after six o'clock, the Prince of Wales' Company and No. 2 Company advanced into the village itself. On the way they ran into two tanks, a Panther and a Mark IV; Captain Sir Richard Powell knocked out the latter with a Piat and the Panther promptly withdrew. Otherwise their entry was only opposed by snipers, one of whom, however, shot and seriously wounded Lieutenant-Colonel Heber-Percy as he was following in the wake of the companies. This man was in civilian clothes and was fortunately caught and promptly shot. The leading troops had just reached the far end of the village when a furious counter-attack was launched against them by infantry and tanks, mainly Panthers of the 9th S.S. Panzer Division. The two companies were caught at a considerable disadvantage; in addition to the loss of their commanding officer they had not yet had time to make defensive dispositions nor to dig in; nor had the Coldstream tanks that were to support them, nor even their own anti-tank guns, had time to arrive. No. 2 Company was cut in half and its commander, Major M. J. Turnbull, an international cricketer and footballer as well as a fine soldier, was killed; the Prince of Wales' Company was completely overrun and also lost a large number of men. A troop of Coldstream tanks rushed up in support at this moment and a game of hide-and-seek ensued between them and the Panthers; the latter seemed unwilling to fight at close quarters and were inclined to withdraw out of sight. However, they never moved far and when, after a great deal of confused fighting, it became obvious that consolidation before nightfall was out of the question Major G. G. Fowke, who had taken over command of the battalion, ordered withdrawal. But it was with the greatest difficulty that Major J. M. Miller finally extricated the remnants of the Prince of Wales' Company. He waited to the very last to superintend and was lucky to get away. His second-in-command, Captain Sir Richard Powell, was less lucky and was wounded and captured unconscious; after a series of adventures and a brilliant escape he was to rejoin the battalion a few weeks later.

By nightfall Major Fowke had succeeded in establishing the battalion on the line of the intermediate objectives. The leadership that he showed on being called upon so suddenly to shoulder the responsibility for a very delicate situation was outstanding. Altogether the battalion had every reason to be proud of the way in which it reacted on this unpleasant occasion. It received its reward the next morning when Montchamp was found deserted by the enemy.

Some credit for the evacuation, however, could also probably be ascribed to the gallant action fought by Captain E. J. Hope with X Company Scots Guards and the supporting section of the 21st Anti-Tank Regiment during the night at Maisoncelles, which lay less than a mile away across a small stream. It was just as well that the seventeen-pounder guns had been sent to join him, because shortly after midnight infantry, accompanied by several tanks, appeared suddenly from the South. The anti-tank gunners were expecting nothing of the kind at that particular moment and were resting, but the layer shot at the leading tank at ten yards' range and it burst into flames. This illuminated conveniently the other enemy tanks and some very close fighting followed, during which Captain Hope had to call down defensive fire almost on top of his own men. Later on, after this attack had been beaten off, an enemy supply echelon sailed into the village and was severely mauled. This latter column was found the following morning to have included a water truck captured from the 2nd Bn. Welsh Guards and a petrol lorry captured from the 2nd Bn. Irish Guards, while the anti-tank section had performed the superb feat of destroying in the dark one Panther and four Mark III tanks; furthermore, the discovery of the German regimental aid post, literally swimming in blood, showed that the attacking infantry had suffered as well. It had been a magnificently fought action, as was recognised by the award of no less than three Military Crosses, to Captain Hope, to Lieutenant A. Drewe and to Lieutenant N. Thorpe; also of the Military Medal to Sergeant Harris, of the 21st Anti-Tank Regiment, and to Lance-Sergeant Mitchell.

It is now time to turn our attention once more to the 2nd Bn. Welsh Guards, the 2nd Bn. Irish Guards and the 5th Bn. Coldstream Guards, the last named temporarily under the command of Major the Marquess of Hartington; it will be remembered that all three battalions harboured near La Marvindière on the night of August 2nd. The following morning the several groups into which they had become divided discovered each other, but they also found that they were virtually cut off, as a considerable stretch of the only available road up was covered by enemy fire, with the result that only armoured vehicles could get through. None the less they pressed forward with the advance, only to find, as has already been seen elsewhere, that the 9th S.S. Panzer Division had arrived and had occupied Estry and Le Busq before them. These two villages lay on a ridge along the top of which ran the main road from Aunay-sur-Odon to Vire; to reach them from La Marvindière it was necessary first of all to go down a slope and then up again on the far side of a stream; the country was such that no approach existed which was not in full view of the enemy. They persisted with the attack all day, but had perforce to withdraw to La Marvindière in the evening after severe losses. About this time contact was made with the 29th Armoured Brigade on the right; the 23rd Hussars and the 8th Bn. Rifle Brigade had succeeded in crossing the Estry–Vire road but were being violently counter-attacked and there seemed no prospect of further progress for the moment on that sector either. An all-round defence was therefore organised and during the ensuing forty-eight hours they had a most unpleasant time, suffering from heavy shelling and mortaring almost continuously and subjected to periodical counter-attacks from all points of the compass.

As if to underline the difficulties, word had come that morning that the gun positions of the Leicestershire Yeomanry were being attacked by Panthers near Point 176, a small road-junction midway between St. Charles de Percy and La Marvindière, which was always referred to as such from the way the map was printed. The regiment had been ordered the previous night to move up at dawn in order to support the battalions at La Marvindière and before the precarious nature of their situation was known. It is true that Major the Hon. B. Brassey, who as second-in-command was responsible for choosing the gun-positions, had qualms and asked for an escort, but none was available and the guns were duly deployed in small fields just South-East of the cross-roads. They engaged a number of targets for some time but when Lieutenant Brisbourne, of P Battery, went forward to observe he saw rather more than he bargained for in the shape of a Panther not more than four hundred yards away. No sooner had he sent back word than small-arms fire opened on the battery position and four more Panthers appeared. Two guns and the Command Post vehicle were quickly hit and the attack soon also involved R Battery in the neighbouring field. As soon as Major Brassey realised the situation he ordered Q Battery, which was closest to Point 176, to cover the withdrawal of the other two. Most of the guns got out all right, but it was not so easy to move the wheeled vehicles, owing to the high banks; a water truck became stuck and an ammunition truck was hit and blown up, and eventually nine in all had to be abandoned. Q Battery was by this time also under attack and fired smoke to cover its own withdrawal; the guns retired one by one and last of all went Captain Winslow, the battery captain.

As Captain Winslow left the first seventeen-pounder self-propelled gun of Q Battery the 21st Anti-Tank Regiment arrived. The minute Brigadier Gwatkin heard that the field guns were being attacked by Panthers he had ordered Major R. I. G. Taylor to take his battery up to help them. At first the German tanks were elusive and the anti-tank gunners had to spend a good deal of time dealing with infantry who were trying to work towards them with machine-guns; but at last Major

Taylor's layer got his chance and knocked out a Panther as it traversed a gateway. After a further hour's shooting at infantry that were still trying to get at them three Panthers suddenly advanced into a field directly in front of Headquarters Troop. Major Taylor, laying his own gun, got the first and Lieutenant Hawker, the troop commander, the second; the third beat a very hasty retreat. Two troops of tanks from the 1st Bn. Coldstream Guards and No. 2 Company the 3rd Bn. Irish Guards arrived in the evening to strengthen the position with a view to opening up the route to La Marvindière once more. Major T. R. D. Batt, M.C., who as squadron commander was personally leading up the tanks, was killed by a sniper when he got out of his tank to investigate a hold-up *en route*. Scarcely had the Irish company commander, Captain E. M. Woods, arrived than he was similarly shot dead while making a reconnaissance. This mixed force held on for the next thirty-six hours subject to constant attacks similar to those experienced by the force at La Marvindière and the Irish Guards lost another brave officer when Lieutenant T. E. King-Harman was killed in the act of charging a machine-gun post. The anti-tank gunners, however, achieved one more triumph. Sergeant Farrow fired three rounds at a spot where he thought that he could see and hear a tank in an orchard and was rewarded with a satisfactory explosion; next day he discovered that he had indeed killed a Panther, but through two stone walls of a cow-byre. For their part in this action Major Taylor and Lieutenant Hawker each received the Military Cross.

It may be imagined that these events along the line of approach did not ease the situation of the battalions at La Marvindière; the bringing up of ammunition and supplies and the evacuation of casualties were equally difficult, and before long there were all too little of both the former and all too many of the latter. The Coldstream had been able to bring almost nothing with them, as they had ridden on the tanks, and they had therefore had to share the supplies of the Irish. The number of wounded was increasing hourly, largely due to the severe shelling. This resulted indirectly in the severe injury of Major Lord Willoughby de Eresby, commander of the 129th Battery of the Leicestershire Yeomanry, which had always worked with the 2nd Bn. Irish Guards. When reconnoitring a way to get supplies up in a Jeep he was caught in a concentration and jumped into a ditch. A tank which was on the far side did not see him and backed, pinning his legs under a track. Both his feet were badly crushed and he joined the many others waiting for evacuation at the Regimental Aid Post. The medical officer in charge, Captain H. A. Ripman, came near to achieving miracles under almost continuous shell-fire. In addition to his normal orderlies he had an extra assistant in a French woman from one of the farmhouses in the village. She nursed the wounded devotedly throughout the battle and with complete disregard of danger.

By the afternoon of August 4th matters had become very serious indeed. It was impossible to spare infantry to clear the road short of evacuating the position; a supply column had been brought through the 29th Armoured Brigade area under arrangements kindly made by its brigadier and was waiting North of the awkward bit of road about a mile away for an opportunity to get through, after having had its leading vehicles destroyed; Captain Ripman had collected the casualties in a farmhouse at the near end of La Marvindière. At that moment an unlucky burst of mortar-fire landed in and around the Regimental Aid Post. There were already fifty casualties and this caused yet more, including the Irish Guards adjutant, Captain A. C. Crichton. Something just had to be done to get them away. At this moment Lieutenant J. A. Fergusson-Cuninghame, a liaison officer from the 5th Guards Brigade Headquarters, arrived in a scout-car and immediately offered to guide an ambulance convoy back and to bring the supplies up if he could be given half an hour in which to reconnoitre a different route. This he did and returned, slightly wounded by a spent bullet which had lodged in his back, but full of enthusiasm. An ambulance convoy improvised out of ammunition lorries was waiting for him under the direction of Major G. A. M. Vandeleur and together they set off at top speed. The Germans opened up with everything they had at the resulting dust but failed to hit anything, and all the wounded got back safely. Major Vandeleur and Lieutenant Fergusson-Cuninghame now set about helping to get the supply column up. They put their scout-cars one at each end of the gauntlet and, calling up a single vehicle at a time, told it to drive at top speed to the next scout-car and after that to carry on in its own time. The Panther traverse was no match for this manœuvre and the whole convoy got in safely. Lieutenant Fergusson-Cuninghame was subsequently awarded the Military Cross for his part in the day's activities.

Although shelling continued monotonously on August 5th, the situation eased considerably subsequent to the capture of Maisoncelles and Montchamp. In the meantime the Grenadier Group had been moved up to St. Charles de Percy and was ordered to sweep the country between there and La Marvindière; they found nothing except for the burnt-out shells of the tanks destroyed by Major Taylor's battery. This raised hopes that the Germans might be preparing to withdraw from Estry and Le Busq, so the 3rd Bn. Irish Guards was ordered to move forward to Les Ecoublets and to clear the road up to Estry with a view to the 15th (Scottish) Division making an attack in two days' time. The 5th Bn. Coldstream Guards was told to seize Le Busq if possible the next day as a preparatory measure.

Lieutenant-Colonel E. R. Hill had just arrived from England to take command of the 5th Bn. Coldstream Guards and he made a careful plan, together with Lieutenant-Colonel Finlay of the Irish Guards. Two squadrons of Irish tanks were to support the attack with fire and the third, that of Major N. S. P. Whitefoord, M.C., was to go forward with the infantry. The advance started at four o'clock in the afternoon and reached the main road on the summit without undue difficulty. But when our troops started to move down the forward slope on the other side they were met with devastating fire. Both forward companies started to lose men heavily; Major Whitefoord was wounded through the knee as he stood up in his tank to try to see over a hedge; Lieutenant F. D. P. McCorkell and his whole crew were killed instantly when by a million to one chance a mortar bomb fell down the turret of his tank and blew it to smithereens. Lieutenant-Colonel Hill decided to hold the Northern part of Le Busq on the near side of the ridge, effectively denying the use of the further part to the enemy, and drew his men back to the line of the road content with an important, if limited, gain of territory.

The enemy's temper and disinclination to yield any further territory was shown even more positively on the sector of the 11th Armoured Division, where a vicious counter-attack was launched that evening on the salient jutting out to the Vire–Vassy road. It was led by the 10th S.S. Panzer Division but included other troops of first-class quality also, and its intention was at least to eliminate the salient completely. Losses were very heavy on both sides but it was eventually driven off after gaining only a few hundred yards of ground.

Although the 3rd Bn. Irish Guards occupied Les Ecoublets without opposition the 15th (Scottish) Division found Estry defended with tremendous determination the next day, August 7th, and was only able to establish itself in the Northern outskirts after severe casualties. It was obvious that the Germans did not intend to let the Vire–Estry line go without a bitter struggle—the decision to launch the now historic Mortain counter-offensive that day made it, as we now know, even more imperative to hold on—and General O'Connor decided that the two armoured divisions should content themselves with holding the line in the centre of the Corps front, while pressure was exerted by infantry on either side. We were therefore told that we could count on forty-eight hours of comparative rest.

Nobody was sorry for this after the exertions of the past few days; despite the so-called rest period after the battles at Caen we had had no real opportunity for doing so to any good purpose since the few days near Bayeux in the middle of July. Although some battalions were still in the line, even they were able to send back small parties of men in turn to enjoy baths and cinemas, let alone some peace and quiet. Fortunately the weather was heavenly—it had been constantly good since the start of the Caumont offensive—and the country was seen to be quite beautiful once the chance was given of looking at it other than in the light of the difficulties it provided against the movement of armour. It resembled the West of England in many respects and was strikingly unlike the landscape that is normally associated with France, valleys such as that of the Souleuvre being strongly reminiscent of the combes of Devonshire. This river incidentally provided admirable bathing, of which many members of the division took advantage in order to get rid of the all-pervading dust of the roads.

There was, however, all too little time for such relaxations before more hard work was required. A renewed attack on Estry by the 44th Brigade on August 8th had to be called off after suffering excessive casualties and that evening we were warned that on the next day we should have to take over a good part of the frontage of the 11th Armoured Division as well as our own, as that formation was being taken out temporarily prior to employment elsewhere. The fact was that plans were having to be altered every few hours to meet the rapidly changing situation. News of the German counter-offensive at Mortain had been coming in dramatically during the past forty-eight hours. At the time it seemed to us incredible that the enemy should really have thought it possible to get through to Avranches at this late hour and so to cut off all the American troops South of that line. It was indeed his obvious target, as has already been pointed out, since all supplies for the advancing Americans had still to come through the comparatively narrow gap between Vire and the sea to the West; but although in theory the appreciation was sound it was not so in fact, as it ignored the relative strength of the German forces and our own. It is of course now known that Field-Marshal von Kluge, and indeed most of the Generals on the spot, disagreed strongly with the assumptions of Hitler and the High Command, but repeated warnings had failed to induce them to abandon their obstinate complacency.

Field-Marshal von Kluge made the best of a bad job and launched the attack suddenly and with the greatest strength in armour that he could muster. Although the possibility had always been realised, the Americans were for the moment taken aback and it had some initial success; but it ended in disaster as it was bound to do. While it did not concern us directly it should be pointed out again that it had an important bearing on the enemy's recent tactics regarding ourselves. Once the Americans had streamed through the Avranches gap the situation in Brittany from his point of view was out of hand, unless they could be cut off from their bases. Our advance, though on a smaller scale than that of the Americans, threatened to remove all possibility of such a counter-blow if we succeeded in penetrating South of Vire. Moreover, a second threat was implicit in that we might also cut off the escape of his troops between Caumont and the Orne, all bridges over this river having been destroyed. In this connection we learned also on August 8th that the whole of the Mont Pinçon area was now in our hands, and thus our forces commanded the entire stretch of territory West of the Orne. Following on this, the long-awaited Canadian attack towards Falaise had begun that morning.

Our flanks were now secure for the first time since the operation started, but unfortunately this meant at the same time that the Germans had to some extent achieved their purpose. They had felt on August 2nd that our threat to them was vital, and the 9th S.S. Panzer Division was rushed up to delay us, followed later by its always faithful colleague, the 10th S.S. Panzer Division. They had no time in which to prepare a line and could not in any case have held one owing to the shortage of infantry; therefore they adopted the tactics of mobile battle-groups which were admirably suited to the country. They were given a suicidal task, and from the evidence it did indeed involve death for the vast majority of them. Though they had the loathsome characteristics inseparable from all S.S. troops they must be given the credit of having been clever fighters and brave men. Despite their skilful defence and the unfavourable nature of the country for attack, VIII Corps could have no doubt broken through, but only by a large-scale operation with considerable air support, and here the question of priority arose. All available aircraft were at this time needed on the American and Canadian sectors, which were considered the most important. It so happened that we found ourselves at the head of the so-called "Sack" in which the Germans were about to be trapped; we were therefore ordered merely to hold the line that we had reached, making at the same time one or two limited attacks in order to tie down the enemy forces.

The 3rd Division had been brought round recently from the area East of Caen, from which it had never yet moved since the original landings, to act on the right flank of VIII Corps in the built-up area round Vire; it now took over the right half of the sector of the 11th Armoured Division. The left half was taken over by the 5th Guards Brigade, with the Grenadier Group on the high ground South of Forgues and the 3rd Bn. Irish supported by the 1st Bn. Coldstream a little further East at Sourdevalle. This was the salient against which the counter-attack by the 10th S.S. Panzer Division had been directed. Very heavy casualties had been suffered throughout its occupation and it was a peculiarly unpleasant position; completely overlooked by German posts on the Perrier ridge, it could only be taken over during the hours of darkness and was subject to continuous shelling. Major D. G. Kingsford was killed in his slit trench during the very first day that the Irish spent there and all who occupied it felt instinctively that it was a place of evil omen. The 5th Bn. Coldstream Guards and the 1st Bn. Welsh Guards, under the 32nd Guards Brigade, retained their positions at Le Busq and in front of the Perrier ridge. The 2nd Bn. Irish Guards continued to support the Coldstream and, since an armoured counter-attack was still a possibility, albeit after the Mortain fiasco a remote one, the 32nd Guards Brigade was recompensed for its shortage of armour by the loan of the 3rd Bn. Scots Guards which, with its Churchills, was allotted to the Welsh.

By the first light on August 10th the relief of the 11th Armoured Division was complete and that afternoon orders were given out for Operation "Grouse" to take place the following morning. While the general object was to continue to exert pressure on the enemy on our front, the immediate purpose was the capture of the high ground on the main Vire–Vassy road in the Boulay-aux-Chats area, to be followed if successful by a further advance to Mont Cerisy and Tinchebray. The 3rd Division and the 2nd U.S. Division beyond them were making similar attacks and the 11th Armoured Division was to be brought in to conform on our left. The main weight of the attack, directed through Chênedolle on Boulay-aux-Chats, was to be made by the 32nd Guards Brigade, which was therefore allotted the larger part of the available artillery support. The Churchills of the 3rd Bn. Scots Guards also were more suitable than our own Shermans for dealing with the dug-in tanks and anti-tank guns that the Germans were known by now to have installed in this area; extremely valuable their support was to prove.

The first phase consisted of the capture of a high ridge between Le Bas Perrier and Pierres, from which cross-fire could be directed against the whole axis of advance. This task was given to the 1st Bn. Welsh Guards, supported by tanks both from the 3rd Bn. Scots Guards and the 2nd Bn. Irish Guards, and it was carried through successfully despite the heavy opposition and the loss of a hundred casualties. The second phase consisted of a simultaneous advance by the remainder of the division to the line Chênedolle–Viessoix. The 5th Bn. Coldstream Guards, supported by another mixed force of Churchill and Sherman tanks, succeeded in reaching Chênedolle after hard fighting, and the two Grenadier battalions cut the main road at Viessoix. But the Coldstream found themselves still in close contact in the late afternoon and only one troop of Grenadier tanks had been able to get through and that by a most unreliable track; they had found progress slow and hard owing to numerous mines and demolitions, while concealed Bazooka teams proved expensive to the tanks.

Meanwhile the 3rd Bn. Irish Guards and the 1st Bn. Coldstream Guards had had the worst time of all. They were to cut across the road to the East of the Grenadiers but their role was adjudged the least important and they could only consequently be spared the support of one field battery. Lieutenant-Colonel Vandeleur pointed out, though in vain, that their start line lay at the top of a forward slope in direct view of the Germans dug in with tanks and anti-tank guns on the ridge opposite; to make matters worse their line of advance was also under direct fire from Chênedolle, not yet captured by the 5th Bn. Coldstream Guards. No covered approach existed to either flank and the attacking troops came under devastating fire of every description the moment they started to advance. To cut a tragic story short, the tanks that ventured forward were all knocked out and the two leading companies suffered seventy per cent casualties, including every officer except one, before reaching their first objective at the bottom of the slope. Among those killed were one company commander, Major Eardley-Wilmot, and Lieutenant Lord E. Fitzmaurice; the other company commander, Major D. A. Reid, was seriously wounded.

Meanwhile the divisions on our right had not found progress much easier and in the evening a halting of the operation was ordered. The Germans, having first used this sector as a defensive flank for their Mortain counter-offensive, were now employing it to protect the withdrawal of the remnants which had survived. Consequently it was manned by first-class troops, as was now shown by the discovery that Chênedolle had been defended by the 9th S.S. Panzer Engineer Battalion, while the area to the West was the concern of the 3rd and 5th Parachute Divisions. We were destined to have a good deal to do with German paratroops in the future and were to find that the mass of mines and obstructions met by the Grenadiers, and incidentally also by the 3rd Division, during this operation was always to be expected of them. The S.S. Engineers were fighting without special equipment in a purely infantry role and it was some consolation for our limited success that such valuable troops had had to be used in this manner; moreover they had incurred crippling losses, as was proved when the following day our men carried out the useful but unpleasant duty of counting the corpses and adding their number to that of the prisoners taken.

The following morning we learned that the pressure on the

Second Army front was to be transferred to the two corps to the East. VIII Corps was to content itself with holding its present front as a firm defensive base. Field-Marshal von Kluge had at last obtained Hitler's permission to withdraw and form a new line behind the Seine, and operations towards preventing this, and particularly with a view to the closing of the trap on the German Seventh Army between Falaise and Argentan, were now well under way. Events were moving to a decisive and dramatic climax and, although it was disappointing at the time to have to perform so passive a role, we were to have our fair share of action later.

We were to fulfil essentially the task of an infantry division and we were told that only the minimum necessary number of tanks should be held forward; these were to be dug in wherever suitable positions could be found, while the remainder were to be held back in reserve with deliberate counter-attack roles. Aggressive patrolling was to take place both by day and night and, as both brigades were short of infantry for their new commitments, the 14th Field Squadron was allotted to the 5th Guards Brigade and the 2nd Household Cavalry Regiment to the 32nd Guards Brigade; both were to function in a purely infantry capacity and for the Household Cavalry it must have seemed the supreme indignity, though they fulfilled the unaccustomed tasks in an exemplary fashion.

For the next two days our patrols continued to report the enemy still holding on, but on August 15th they found incipient signs of withdrawal and by the following day our front was entirely clear save for numerous mines and booby-traps. Despite every precaution some casualties were suffered by the division from these infernal affairs and many of us were also sad to learn of the death near by, when his scout-car was blown up by a mine, of Brigadier Sir Walter Barttelot, then commanding the 6th Guards Tank Brigade, and until recently commanding officer of the 4th (Tank) Bn. Coldstream Guards.

That day, August 16th, the Secretary of State for War, Sir James Grigg, and General Montgomery lunched at Divisional

Headquarters; in the evening the division learned that it was to revert to normal grouping and to go into Army Reserve. So, while the flower of the German Army was destroyed in its thousands during the next week, our tasks were of the most menial. The sappers were indeed fully employed on mine-lifting and bridge-building in order to open the main roads to traffic but, apart from the few men required to give them local protection in these tasks, the activities of the remainder of the division were largely confined to the disposal of the dead and rotting cows, of which there were many hundreds in the district. It was a most necessary job from every angle, but not one over which great enthusiasm could be expected.

During this period General Montgomery held an investiture at Divisional Headquarters on August 20th and three days later the Major-General Commanding the Brigade of Guards, Lieutenant-General Sir Charles Loyd, visited all units.

Attention meanwhile was focussed on the replacement of casualties both of men and vehicles, and on the maintenance of those of the latter that had survived. Losses had unfortunately been fairly heavy, and it was the first real opportunity for such work that we had had since landing in France. The reinforcement situation necessitated one important change in the order of battle of the division. X Company Scots Guards, which had formed part of the 3rd Bn. Irish Guards ever since that battalion had joined the division at Malton, was transferred to the 1st Bn. Welsh Guards, since the Irish Guards replacement position happened to be a good deal stronger than that of the Welsh. All concerned were very sad when the moment for the company's departure from the Irish came, since the arrangement had worked particularly smoothly and happily throughout. Lieutenant-Colonel Vandeleur got up a great party for them with all kinds of wonderful and rare things to eat and drink, complete to the tune of pipes, and he made a heartfelt farewell speech. But, despite the natural sorrow felt on all sides, X Company was to find its relations with the Welsh no less happy.

Casualties were the cause also of important staff changes. The

G.S.O. I, Lieutenant-Colonel P. R. C. Hobart, was summoned away to take command of his own battalion, the 1st Royal Tank Regiment. It had always been realised that he could not remain permanently, as he had only been loaned to us for the initial period in view of his operational experience; the division had profited greatly thereby, and we were all very sorry to see him go. Major J. D. Hornung, M.C., Brigade Major of the 32nd Guards Brigade, was appointed in his place; originally adjutant of the 2nd Bn. Irish Guards, he had served in the division since its inception, apart from one brief interlude on the staff of Combined Operations, and no more suitable or popular choice could have been made. He was in turn succeeded by Major the Hon. Michael Fitzalan-Howard, M.C., who, as a squadron commander in the 3rd Bn. Scots Guards, had taken a gallant part in the Le Bas Perrier action in our support only a few days previously. His elder brother, Major the Hon. Miles Fitzalan-Howard, M.C., had already for some time been Brigade Major of the 5th Guards Brigade, providing a situation that must have been very unusual, if not unique, in any division.

Chapter Four

THE ADVANCE TO BRUSSELS

ON AUGUST 23rd the whole division was told to move on the following morning, but not for operational reasons. It is doubtful if any of us were sorry; though the danger, the smells and the noise were all memories of the past, the whole locality was too redolent of unpleasant associations. Our new homes were only some fifteen miles away, near Condé sur Noireau, and we were fairly concentrated so that everybody could visit their friends and partake together of any of the amusements provided, of which there were quite a few. But apart from this the real reason for the move lay in the fact that new operations were already being decided, now that the Normandy campaign was rapidly drawing to a close, and it was considered more convenient for us to concentrate nearer to VIII Corps Headquarters, now situated on the slopes of Mont Cerisy, for planning and administrative purposes.

We were told to enjoy real rest during the next few days, particularly as it was not envisaged that we should get much of it once the next operation started. Our surroundings were ideally conducive to the purpose, since we had passed through into a part of the country that the Germans had had to leave at top speed. Although the centres of the towns and sometimes even simple road junctions presented tragic spectacles, the farm lands in between were quite untouched; and very rich farms they mostly were, with owners who were only too anxious and willing to let us have any milk, butter, cheese and eggs that there were to spare. Hitherto the few houses that were still intact had either been evacuated or filled with refugees, and for the first time we had the opportunity of meeting French people in normal surroundings. They too were mostly meeting British soldiers for the first time, and on the whole both parties were pleased with the encounter. The 3rd Bn. Irish Guards even went so far as to organise an afternoon party with a circus for the local children, which was an uproarious success, partially helped by the weather which was now glorious again after having broken during our last week near Vire. While we were experiencing this carefree, pastoral, existence the Seventh German Army was meeting its doom in the Falaise "pocket" between that town and Argentan, and on August 19th the neck of the "pocket" was finally closed when American troops from the South linked up with the Polish Armoured Division from the North fighting on the left of the First Canadian Army. This presented the Allied Air Forces with targets probably unparalleled in the whole war and in a few days all resistance was at an end.

On August 27th we received a warning order that we were to come under the command of XXX Corps and to move the following day to L'Aigle; this was no longer a matter of the few odd miles to which we had grown accustomed, as our destination was some seventy miles to the East and more than half-way to the Seine.

While the division was moving up, a matter of some considerable difficulty as half the possible roads were impassable owing to demolished bridges and blocked towns, resulting in appalling traffic congestion, the General flew up to see our new Corps Commander, Lieutenant-General B. G. Horrocks, at his Headquarters near Vernon on the banks of the Seine. The 43rd Division had carried out a fine crossing operation of the river here two days previously and the 11th Armoured Division, the 8th Armoured Brigade and the 50th Division were in the process of moving over the two Bailey bridges which had just been built. General Horrocks was most anxious to push on to the River Somme at the earliest possible moment and asked when the division could be up; as it was still over a hundred miles away, the answer had to be that the earliest time for its concentration North of the river was on the night of August 30th. "Then we will start tomorrow," said General Horrocks, "the 11th Armoured Division directed on Amiens and the 8th Armoured Brigade on Beauvais.

You will come on as quickly as you can, moving by night if necessary, and pass through the 8th Armoured Brigade to seize the crossings over the Somme at Corbie." Our right flank would be protected by the 2nd U.S. Armoured Division, which was to conform with our advance on moving out of a more Easterly bridgehead over the Seine at Mantes.

The resultant orders that reached the division were quite short but they were in dramatic contrast to any that had been previously given. It was an exciting moment, as everybody realised that we should at last for the first time be carrying out the mobile operations for which we had been training for three years. Curiously enough, though, experience gained in the preceding weeks led us to adopt a different organisation from any that we had ever practised; during the years of training we had found increasingly that under European conditions, as opposed to those of the desert, tanks and infantry needed to work in close co-operation down to the lowest level if the best results were to be achieved. It has already been pointed out that, in the later days of Normandy, the 5th Guards Brigade had usually been loaned one infantry battalion in exchange for one armoured battalion allotted to the 32nd Guards Brigade, but for the forthcoming operations it was considered best that each brigade should control an equal proportion of infantry and armour. Under the old organisation this would have been impossible to arrange, but the decision to give once more an armoured car regiment to each armoured division, which in our case involved the reversion of the 2nd Household Cavalry Regiment to divisional command after some two years' absence as Corps troops, provided the solution—the 2nd Bn. Welsh Guards was no longer needed for specific reconnaissance purposes, and each brigade could be provided with two armoured and two infantry battalions. As each regiment other than the Scots Guards, which was only represented by X Company, had one battalion of each type, four regimental battle groups were formed; these groups were in future allotted to each brigade as convenient, but for the present operation and in the normal course of events the 5th Guards Brigade received the Grenadier and

Irish Groups and the 32nd Guards Brigade the Coldstream and Welsh Groups.

The Grenadiers led the divisional column; they started to cross the Seine on the afternoon of August 29th and by mid-day the next day the whole Group was complete on the further side. Orders were immediately given to re-form and to move on through Gisors behind the 8th Armoured Brigade in order to push through to the Somme on the following morning. The roads were very crowded but they reached and passed Gisors. At dusk they harboured in the fields by the roadside immediately behind the 8th Armoured Brigade, which had been held up by Germans holding a defile on the main road near Auneuil, twelve miles short of Beauvais. Everybody was very tired after three days of almost continuous movement and hoped for a good night's rest, but at half-past ten all hopes of this were rudely shattered. Orders came to reconnoitre a route at once by which the opposition at Auneuil might be by-passed, with the object of resuming the advance at two o'clock in the morning.

An alternative road was quickly found and the Grenadiers duly led off at the appointed hour. Ahead of them went the Household Cavalry, fanning out over a wide front both to get information and to discourage and disorganise still further the few Germans who were still around. Beauvais was reached without incident at dawn and soon after mid-day one of the armoured car patrols reported that it had seized an intact bridge over the Somme at Corbie, a few miles South-East of Amiens, and that the demolition charges had been removed.

This was superb news. The Grenadiers were told to push across and to establish themselves in a firm bridgehead before dark. The rest of the division, now altogether across the Seine, would meanwhile concentrate between Beauvais and the Somme and the whole would move forward on Arras next morning.

The ground rose fairly abruptly on the far side of the river at Corbie and some Germans were known still to be there. Lieutenant-Colonel Goulburn decided to send the King's Company–No. 2 Squadron Group through first, directed on the ridge to the left of the main road; No. 2 Company–No. 3 Squadron Group was to follow and to make for the ridge to the right, thus securing all ground that commanded a view of the bridge. There were quite a few Germans around and they had one anti-tank gun, which was well concealed and knocked out two tanks of No. 3 Squadron before being itself destroyed. Some of them in particular were advantageously positioned behind the tombstones of a graveyard, but when our infantry deployed the opposition soon melted away, providing some prisoners who were unable to tell us anything of interest.

That night we heard that our success had not been an isolated one. The 11th Armoured Division was also across the Somme, having seized Amiens and found all the bridges there intact. We had no news of the Americans on our right but at least we could count on complete security on our left when we advanced the next day.

To most of us this day brought for the first time a full understanding of what freedom after four years of slavery meant to the inhabitants of the occupied countries. Not that the people of Normandy had not mostly been happy and grateful, as one discovered when one talked to them, but war had gone on too long and at too close quarters for the first flush of enthusiasm still to be present. Here, however, liberty had come with one fell swoop, and it became difficult during this phase to get through any town because of the crowds of radiantly happy and cheering civilians who clustered round the vehicles not only to exchange greetings but to offer fruit, vegetables, wine, flowers, in fact any local produce on which they could lay their hands. It was on this day too that we began to feel a real admiration for the men of the French Forces of the Interior. To a guardsman they may not have been much to look at, but they had had to work under difficult and exceedingly dangerous conditions throughout the occupation and they now proved invaluable to us if only because of the assistance they gave in taking all prisoners off our hands. It is in fact doubtful if the momentum of our advance could have been maintained without them, as there were Germans in every wood and almost in every bush. These were hopelessly disorganised and often only too anxious to surrender, but they could not be left in shoals along the whole line of our communications, nor could we spare anyone to leave behind to look after them. This the French did for us, not only taking charge of all our prisoners but sending out parties in all directions to round them up. Their handling of them was perfectly orderly and correct, if not unduly gentle, and we neither saw nor heard of any cases of excesses; considering the indignities and sufferings that many of these men had had inflicted on their families and themselves we marvelled that their conduct towards the hated enemy could be so exemplary.

This was by no means the limit of their help, however, for as we proceeded we occasionally saw stakes and brushwood by the sides of the road or of tracks; this was their way of showing where the Germans had laid mines, and it was undoubtedly instrumental in saving many lives.

We came to learn, too, before long, that they had given us even more notable assistance that day; they had removed the charges laid by the Germans in the bridge at Corbie and moreover had shot a party of them who had come to set them off. To them therefore a large share of credit for the capture of that bridge was due.

At first light on September 1st we were off again, as Arras had to be captured and there was no time to be lost. The 2nd Bn. Welsh Guards led behind a screen of armoured cars in its proper role of divisional reconnaissance, since we were now in the familiar Somme country which we had constantly studied as ideal for the armoured battle. March tables and the limitations imposed by them were things of the past and Lieutenant-Colonel Windsor-Lewis pressed on at full speed. A few self-propelled guns opposed him and he lost one or two tanks, but neither he nor his men were in any mood for delay. They certainly wasted no time and quite early in the morning reported the capture of no less than the Commander of the entire Somme defences. Soon after eleven o'clock came even more exciting news, that they were already positioned on the high ground immediately north of Arras. The 5th Guards

Brigade quickly joined them there, while the 32nd Guards Brigade was told to occupy the town. The Coldstream Group first entered, led by the tanks of the 1st Battalion now commanded by Lieutenant-Colonel R. F. S. Gooch, M.C. The occupation was soon effected, in the course of which some sharp exchanges occurred. As soon as Lieutenant-Colonel Hill and the infantry of the 5th Bn. Coldstream had time to join the tanks of the 1st Battalion in the Grand' Place, the group was ordered to move on to the high ground beyond and leave the further occupation of Arras to the 1st Bn. Welsh Guards, which had a very special reason for gratification in that the battalion had been the last to leave the town in 1940. It was greeted by a wildly cheering population which became quite delirious when it realised the actual identity of its liberators. The occasion must also have been particularly moving for the General, for it was here that he was wounded and won his Military Cross in the first world war.

The 11th Armoured Division had moved forward simultaneously on our left to take up its position on the continuation of the high ground to the North-West, including Vimy ridge of last war fame. XXX Corps was therefore on its objective, which consisted of the district forming the watershed between the Somme valley and the plain of Flanders, from where it could dominate the whole of North-Eastern France. Not only was it now possible to strike at will across any spot on the Belgian frontier, but the fate of the Channel ports was sealed, even if they might individually hold out for some time, and with them the numerous V.1 launching sites, products of which had been distressing so many of our families during the preceding weeks.

The full disintegration of the German forces resulting from the recent advances, which had become increasingly apparent to us, was meanwhile strikingly confirmed by the news we got that afternoon of the capture on the previous day by the 11th Armoured Division of General Eberbach, the Commander of the German Army conducting the retreat. He had been made prisoner South-West of Amiens with his entire tactical Headquarters, and the very fact of their presence in so vulnerable an area clearly showed the complete lack of information from which they were suffering. Among the documents captured was an Operation Order providing for the defence of the Beauvais line till the day after this very one on which we had reached Arras; we must actually have already been through this line at the time when it was being written. It had apparently been the German intention to stage a series of delaying actions of the type so often met with in Normandy, in order to give to the troops selected to man the Somme line the time and opportunity to arrange for a wholesale demolition scheme and for an extensive defence system. A special Corps Headquarters "Somme" was formed, with all available engineers under command, for the purpose of manning and administering this line, and it was the commander of this force whom we had captured earlier that day. Our divisional commander had dispensed with the usual procedure of interviewing senior enemy commanders on the ground that anyone who had achieved so pitiable a result could not possibly have any information of value to impart. Altogether there seemed no doubt that the Germans felt quite confident that the line of the Somme could be held and that they could successfully keep us at arms' length while it was being fully prepared for defence. They appear to have appreciated that the American threat further East was the more serious one and that, while they were dealing with this as the first consideration, no great difficulty need be anticipated with regard to the pinning down of the British forces in the Lower Seine valley. By now they had no doubt realised that they had made a gross miscalculation, but it was far too late for any action to be taken, even had their organisation and communications still been capable of functioning. Break-throughs are often written about and discussed, but this was for once an occasion when one had genuinely been accomplished.

Only one small pocket of resistance had been discovered, at Albert; this was a large store depot lying a few miles to the East of our centre-line. Owing to its proximity and because it was reported to be strongly garrisoned, the Grenadiers had despatched No. 2 Company and No. 3 Squadron group to deal with it but, after losing two tanks, they were told to content themselves with masking it pending the arrival of the 50th Division, which was following immediately behind us to consolidate and to safeguard our supply lines. In general, however, the situation was so wholly favourable that the General felt justified in sending the Irish Group forward a further fifteen miles to occupy Douai and the crossing over the River Scarpe just beyond. They were involved in some fighting on the outskirts of the town, but by dusk they had successfully carried out their mission.

The following morning, September 2nd, the whole division concentrated behind the Irish, West of Douai, and battalions had a few hours in which to do some much-needed maintenance. It must be admitted that by now we were feeling supremely confident and our only wish was to continue the advance as quickly as possible, but we were told that we had already gone so far and so fast that we were in danger of outrunning our supplies. The strain at this time on all the administrative departments in the division in order to keep up the momentum of the advance was terrific. Staff Officers often spent the entire night on their wireless sets arranging for lorries to bring up extra petrol and other almost equally urgent requirements. The task of those ordered to bring up the supplies, moreover, was made no easier through our having long ago run off all maps issued to us. For some reason only a woefully inadequate number of exceedingly small-scale sheets of our present area was available, and these not unnaturally had to be allotted to the fighting troops. None the less it can truly be said that we were never delayed for one minute by lack of supplies, though on one memorable day the Jerrycans of petrol had to be thrown from a moving lorry on to the Grenadier tanks as they left their harbour area.

Although it did not affect their operational capabilities, it should be remarked in passing that by this time most of our vehicles looked more suitable for the Lord Mayor's show than for use in battle, so covered were they with flowers and streamers and with chalked-on messages of welcome. Of the latter the "V" sign was the most popular of all; it was completely spontaneous in every village and there can be no question but that its use in broadcasts played a very large part in building up resistance. But anybody who could get near a vehicle in safety could please himself, and there were many variants, one of which led to an incident which is worthy of record. On one of these days the scout-car of the General's Aide-de-Camp, Captain the Hon. A. Tryon, had had "Vive la R.A.F." inscribed in large letters on its side. While the concentration of the division was in progress two British fighters hovered enquiringly overhead, circled round to get the sun at their backs and then came in with all guns firing. It was a magnificent sight and there was ample excuse, as our advance had been so phenomenally rapid, but three ammunition lorries went up and with them a great deal of abuse. Captain Tryon, without a word, walked over to his scout-car and added the inscription "Less two Spitfires".

We were now in the industrial district of Northern France and met with an increasingly fervent welcome, but the reason for the even greater joy of the inhabitants at seeing us was painfully apparent. Here, as everywhere, masses of German transport had been shot up by our aircraft as they fled and, as so many of the vehicles were horse-drawn, many horses were lying dead beside them. But whereas, in the rich farming districts through which we had so far passed, we had often before seen their bodies by the wayside, nothing was left here but skeletons. Hitherto we had been inclined to feel that the stories of starvation in Europe, as pictured by our propaganda, had been grossly exaggerated, but no starker evidence could have been provided of the genuine shortage of food from which these unfortunate people must have been suffering.

At about mid-day on September 2nd the Army and Corps Commanders came to see our General and Major-General Roberts, the commander of the 11th Armoured Division; together they had a conference about the next day's advance in a farmhouse on the outskirts of Douai. The plan was ambitious enough in all conscience. If conditions were favourable, airborne troops were to be dropped to seize various key bridges across the

Belgian frontier, particularly at Tournai, together with strong points on a larger plan to cut off the Germans retreating from the coastal areas. The 11th Armoured Division was directed on Ghent and Antwerp, while we were to make for Brussels, the time of our advance depending on the completion of a bombing programme arranged in co-ordination with the airborne landings. For this reason explicit orders were given that no troops were on any account to cross the Belgian frontier; moreover, an urgent message reading, "All ranks will immediately dig slit trenches and hold ground-to-air recognition signals readily available" caused considerable consternation among those who had not yet been aware of the plan.

The General gave out his orders just as darkness was falling, and they did not take long. "My intention is to advance and liberate Brussels," he said, adding, "That is a grand intention." His manner was inspiring to the extent that all who attended the meeting left with the certain knowledge that they could pass on the same spirit to their own order groups. Speed was essential and any serious opposition was to be by-passed, while we were to move on two centre-lines. As this was only the first of many times when we advanced thus in brigade groups on more or less parallel routes, it may be as well on this occasion to give the detailed order of march. While this was never precisely the same in any two instances, it varied only in small particulars according to the needs of the moment, and the following can be regarded as typical.

On the left centre-line the order of march was one squadron of the Household Cavalry, the Grenadier Group, the 5th Guards Brigade Tactical Headquarters, the Coldstream Group, one self-propelled anti-tank battery and the Leicestershire Yeomanry, followed by the 5th Guards Brigade Main Headquarters and supporting troops. On the right centre-line came two squadrons of the Household Cavalry, the Welsh Group, the 32nd Guards Brigade Headquarter Group, including one self-propelled anti-tank battery, the machine-gun Company of the Northumberland Fusiliers and the West Somerset Yeomanry; then the Irish Group, the 21st Anti-Tank Regiment (less two batteries), Divisional

Headquarters Group and the Sapper Companies. Following immediately behind on both routes and in support of the division—which was not normal and only due to exceptional circumstances—came the 231st Infantry Brigade Group, temporarily divorced from the 50th Division, under its Welsh Guards commander, Brigadier Sir Alexander Stanier. Included with it was the 1st Belgian Brigade, which had been rushed up from Le Havre at the last moment. The route on the left lay through Pont-à-Marcq, Rumes, Tournai and Lessines, that on the right through Orchies, Lesdain and Antoing, subsequently following the Route Nationale from Leuze to Brussels. The distance was about seventy-five miles by each route and all left the conference with determination to reach the objective, coupled with a curious inner conviction that somehow it would be achieved, despite the ever-shortening September daylight. In defiance of the inherent improbability of it, the only excitement lay in which Brigade would get there first. The 5th Guards Brigade had a rather twisty and complicated route throughout, while the 32nd Guards Brigade, after an even more difficult start, had one of the main roads into Brussels for the latter part of its journey; a great advantage, particularly with the fast Cromwell tanks of the Welsh Guards in the lead. On the other hand, being the main road, it was likely to be more strongly defended, and the chances were therefore regarded as pretty even. Obviously much would depend on demolitions, but we all felt that it would need considerable opposition to hold us up in a role which we had both practised on exercises innumerable and fought so often in our dreams.

Our only worry concerned the hour at which we could start and, anxious and ungrateful though it may seem, seldom can a more united prayer for unfavourable air weather have been invoked. It may have been the result of a feeling of over-confidence on our part, but, in the present state of the enemy forces, such an expenditure of airborne troops seemed a waste of time and the proposed bombing a senseless sacrifice of lives. If we left at our own hour, which naturally enough was dawn, we considered that we had a good chance of reaching Brussels in the day but, if we had to put it off, the hours of daylight would be too scarce, apart from the fact that the Germans would by then be warned and have time to organise obstacles in our path. It was therefore with profound relief that we learned towards midnight that the storm which had sprung up would prevent the landings and that we were to rely on ourselves and leave when we pleased.

The Household Cavalry crossed the start line at ten minutes to seven on the left and precisely at seven o'clock on the right with the difficult task of screening both brigades. The Welsh Guards crossed at twenty-five minutes past seven on the right and the Grenadiers, who had met slight opposition on the way, at eight o'clock on the left. After that the story was much the same on each centre-line—plain sailing for some miles at a stretch, with occasional small enemy pockets of resistance in towns or at cross-roads consisting of a few anti-tank guns with supporting infantry. The armoured cars were often able to deal with the smaller strong-points themselves by outflanking and shooting them up from the rear; the more important ones they reported and by-passed, leaving them to be dealt with by the combined tank and infantry forces of the leading regimental group in question.

It was not just a ninety-mile pleasure drive and some of the strong-points were stoutly defended. The 32nd Guards Brigade received its first set-back when it heard that a bridge on its route short even of the Belgian frontier had been demolished, but the armoured cars were not there for nothing; within five minutes they had found a way round and were moving again and by ten o'clock they had reached the main road. The Grenadiers had meanwhile met their first strong-point near Pont-à-Marcq, consisting of eight anti-tank guns with infantry. This caused them some delay before they succeeded in liquidating it for the loss of two tanks, by which time the Welsh were similarly held up at Leuze. Their tanks tried to force a way through, but the anti-tank guns were too much for them and the infantry had to deploy, entailing an hour and a half's delay. By the time Leuze was clear the columns were pretty well abreast. Rivalry between the two brigades was becoming increasingly keen and it was at this moment that the General was persuaded to decide on a winning post. He chose the spot where the two routes met, just beyond a railway bridge within the confines of Brussels.

For the next thirty miles both columns moved on unchecked but then the Welsh reported that they were once more held up, this time at Enghien; the Grenadiers, on the other hand, raced on, and for a time it looked as though they must win. Enghien did not, however, prove so stubborn a spot to deal with as had Leuze, and in less than an hour the road was clear again. The Welsh tank crews had profited by the halt to do a little very necessary maintenance, and now Lieutenant-Colonel Windsor-Lewis announced that, with Brigadier Johnson's permission, he intended to head straight for Brussels at maximum speed, even if the pace should prove too much for some of the vehicles and should lead to their collapse on the way. It should be mentioned that Cromwell tanks, with which the Welsh alone in the division were provided, were capable of going fifty miles an hour on an excellent road such as this one was, a speed of which many other military vehicles were not capable and for which reason they had up to now held themselves back a little. It was an unorthodox suggestion, in that it might interfere with the tactical arrangement of the column, but under the circumstances permission was readily granted.

The 5th Guards Brigade had by now got within ten miles of the capital, but suddenly encountered unexpected opposition at an important road and railway crossing. Neither the armoured cars nor the Grenadier tanks were able to deal with the anti-tank guns sited there, and there was nothing for it but for the infantry to deploy. When the Welsh heard this, they promptly replied that they would see if their tanks could not with persuasion achieve sixty miles an hour, rather than a mere fifty.

What pace they actually went is not recorded, but there were certainly many stretches along which the following troops at any rate fully achieved it. Occasionally a carrier or a self-propelled gun for which the pace had proved too hot was passed, but it seemed almost as though the vehicles understood what was wanted of them, and were determined to accomplish it, for few of them did in fact fall by the wayside. Far greater in number were the evidences of the achievements of the leading troops—burning trucks and cars, overturned carts with luckless dead horses which had been stolen from farms and Germans still lying where they had been killed, small parties of prisoners in the capable hands of the patriots who were armed with weapons of every type, rifles, shot-guns, knives, bayonets and invariably stick grenades stolen from the Germans. The armour was moving so fast that these latter proved invaluable not only in guarding prisoners but in clearing snipers and holding bridges until the 231st Brigade could take over and clean up the area as far as was possible in such a rapid advance. In addition the local inhabitants on their own initiative turned out with spades to repair roads where the tanks had turned, while those who could find no useful job lined the roads and cheered until we thought their lungs would burst. An armoured division on the advance is always an impressive sight, but at the pace at which we moved that day our progress may well to them have seemed awe-inspiring.

The Welsh had one more engagement at the little town of Hal only a few miles short of Brussels, but it did not delay them long and just after eight o'clock they reported that they had crossed the road junction designated as the winning post. At the same moment the Grenadiers were entering the outskirts of the city after successfully dealing with the anti-tank screen which had held them up. So both brigades reached the city as darkness was falling to be greeted by the inhabitants in a manner which can surely never have been equalled. As we approached our pace gradually slackened until it was literally reduced to a crawl. But this time there was no need to worry; it was no enemy opposing our entry, only hordes of Belgians careering madly about in such a frenzy of joy that movement was almost impossible. The news of our imminent arrival had obviously spread like wildfire and the crowds all surged by instinct towards the road by which we were making our entry. All emotions are infectious, to an increasing degree according to the numbers of people involved, and as Brussels was immeasurably the largest town that we had entered so were the joy and enthusiasm with which we were greeted proportionately greater than any we had met before. Everybody was crazy in a delirium of happiness that knew no bounds. Effigies of Hitler were burning round which they danced, the usual gifts of food and wine, the display of flags and bunting and the cheers were not only more overwhelming than ever before, but the normal handshakes of gratitude were more often than not amplified with embraces. Most frequently it was the children who were held up to be kissed, but young ladies and old ladies, some pretty and some not at all, and even on occasions gentlemen, some of whom had beards, all competed to welcome their liberators with embraces in which one felt were pent-up all the sufferings and emotions of the past four years. It was as un-English a scene as could be imagined, and yet so natural and touching did it seem at the time that scarcely one of us could feel shy or embarrassed or even flinch, other than perhaps mentally, at the enforced attentions of the occasional bearded old gentleman.

And yet, amid all these scenes of unbridled enthusiasm, it was in many ways the most orderly and easily controlled crowd imaginable. The city police were lining the streets in an effort to keep the way open for us, and there was no question of any resentment over any restraint imposed by them. Although the people clambered on to our vehicles in their dozens, if one of us had occasion to go up or down the column on duty in a scout-car or jeep, there was not the slightest difficulty in inducing the odd half-dozen passengers to leave—once the reason for asking them to do so was explained to them. It must be rare to get the impression that vast crowds of people are, collectively, lovable but the crowds of Brussels certainly were that night.

Brussels is a big city and an armoured division could easily get lost in it. The General had therefore allotted areas of responsibility beforehand, consisting of key-points controlling the approaches to the centre; but by the time we were well within the city it was already dark and the difficulty of finding our exact destinations in view of the fact that we had not been issued with a single detailed map began to seem insuperable. The Welsh

Guards consequently enquired in due course on the wireless as to whether they should proceed any further. They were on the Boulevard de Waterloo and, though nobody knew exactly where that was, it seemed well in the centre and very appropriately named; moreover their leading elements were involved in some shooting with a small group of Germans fighting a rearguard action at the Porte de Namur, only about three hundred yards further on, while a colossal building was burning furiously to their left. Certainly it seemed prudent to call a halt, and Brigadier Johnson told them to organise a close harbour area there for the night. He joined them himself soon afterwards with his headquarters and the location had perforce to be sent back in most unmilitary fashion by the name of the street instead of by coded map reference.

The Irish Guards had meanwhile been told to wheel round to seize the Eastern approaches, which they successfully did after dealing with an enemy position at a cross-roads on the way. By now the 5th Guards Brigade was equally astride the roads leading in from the North and West, while Brigadier Gwatkin was preparing himself, with his headquarters, to sleep the sleep of the just at the Royal Palace of Laeken, where Queen Elizabeth of the Belgians had been on the steps to welcome the Grenadiers on their arrival.

All subsequent evidence tended to show that the Germans had not expected to have to give up Brussels so soon and that they were hustled out of the capital by our advance. Demolition charges on the main bridges were never fired, while they had no time in which to remove or destroy a large number of highly incriminating documents. They cannot have enjoyed the falling of these into our hands, and the burning building on the Boulevard de Waterloo proved to be the Palais de Justice, set on fire with the express purpose of destroying them, though the effort was largely unsuccessful. They would probably also have liked to remove some of the excellent wine that the Gestapo had collected for their delectation in the cellars. What could be more right and proper than that we should share some of this looted store with the people of Brussels and toast victory in it together? That was what they thought and we were in no mood to disagree, as case after case was deposited on the pavements in the lurid glare that came from the blazing building. It is a curious fact, and a pertinent one that demands study by prohibitionists, that, though an enormous amount must have been consumed, no case of drunkenness was recorded, nor did any man fail in his duty either during the course of that night or of the following morning.

It may well be asked whether we did not pursue very unorthodox tactics in entering and occupying a large city during the hours of darkness, after an advance of a quite unusual length. Admittedly our general object might have been equally well achieved by merely blocking all the approaches, but our orders were explicitly to capture Brussels itself. The long dash forward with this express purpose in view was obviously dictated largely by political and psychological considerations, and the General therefore took the view that at least a portion of the division ought to get right through to the centre of the city. Undoubtedly a risk was taken, but not an unduly great one in view of the known disorganisation of the Germans and the universal good will of the citizens. Its tonic effects on all the inhabitants of the Belgian capital alone made it seem to us well worth while. Bearing all this in mind, there can be little doubt but that the decision was eminently right.

Chapter Five

FORCING THE CANAL LINES

THE MORNING following the entry into Brussels was spent mainly in clearing up the few remaining enemy, a task in which the Armée Blanche assisted most joyfully and successfully. But there are two aspects to the business of liberating a capital city. One is to ensure that the enemy leave and do not return; the other, admittedly less essential but nevertheless very desirable, is to show to a population who are extending a delirious and whole-hearted welcome something to symbolise the event. The General therefore made a state entry that afternoon. He drove past the tomb of the Unknown Warrior on to the historic Hôtel de Ville in the Grand' Place, where he officially handed back to the Burgomaster his beautiful city; he stood up in his Command Tank as he drove, escorted as ever by his troop of Cromwells and by a troop of the Household Cavalry, who had played so important a part in the previous day's advance. The Belgian Brigade followed in a triumphant return to their capital after four weary years, and finally came the rest of Divisional Headquarters with the giant Armoured Command Vehicles more than ever resembling elephants in some circus procession. The crowds were so dense that it was only with difficulty that the column kept on its appointed course. Very few inhabitants can have stayed indoors that day, almost every house and certainly every child carried a flag, and the tanks and following vehicles soon began to look as though they were competing in a *concours d'élégance* on the Riviera, so festooned did they become with the flowers, streamers, fruit and other objects that were thrown at them. It was an unforgettable scene; it was at the same time a wonderful tribute by the populace to the British and Allied Armies and a magnificent homecoming for their own soldiers.

After the ceremony at the Hôtel de Ville, and as the column

approached the Royal Palace near which Divisional Headquarters was to be set up, five shells landed nearby in the Palace gardens. The results could have been horrible but providentially nobody was hurt and they proved to be parting shots. The incident brought home, however, the necessity of ensuring against the enemy's return. Not that the battalions had been wasting their time; patrols had gone out in the early morning and as soon as their reports began to come in it became obvious that infantry with a few tanks and eighty-eight-millimetre guns were still to be found over a wide area to the East. The 32nd Guards Brigade moved out to the Parc de Woluwé on the Eastern outskirts of the city and the Welsh Group was ordered to assist the Irish Group in blocking the approaches. Its troops did this effectively and rounded up a number of prisoners during the ensuing two days. They also combined business with pleasure to the extent of installing their Headquarters in an extremely luxurious golf club on the edge of the Forest of Tervueren, where in their capacity of honoured guests they were treated to every kind of comfort and delicacy. The words "Welsh Guards" remained a talisman to members of that Club for months afterwards, and may very well do so yet.

The Irish Group had already set up Headquarters at Auderghem in the early morning and most of its troops were employed in blocking the main roads to Wavre, Hoeylaert and Waterloo, but one Squadron-Company Group had been ordered forward during the night to Schaerbeek. This was a village just off the Louvain road and next to the Brussels airfield, which was reported still to be in the hands of the Germans; daybreak showed that this was indeed the case, as four dual-purpose guns could be seen well dug-in about seven hundred yards away. A battery of the Leicestershire Yeomanry was asked to shell the airfield for five minutes prior to an assault by an infantry platoon and a troop of tanks; but the shelling only put one gun out of commission and another opened up from behind, followed by some heavy mortars from further to the East. It was obvious that something more forceful would be needed and the 84th Medium Regiment was asked to provide a regimental shoot, pending which the tanks would keep the heads of the enemy down. The regiment kindly obliged with unerring aim and the whole of No. 1 Company, led by Major G. E. Fisher-Rowe, went into the assault supported by a troop of tanks. The company was at the time composed largely of recruits, for whom it was an ideal inoculation. They threw grenades and shot at everything they could see and Germans came out to surrender wholesale, including six officers.

A small force which was despatched later in the day with the object of assisting the Armée Blanche in clearing Waterloo was less successful. The Germans were unexpectedly found still to be holding the place in some strength and although one enemy tank was destroyed we ourselves lost a tank and a scout-car with their crews. It never pays to take risks when dealing with Germans.

The 5th Guards Brigade had no need to change their Headquarters. Their responsibility was the protection of the Northern side of the city and their situation in the Royal Laundry at Laeken was ideal for the purpose. The Coldstream Group carried out the task with its tanks comfortably based on the Koekelberg Brewery.

Meanwhile striking advances had been made by all our allied formations. The First Canadian Army was pushing up the coast and had reached the mouth of the Somme on September 3rd. All three armoured divisions of the Second British Army were in line with the 7th Armoured in Ghent on the 5th, the 11th Armoured in Antwerp on the 4th, though the dock area was not cleared for a further few days, and ourselves, as we have seen, in and through Brussels on the 3rd and 4th. On our right, the First U.S. Army had reached the general line Namur–Tirlemont, thus affording us flank protection.

The Commander-in-Chief, who had been promoted to the rank of Field-Marshal in recognition of his brilliant Normandy victory, now issued orders for the advance to continue to the Rhine and for the Second Army to threaten the Western face of the Ruhr. With this in view, XXX Corps, who were to lead, was to position the Guards Armoured Division in the Eindhoven area of Holland. This manœuvre would entail the passage of two canals, the Albert and the Meuse-Escaut.

In furtherance of these orders, the Grenadier Group had already been ordered to capture Louvain, some fifteen miles to the East and an important centre of communications; loth though the men were to leave Brussels, some of them remembered the night four years before when they were ordered back from this very town and they were keen to return to it as liberators. The main road was believed to be covered by the guns on the airfield which the Irish were at this very moment preparing to attack and, when Lieutenant-Colonel J. N. R. Moore, who was with the Advance Guard, found that this was indeed so, he decided to take an alternative road to the South through Tervueren. Great difficulty was experienced in making this change owing to the holiday mood of the population; they tried to join in every conference at this time and when Lieutenant-Colonel Moore got back to the group commander, Lieutenant-Colonel Goulburn, their insistence was such that a motor platoon had to be put round them to keep the crowd back while they made their plan. Apart from this it was a curious way in which to go out to a battle, as all the tanks were covered with flowers and there were even civilians on some of the accompanying vehicles.

No opposition was encountered on the way but Major E. J. S. Ward's Squadron of the Household Cavalry, which had been sent on ahead to seize the bridges over the River Dyle in the centre of the town, was fired upon on approaching the outskirts. As the armoured cars sped through the streets they were shot at by Germans from windows and roof-tops but Lieutenant T. Hanbury, whose troop was directed on the bridge carrying the main road, quickly reached it and found German sappers feverishly at work underneath. They were promptly shot. Lieutenant Hanbury's plan was to hold the near end of the bridge himself, while his corporal of horse held the far end; the section of sappers who had accompanied the troop would then remove the charges. Corporal of Horse Thompson made for a small bridge close by, in which a hole had been blown; under heavy fire he dismounted from his car, collected a door from a nearby house, spanned the gap and crossed successfully. A battle royal now ensued; the Germans reacted vigorously, attacking both ends of the bridge, and the armoured cars fought back, while the sappers worked steadily under a hail of fire until all the charges had been removed. Lieutenant Hanbury received the Military Cross, and Corporal of Horse Thompson the Distinguished Conduct Medal, for this gallant exploit.

While the sappers were still at work the leading Grenadiers, No. 2 Company–No. 3 Squadron Group, arrived and sent strong patrols up the main roads leading to the railway station on the far side of the town, which they soon reached despite spasmodic sniping which caused a few casualties. Sergeant A. R. Killick was very badly wounded by a bullet which entered his head at the cheek-bone and came out again behind the ear. Under normal battle conditions he would have stood no chance of recovery but as luck would have it he fell about a hundred yards from the operating theatre of the leading brain-specialist in Belgium; he was operated on within minutes and was off the danger list within a few days.

It was now about seven o'clock on September 4th and Lieutenant-Colonel Goulburn, after a reconnaissance, decided on the dispositions to be taken up for the night. One infantry company was left guarding the main bridge and two others took up positions covering the vulnerable approaches on the far side of the town. Headquarters and the remainder of the group found a gritty resting-place in a dust-field on the Western outskirts. Some of the disappointment at the sudden departure from Brussels was somewhat alleviated when some officers from the echelons, which were still in the capital, arrived with cases of champagne for distribution.

The next day was spent in clearing the surrounding countryside. In the early afternoon a composite force consisting of No. 4 Company–No. 1 Squadron and a troop each of anti-tank and field artillery was sent to Aerschot, about twelve miles to the

North-East. It met no opposition and took up defensive positions around the town, falling in subsequently in front when the group passed through on the following day.

On that morning, September 5th, the remainder of the 5th Guards Brigade Group was warned to be ready to move up to Louvain while the rest of the division remained around Brussels; but after luncheon orders were received that the whole division was to continue the advance and a conference was summoned by the General that evening at nine o'clock. Just before it was due to begin a paraffin lamp on the table in the tent which joined Armoured Command Vehicles 1 and 3 and which formed the Operations Room started to splutter and set fire to the talc of the huge Operations map. Nothing is more inflammable than talc and, despite the presence of mind of some officers who immediately tore it down and trampled on it, the roof of the tent had already caught fire within a matter of seconds and two minutes later both vehicles were blazing. The staff officers watched the destruction of many of their personal belongings with remarkable calm and the conference was nevertheless held almost punctually in the mess tent, albeit somewhat interrupted by the noise made by the Sappeurs Pompiers in their vain attempts to extinguish the flames devouring the "nerve centre of the Guards Armoured Division". Subsequently we saw several accounts in the newspapers, one of which read: "As I write by the light of the great bonfire which the populace have lit in the Palace Gardens to celebrate . . ."

The orders were to continue our easterly advance and to seize crossings over the Albert Canal. On September 6th, the 5th Guards Brigade was therefore told to make for the bridge South-West of Oostham and the 32nd Guards Brigade for that at Beeringen. The Grenadier Group led the 5th Guards Brigade column and proceeded without a hitch as far as the canal; but, as the Household Cavalry contingent preceding them was about to cross, the bridge was blown up and it was seen that the far bank was held in considerable strength with at least two anti-tank guns present. While the leading companies deployed to watch the canal a reconnaissance was made on either side and a railway bridge discovered that was passable to troops on foot. A plan had just been made for a crossing of this bridge, to be followed by an attack from the flank and rear on the enemy holding the main road-bridge approaches, when orders came to suspend operations as the 32nd Guards Brigade had meanwhile secured their bridge, over which it was intended to pass the whole division.

The 32nd Guards Brigade, led by the Welsh Group, had equally met no opposition of any kind on the road through Diest to Beeringen, although reports were received from the Armée Blanche of tanks and infantry on the right flank; these subsequently proved to be well-founded as for some time a small body of them succeeded in cutting the road between Louvain and Diest in our rear and in inflicting some casualties on the Dutch Brigade that was following us. First reports that the bridge at Beeringen was intact were found to be false, but the German attempts at destroying it had been only partially successful. The central span had been cut, but not very effectively, while the side spans and piers were virtually undamaged. In theory a crossing on foot was perfectly possible, though in practice it was prevented by fire from the far bank.

The Welsh were making a plan to cross by boat and assault the bridge from the far side when a very brave Belgian, waving a white handkerchief, raced across to tell them that the Germans were leaving the village. The Prince of Wales' Company thereupon charged precariously over and established a bridgehead by half-past five in the afternoon. The 615th Field Squadron now set to work amid pouring rain to rebuild the bridge, watched by a large crowd of civilians from both sides of the canal and helped by a few prisoners; they were not all impressed against their will as one of them told a senior officer in no uncertain terms to get out of his way as he was interfering with the rapid completion of the task. At the same time local bargees, not to be outdone, marshalled their barges and anchored them across the river a couple of hundred yards to the North in order to provide an alternative means of crossing.

By four o'clock on the morning of September 7th the repairs to the bridge were complete and No. 1 Squadron crossed. But considerable opposition was soon met and it became evident that the bridge had only just been completed in time and that we had gained a very real advantage by pushing on with all possible speed. Enemy reinforcements had now reached the outskirts of Beeringen in some strength and harassing fire began to come down on the approaches to the bridge. This was directed from some slag heaps—for we had entered a mining district—to the North of the town, which afforded an uninterrupted view over the exceedingly flat countryside. The unarmoured vehicles of the infantry suffered several hits from what was fast becoming severe shelling and soon the bridge was no longer safe for light traffic. Notwithstanding this, as our orders were to brook no delay, the Welsh Group were told to force their way on and seize Helchteren with, if possible, Hechtel also, while the 3rd Bn. Irish Guards completed the clearing of Beeringen on foot. Helchteren was captured by No. 4 Company and No. 3 Squadron after a fight in which two anti-tank guns were destroyed and considerable casualties inflicted, but opposition stiffened as Hechtel was approached. The leading group encountered, for the first time since Normandy, enemy advancing to meet them and a small action was fought on the outskirts of the village; as it appeared strongly held they withdrew to Helchteren as night fell.

The Irish Group in the meantime was having a far from pleasant time in Beeringen. In addition to the task of consolidating a firm base in the town orders had been given to attack and capture the slag heaps that were providing the enemy with observation. The necessity for this became increasingly evident as the shelling continued to get heavier and more accurate. Casualties were fairly heavy and particularly so among officers owing to the need for reconnaissances along the streets. Captain W. R. R. S. Bruce was killed and Captain R. B. H. Ingleby and Lieutenant Lord Plunket wounded; also wounded most unfortunately was Major R. Eames, commander of the 439th Battery of the West Somerset Yeomanry. Major Eames had always worked with notable success with the

Irish Group and, just before he was wounded, he had found a convent window affording a perfect view of the slag heaps and also of the main road running North past him towards Bourg Léopold. At least three German armoured vehicles could be seen moving up and down the road and it was decided to shell them before launching the attack in the hope of scoring one or two hits or at least of frightening them away from our axis of advance. This shoot was a delight for the watchers as two of the tanks went up in a sheet of flames and the rest disappeared.

The attack went in at five o'clock and was made by No. 4 Company under Major M. V. Dudley, with a weak squadron of tanks under Major D. R. S. FitzGerald and supported by the West Somerset Yeomanry and a battery of the 64th Medium Regiment. Due largely to carefully directed fire from the machine-guns of the Northumberland Fusiliers and also from their own Bren gunners the advance by the infantry proceeded steadily for the first half of the distance but was then held up by enemy carefully sited on a reverse slope. The armour had meanwhile been halted by boggy country and small streams not passable for tanks; but, when they found a way round to the left, they were able to dispose of the Germans in their slit trenches, whereupon numbers came forward waving white handkerchiefs and only too anxious to give themselves up. By dusk the mine offices were in our hands and patrols were climbing the slag heaps. The operation proved well worth while as the shelling afterwards became both sporadic and inaccurate.

That was a depressing evening for most of us, spoiled as we had recently been with too easy successes. Progress beyond the Albert Canal was obviously going to require stiff fighting and all that we knew of the situation on our flanks was that our bridgehead was the only one that had yet been obtained, although the 50th Division was at that moment engaged in fighting for one on our left. Information further afield was completely lacking and at no stage either previously or subsequently during the campaign did we know so little about the general progress of operations. One comforting inference could, however, be drawn from the sudden departure of H.R.H. Prince John of Luxembourg; as an officer in the Irish Guards he had been serving at the 32nd Guards Brigade Headquarters since the early days in Normandy but was now summoned to attend the official entry into his capital.

Prisoners had been coming in well and we soon received from them proof that the Germans had intended to hold the Albert Canal as a main defence line at all costs. The task had been given to the 719th Infantry Division, who had started to leave the Hague for Brussels on September 2nd; they had necessarily been diverted on the way and, while reaching the line of the canal further West just in time, had been beaten by us at Beeringen by a short head. Nevertheless they quickly set to work to bring reinforcements to make a ring round our bridgehead and seemed as determined to contain us as we were to force our way on.

The following morning, September 8th, the Coldstream Group crossed the canal with orders to take over the colliery area from the Irish and, after clearing it thoroughly, to push on through Beverloo and Heppen with the object of capturing Bourg Léopold, the Belgian counterpart of Aldershot. At dawn their leading companies passed through the Irish Guards in the battered streets of Beeringen and took up positions beyond the slag heap in accordance with the plan. Then difficulties began; a German gun started firing straight down the road, and two tanks and several lorries were hit before they could take cover; and, while Lieutenant-Colonel Hill was waiting for the barrage to begin, the news came that there would be no barrage—the infantry would have to attack on its own. So Major C. H. Feilden and Major Lord Hartington started off, No. 1 Company on the left advancing through close-set fir plantations, No. 3 Company on the right having to climb over factory walls and through railway yards. In the absence of artillery support they did not find the opposition easy to deal with and by ten o'clock, though Lord Hartington had reached his objective, Major Feilden had not been able to make progress against the German machine-guns and his losses had been heavy. The commanding officer therefore sent No. 4

Company commanded by Major J. Chandos-Pole to sweep round to the left and come in on the German flank. The company had a tough fight, as only bayonets and hand grenades could prise the Germans out of their deep trenches, but by eleven o'clock the way was clear and No. 1 Company moved on to their objective.

The next phase of the attack was the capture of Beverloo by No. 2 Company and No. 3 Squadron. Half a mile of open ground lay in front of the village where the Germans held out with infantry and self-propelled guns; but the artillery was now available, and under cover of smoke the guardsmen fought their way into the village with No. 3 Squadron in support. The tanks on the left ran into trouble but Lieutenant I. L. Jardine took the reserve troop up to help and in little more than an hour Beverloo was clear. Three anti-tank guns were captured and a hundred prisoners were sent back to battalion headquarters.

The Germans still held out a mile further on, in the straggling village of Heppen, and the commanding officer called up No. 1 Company for the third phase of the attack. So far all had gone well but Lieutenant-Colonel Hill modified his original plan. He chose the station half-way to Heppen, where the railway crosses the road that leads to Heppen from Beverloo, as an "intermediate objective" and at three o'clock launched No. 1 Company with No. 1 Squadron to attack it. Moving through the woods on the left of the road, Major Feilden reached the station without difficulty but there he found a Panther tank on the level-crossing. His own tanks could not reach him: advancing over the open fields to the right of the road they had come under accurate fire, and could make no progress. The squadron then tried to drive straight up the road and at once had two tanks knocked out; four others, taking to the soft ground by the roadside, became hopelessly bogged and the remaining six tanks had to put down smoke and withdraw.

The commanding officer nevertheless now decided to attack Heppen village with a company-squadron group as soon as sufficient artillery support could be arranged. This took time and the light was already failing before No. 4 Company supported by No. 2 Squadron neared their objective, advancing round the left of No. 1 Company in Heppen Station. Major Chandos-Pole started at four o'clock and led his men through the woods to the railway line without meeting opposition; but the moment he crossed the railway track the Germans opened fire from the backs of the houses on the road. Two of these houses were captured, but Lieutenant S. E. Argyle was killed, Major Chandos-Pole himself was seriously wounded, and wireless contact was lost with battalion headquarters. The squadron had not been able to use the company's line of advance and had to swing still further out to the left. Dusk was beginning to fall by the time the squadron reached the company and a well-hidden German gun soon destroyed two of Lieutenant P. W. Loyd's troop as he led his tanks over the railway, but the squadron pushed on through the twilight woods to come into Heppen from the west. It was nearly dark when Lieutentant Loyd entered the village and a Jagd-Panther, waiting in the shadows, sent the leading tank up in flames. In the light thrown by the burning houses any tank entering the village was an easy target for this lurking enemy and there was nothing at this late hour for them to do but to recross the railway and return to Beverloo. Meanwhile no contact had been made between No. 4 Company and Battalion Headquarters. The night was now very dark, but Captain T. I. D. Eastman, the company second-in-command, asked permission to go forward in a carrier over ground which he had never seen and which the Germans were known to occupy to find the company and bring back the remnants. This he successfully accomplished and for his achievement was awarded the Military Cross.

That night the 1st Battalion suffered several casualties by shell-fire, among them Major the Hon. C. M. K. St. Clair, and the next day No. 1 Squadron was amalgamated with No. 3 under Major the Hon. H. R. Allsopp. In the morning Lieutenant-Colonel Hill prepared to renew the attack on Heppen. More artillery was brought up and under a heavy barrage Captain the Hon. D. M. G. J. Willoughby and Major Lord Hartington took their companies into the assault. The struggle was short and bitter; the companies set out at a quarter to nine and in half an hour all was over. Lieutenant K. H. Irgens and several men of No. 2 Company were killed by anti-tank fire from Bourg Léopold before they reached the start line and on the right No. 3 Company met even stronger opposition. Lord Hartington was shot through the heart and instantly killed; Lieutenant the Hon. J. U. Knatchbull, his only platoon commander, was badly wounded: it was left to Company-Sergeant-Major Cowley to rally the company, fight his way into the village, and repulse an immediate counter-attack, thereby winning the Distinguished Conduct Medal. The 1st Battalion came up immediately behind the leading companies to help to clear and hold Heppen and found it already full of German dead; the barrage had caught them as they were forming up for a counter-attack on Beverloo. Another counter-attack, launched along the banks of the canal, came in among the store lorries and cookers of F2 echelon but the storemen and cooks, supported by the tanks of Lieutenant Loyd's troop, repulsed it without undue difficulty.

Thus the group had accomplished three parts of its four-fold task. Bourg Léopold had not fallen but on the first day alone nearly one hundred and fifty prisoners had been taken and in the evening of September 9th the 15th/19th Hussars came up to Beverloo and Heppen and the Coldstream were withdrawn to the South bank of the canal. No. 3 Company was temporarily dissolved and its surviving members distributed among the other companies; even so the remaining three rifle companies were seven officers and sixty men under strength. The Coldstream Group received the congratulations of the corps commander for their efforts and the divisional commander was afterwards to say he thought their battle was the key to the whole subsequent operations.

The Irish Group had meanwhile taken over Helchteren and set to work to clear the neighbouring woods in order to enable the Welsh Group to concentrate on Hechtel. This operation led to a very confused battle which persisted sharply throughout the night and resulted in many casualties. Captain J. L. L. Savill and

Lieutenant M. A. Callender were both seriously wounded and Lance-Sergeant Radcliffe, Medical Sergeant of the 2nd Bn. Irish Guards, a very gallant man who had been responsible for saving many lives in past actions, was killed. The immediate defence of the Beeringen bridge was relegated to the Royal Netherlands Brigade Group, but was still no sinecure because, as we have seen, an ambitious enemy force attempted to get through along the canal bank from the North-West on the morning of the 9th. Some of them succeeded in getting as far as the barge bridge and destroyed some thirty administrative vehicles of the 8th Armoured Brigade before they were eliminated. This Brigade was attemping to push through to the assistance of the 50th Division, who had formed a small bridgeless bridgehead further West, but they could not do so until the Coldstream had gained ground as already related.

Apart from the attempt to reach the bridge, it became apparent during the course of September 9th that many enemy reinforcements had arrived. Pressure on the Coldstream Guards from the direction of Bourg Léopold had been maintained throughout the day, despite the news of its capture on the B.B.C. at one o'clock, and the Welsh group found conditions at Hechtel no easier. A footing had been obtained in the Southern part of the town, but the Germans still held the Northern part and infiltrated back during the hours of darkness. Major J. D. Spencer, whose squadron was holding positions covering one of the main roads, was killed during the confused fighting in the early hours of the morning and Major G. Hollebone, who had done excellent work commanding the 374th Battery, West Somerset Yeomanry, in support of the Welsh Group since Normandy, was wounded. Major Spencer was not a young man and could easily have gone through the war in an honourable manner without taking upon himself the hardships and risks of active service. He was very much beloved by all under his command, who knew him affectionately as "Uncle John", and he was a great loss to his battalion. Later in the morning the Germans proceeded to put in a strong attack from the East. Two platoons of X Company Scots Guards were temporarily isolated and suffered severe casualties, Lieutenant I. N. Thorpe, M.C., being killed and Lieutenant A. D. G. Llewellyn wounded and taken prisoner, but it was finally driven off and three Jagd-Panthers were destroyed. One of these twice missed a Welsh Guards tank, commanded by Lieutenant H. Griffiths, who then lay in wait for it for half an hour until the monster came rumbling down the road to be shot by its intended victim at fifty yards' range. For this achievement, added to much distinguished service in the past, Lieutenant Griffiths was awarded the Military Cross.

During the first three days after crossing the Albert Canal the position of the division was distinctly vulnerable; it was isolated and its troops were extremely spread out, with Germans reported in every wood on the map. But on the afternoon of the 9th the 11th Armoured Division started to come through in order to clear our right flank and by the following morning there were enough troops across the canal to allow us to turn our attention once more to our proper role of pushing on. General Horrocks, the Corps Commander, gave orders for the capture of a bridge over the Escaut canal, about ten miles North of Hechtel, at any risk and any cost. The Coldstream and Welsh Groups had had a gruelling time and the latter in particular were unable to disengage at Hechtel, but the other two groups were available. Undeterred by the fact that the only two roads were blocked respectively at Bourg Léopold and Hechtel, the General made a plan to move the Grenadiers and Irish straight across the Aldershot-type country between them, the chance of a surprise capture of a bridge far outweighing in importance any possible threat to our communications.

A troop of Household Cavalry, with their usual uncanny knack, soon found a way through. They followed a rough track among the sand-dunes which crossed the main road to Bourg Léopold a mile West of Hechtel and rejoined the centre-line about two miles to the North. Before doing so, however, the track crossed a small boggy stream with only a narrow bridge over which all traffic would have to pass. Difficult wooded country lay ahead and they were fired on in a cutting soon after rejoining the main road. Nothing daunted, they moved to the East through Exel and Overpelt until they were approaching the bridge at De Groote Barrier, which carries the main road to Holland over the canal. The troop leader, Lieutenant J. N. Cresswell, appreciated that if his armoured cars appeared suddenly near the bridge the enemy might blow it up; he therefore left them forming a strong-point, while he with a corporal went forward on bicycles borrowed from local inhabitants. A great factory overlooks the bridge, standing about half a mile away to the East. Lieutenant Cresswell succeeded in reaching the roof, from where he could see that it was intact all right; he could also see that it was strongly held and was able even to spot the positions of four eighty-eight millimetre guns defending it. He lost no time in reporting this exciting news and the Grenadier Group was promptly told to lead off, to be followed by the Irish Group until the small bridge was crossed. After that the Grenadiers were to follow the main axis and the Irish were to move along the route already taken by the armoured cars. Whichever of the groups succeeded in reaching the area of the canal first was ordered to attempt to rush the bridge. It was a bold plan, but the enemy were very disorganised and the defenders knew that theirs was the last remaining bridge and that many of their troops and some tanks still remained on the wrong side. The fateful decision to blow up a bridge also often does not depend on the initiative of the immediate local commander but on the order of a superior officer far away and not necessarily in touch with the local situation. The stakes were high and the gamble well worth while.

Shortly before ten o'clock that morning, September 10th, the advance started under cover of an artillery concentration and smoke-screen. The leading group was held up and lost one tank at the small stream, its commander, Lieutenant Sir Howard Frank, being killed, but it quickly forced its way across the bridge, destroying two self-propelled guns and taking several prisoners; it then concentrated on the main road running North from Hechtel and passed a patrol of Household Cavalry through. But progress up the road still proved difficult; after moving forward about a thousand yards, this patrol was fired on by a self-propelled gun and as there were thick woods on either side further advance except on foot was out of the question. A sweep with infantry induced the anti-tank gun to withdraw half a mile and after repetition of the manœuvre open country was reached. But any tank was fired at immediately it edged forward and it was evident that a direct attack on the road and railway crossings a mile South of the canal, which were obviously the main centres of enemy resistance, would be very difficult and expensive in default of artillery support; so at about three o'clock the King's Company and No. 2 Squadron were sent round in a wide sweep to the left and reached the railway line about a mile West of the road, after traversing very difficult country but without meeting any opposition. Here the infantry got out and moved off on foot along the railway supported by the tanks. Very soon a considerable amount of equipment and transport could be seen on the road. The enemy's attention was clearly distracted by the remainder of the group on the main road to the South; so the King's Company, ably backed up by the tanks, dashed in and did great damage to a completely unsuspecting enemy with no loss to themselves. Two tanks and several anti-tank guns of various sizes, together with their equipment and many vehicles, were destroyed and the crews either killed or made prisoner. The road was by now completely blocked by blazing vehicles, but the company consolidated as close as the exploding ammunition would allow and one platoon was sent up the road to secure the main cross-roads, which it did without further opposition. But no tanks could get forward until the wrecks could be cleared and meanwhile news came that the Irish Group had already reached the crucial bridge.

After a tiresome morning spent by No. 4 Company–No. 2 Squadron Group in trying to cut across country more to the East, an attempt defeated more by the ground than by the enemy, who lost five self-propelled guns and tanks, the Irish had followed the Grenadiers as far as the main road. Here they branched off East to Exel, which they reached at six o'clock and where they found a troop of tanks and a motor platoon of the Grenadiers, which Lieutenant-Colonel Moore had taken and placed there with the express purpose of ensuring that it would be clear for them. Moreover they found that a new German military road, not marked on the map, had been recently built leading North to Overpelt, and this enabled them to make up handsomely for lost time. By seven forty-five the original Household Cavalry patrol had been reached in the factory area just South-East of the bridge; from this vantage-point it could distinctly be seen to be still intact and still strongly defended, though the defenders could be expected to have had most of their attention focussed on the battle still going on with the Grenadiers on the opposite flank. The failing light was all in our favour and Lieutenant-Colonel Vandeleur ordered No. 1, Major D. A. Peel's, Squadron to attack and rush it as soon as possible, supported by No. 2, Captain J. A. H. Hendry's, Company. The sapper party to accompany them was of a rather unusual composition, since Captain R. Hutton, of the 615th Field Squadron, had somehow got separated from his troop and could only muster his driver, his wireless operator and his orderly; none of these had any knowledge of demolition technique and to them were added four guardsmen who were assuredly even less expert but who were unofficially made sappers on the spot. There could be no question of artillery support as the guns were out of range.

Major Peel decided to send Lieutenant D. A. Lampard's troop to patrol slowly forward towards the cross-roads immediately South of the bridge, accompanied by Lieutenant J. Stanley-Clarke's platoon. The remaining tanks of the squadron took up positions enabling them to keep up a continuous fire at the bridge and its approaches, in order to discourage the defenders. Gradually the troop edged its way forward, destroying one eighty-eight-millimetre gun on the way, until it was established among the houses at the cross-roads. Lieutenant Lampard had been told to make his own plan for the actual assault and he now agreed with Lieutenant Stanley-Clarke to cover his platoon up the main road to within a hundred yards of the bridge, when a green Verey light would be fired. This was to be a signal for all guns to fire only on the bridge; and when the infantry were ready for the final assault a red Verey light would be fired as a signal for all fire to cease and the leading tanks to charge. It was eight-thirty when the green Verey light went up, and for two minutes very heavy fire came down on the bridge, after which the red light followed and the tanks charged. One of the troop had jammed its gun shortly before and a second now hit the corner of a house and stuck, so only two tanks actually made the assault, that of Sergeant Steer in the lead and Lieutenant Lampard's own. These rushed straight across the bridge and halted in fire positions on the North side, the infantry doubling close behind and lying down around them. Major Peel at once ordered the rest of the squadron and company across to join them, while Captain Hutton and his party immediately set to work to make the bridge safe. Sapper Davies, his wireless operator, and two guardsmen cut all wires and fuses on the near side and Sapper Smith, his orderly, and the other two guardsmen those on the far side, while Captain Hutton himself found and destroyed the electric circuit. This was quickly done, and as a further squadron-company group came up in support a German stepped up to Lieutenant Stanley-Clarke and patted him on the back, congratulating him on his boldness with the words: "Well done, Tommy, well done."

The bridge was immediately christened "Joe's Bridge", and nobody is exactly sure as to how this occurred. But by a happy coincidence the name honoured both Lieutenant-Colonel Vandeleur and Captain Hutton, whose troop was always called Joe's troop. Anyway, as such it was officially signed the next day and so it appeared in all subsequent operation orders, even up to Army level.

The feat had indeed been a fine one and must have been peculiarly startling and disconcerting to the Germans. The main defence of the bridge had consisted of eighty-eight-millimetre guns brought down on purpose from airfields in Holland and sited in an anti-tank role. They had only arrived the previous day and the troops had been given a tremendous lecture by a senior officer on the vital nature of their task of denying the use of the bridge to ourselves. This was found to have been very fully prepared for demolition with charges totalling a weight of two thousand pounds, and with the cross-roads to the South also strongly defended the enemy no doubt considered that everything was well covered. The measure of his surprise and consequent disorganisation was illustrated clearly enough by the fact that the Irish Guards only suffered three casualties, none of them fatal.

Further evidence of this was forthcoming in the lack of any immediate attempt to recapture the bridge; this could have come from either direction as considerable enemy forces, including some tanks, were still on the South side of the canal. Two motor companies were sent up to thicken the defence by the Grenadiers, with whom contact had quickly been established, but the night passed without incident. At first light patrols were pushed out to the South-West towards Lommel, which the Germans were still thought to hold, and surely enough about a company of infantry was there with several self-propelled guns. Almost simultaneously with the receipt of this information the quietness of the early morning was broken by sudden firing and a six-pounder gun just near Group Headquarters was hit and the crew killed. Other casualties followed quickly and the adjutant of the 2nd Bn. Irish Guards, Captain R. S. Langton, was wounded while helping to carry a stretcher. One of the enemy guns was now spotted and promptly engaged and destroyed by Major Peel; but a second one was still shooting far too accurately to be pleasant and he went forward to try to locate it. On his way he was killed by a direct hit from a shell, a particularly tragic loss after his superb handling of the assault the previous evening. Also killed that morning was Captain E. E. Rawlence, transport officer of the 3rd Bn. Irish Guards, who tried to stalk the same offending gun with a Piat. But revenge was soon taken by one of our seventeen-pounders; the shelling slackened and it became apparent that the enemy attempt to recapture the bridge, as it afterwards transpired that it was, had failed. Moreover, Lommel was itself by now in process of being attacked by the King's Company, supported by a troop of tanks and two troops of the 21st Anti-Tank Regiment. They destroyed one self-propelled and four eighty-eight-millimetre guns and inflicted heavy casualties. By the early afternoon they were in undisturbed possession of the village, while our aircraft were dealing with the remaining Germans fleeing North across its bridge. At two-thirty it was blown up, leaving us possessors of the sole passable bridge across the Escaut Canal.

Meanwhile, however, our main axis was still not open. While Bourg Léopold had finally been occupied without difficulty, the Germans had continued to reinforce Hechtel even after it was almost surrounded. So strongly was it held that our own troops were in the end ordered to withdraw from the part they were holding during the night of September 11th, so that a really heavy concentration of 4·2-inch mortars and artillery could be brought down on it the following morning prior to an assault by the Welsh group. As our own guns were by now deployed further forward to cover the bridgehead, we got for this purpose the support of the mediums of the 11th Armoured Division.

Soon after daybreak the concentration came down; prisoners subsequently testified that it was indeed heavy and that the mortar bombs, of which no less than nine hundred were fired, were especially effective. Immediately afterwards the infantry attacked, supported by tanks which fired at any house suspected of holding Germans. The village, although small in population, covered a considerable area and the majority of the houses had cellars ideal for harbouring defending troops. Considering the difficulties of this type of fighting and the obstinacy of the garrison the assault was a highly successful operation and moreover was carried out with comparatively light casualties. Shortly after mid-day the last resistance was overcome, and the garrison was found to have been even larger than had been suspected. Six hundred prisoners were taken, of which two hundred were wounded, and at least a hundred and fifty dead were actually counted; their total casualties in the four days' fighting were said to have been nearly a thousand. The force was found to have consisted of paratroops and raw recruits of the Hermann Goering Training Battalion in about equal proportions, the whole commanded by a Captain Müller, who must be given the credit for organising a magnificent defence with distinctly mixed material. He had had to rely mainly on the paratroops, many of whom had seen service in Russia and Italy and who formed the backbone of the very tough resistance, as the others were young and untrained. Sad to relate Captain Müller had other qualities less attractive than military courage and initiative; like so many Germans he was a bully, and even some of his own men talked of his brutal behaviour to civilians. Subsequent enquiries led to the discovery that eleven villagers had been despatched at his orders for no apparent reason other than that they had incurred his displeasure. Those that had not died from a burst of machine-gun fire had been finished off with grenades, and the grisly remains were duly discovered in a cellar. Many weeks later we heard that the Belgian authorities had had little difficulty in proving the facts and that Captain Müller had been convicted as a war criminal.

The clearing of the main road to the bridgehead eased the whole situation at once. In particular the 15th/19th Hussars was put under command of the 32nd Guards Brigade as close support to the Irish and Coldstream infantry battalions, enabling the entire armour of the division to be withdrawn to refit. This force had to withstand a spirited counter-attack on the morning of September 14th. It was mounted in considerable strength, having regard to the condition of the enemy forces, and came in both from the North, where it was supported by some self-propelled guns, three of which were captured, and also from the North-West. Here the country was thickly wooded and the attack was made solely by infantry, but they infiltrated with Bazookas right up to the positions held by the Irish, who were involved in hard fighting before they were driven off. The Coldstream also had a tough morning and both battalions were most gallantly supported by the Hussars but, though two tanks were destroyed, our casualties were not unduly severe, while the enemy lost a hundred and seventy prisoners alone. We heard from some of them that they had been told that "the bridgehead was manned by the

Guards, who were very much below strength after crippling losses and whose morale had suffered as a result". Truth to tell, most of them were not taken in and admitted frankly that they realised from the start that their task was an impossible one.

This may be the moment to attempt to explain how the Germans succeeded in putting up the fight that they did—and our experiences were reasonably typical—during the period immediately following the complete collapse of their armies in France. Proof was once more given that the German is essentially a good soldier, if he is given leadership; the latter cannot have been easy to provide at short notice, but the problem had been solved in characteristic fashion. Under the grandiloquent title of the First Parachute Army, to which the defence of the Albert Canal had been entrusted, was gathered an extraordinary collection of oddments as and where they could be found. Certain small units were incorporated, but mostly they were individuals making their way back and who were impressed quite arbitrarily, together with a large number of air force ground troops whose services were no longer needed on airfields. Their quality was naturally very variable, but, when a proportion of seasoned troops was included, as at Hechtel, it proved to be very good indeed. Experienced and tough commanders were allotted, on whose ability to weld each ill-assorted unit into a competent whole everything depended. The main weakness lay in the lack of support, little being available other than self-propelled guns and static eighty-eight-millimetre guns from airfields. There were also occasional tanks, but even if there had been more they could not altogether have made up for the lack of artillery and mortars. For this reason, while they could delay us by holding some nodal point suitable for defence as they did at Hechtel and elsewhere, they were unable to affect our main plans.

On September 15th, the day after the counter-attack, the 231st Infantry Brigade took over the defence of the bridgehead and the whole division was concentrated behind the canal to get ready for the next surge forward. Replacements of all sorts were badly needed after the rapid advance and hard fighting since the beginning of the month and this time, owing to the enormous distances covered, the Services faced a greater task than ever before.

At this time the corps commander visited all the battalions and met as many officers and men as possible. Since joining XXX Corps the division had been in action and on the move almost continuously and General Horrocks had had no previous similar opportunity. He congratulated the battalions on the success of their recent engagements, which he described as "brilliant"; this was, he added, a word he seldom used.

Chapter Six

THE ARNHEM OPERATION

MUCH HAS been written already about the Arnhem Operation. The Guards Armoured Division was only one of several participating in this most exciting and daring venture. While making every effort to focus attention in this narrative on the part played by ourselves, our actions were nevertheless so closely interrelated with those of others that some account both of these and the general plan will be essential if the story is to be fully coherent.

It will be remembered that it had been Field-Marshal Montgomery's intention to advance to the Rhine and for the Second Army to threaten the Western face of the Ruhr. He now came to the conclusion that a better "thrust line" for his forces would be by way of the general area Grave–Nijmegen–Arnhem, because, although this axis involved the additional obstacle of the Neder Rijn as compared with the more Easterly route and would take us to an area further removed from the Ruhr, it gave due weight to three other factors; we should outflank the Siegfried Line, we might hope to achieve surprise, and our airborne forces would be operating within range of their home bases. This last consideration was very important because it had been decided that for this operation, to which had been given the peculiar name of "Market Garden", the Second Army should have placed under its command the Airborne Corps commanded by Lieutenant-General F. A. M. Browning, a Grenadier Guardsman.

The intention therefore was to drive through to the Zuider Zee while at the same time the German troops in Holland, estimated at two hundred and fifty thousand, would be cut off and the freeing of the desperately needed Dutch and Belgian ports accelerated. By profiting from the present German disorganisation and with a certain amount of luck it was reckoned just possible that in this way the war might be over by Christmas. It was a great gamble, and it very nearly came off.

The gamble lay mainly in the difficulty of the country that had to be traversed. Three major and many minor water obstacles had to be crossed and most of the country through which the ninety-nine miles of road between the Dutch frontier and Nunspeet, on the shores of the Zuider Zee, passed was wholly unsuited to armoured warfare. Along many stretches it was impossible for a vehicle of any type to leave the road at all.

The problem of the water obstacles was to be surmounted by the employment of the largest number of airborne forces ever yet used, without which the operation could not even have been contemplated. If the weather was good and they succeeded in seizing and holding the passages over the water obstacles it was reckoned that the ground troops should be able to break out and compete with the other difficulties within the time during which the airborne troops could hold out on their own. Although the weather was not good and the original plan to seize one of the main bridges, that at Arnhem, did not succeed, the project only failed by the margin of the few miles of marshy country south of that town, beyond which there were no further natural obstacles.

The airborne forces under the command of the Airborne Corps consisted of the 1st British Airborne Division, which was to seize the crossing over the Neder Rijn at Arnhem; the 82nd U.S. Airborne Division, which was to seize the crossings over the Waal at Nijmegen and over the Maas at Grave and also the high wooded ground South of Nijmegen; and the 101st U.S. Airborne Division which was to occupy Eindhoven and secure the bridges over the various canals between there and Grave. The land troops were to be led by XXX Corps, which was to advance straight through on a single axis to the area between Arnhem and the Zuider Zee. VIII and XII Corps were to support it, advancing more slowly towards the Maas and safe-guarding the right and left flanks respectively.

The advance by XXX Corps was to be led by the Guards Armoured Division, which was to make the break-out and push straight through at maximum speed. The 43rd Division was to follow and, if all went well, was to occupy the gap between ourselves and Arnhem; as a secondary task it was to be prepared to carry out an assault crossing and bridging operation in the event of any of the three main bridges having been destroyed. The 50th Division was to continue to hold the existing bridgehead, advancing to join the 43rd Division North of Arnhem when the situation became sufficiently clear. The 8th Armoured Brigade was to form three regimental groups to support the American airborne troops in keeping the axis open in the Grave, Veghel and Eindhoven area. The limitation to a single supply route for so vast an operation presented the administrative staffs with a whole set of difficult problems quite apart from the risk of enemy attacks on it. In addition there were two very large and vulnerable groups, a bridging group which might extend to some five thousand vehicles, many of them extremely cumbersome, and the administrative transport of the airborne forces of at least two thousand vehicles. Both had of necessity to be fitted in ahead of a great many of the fighting troops, and the whole order of march had to be very fluid in order to be able to meet all possible contingencies.

For some days the outline plan had been known to the General and certain senior officers, and on the morning of September 16th a conference was held by General Horrocks in the theatre at Bourg Léopold. If the weather remained favourable the operation would start the following day and orders were given throughout the division by nightfall. The 5th Guards Brigade was to lead and capture Valkenswaard the same evening; at first light on the 18th the advance was to continue and carry straight through. From Valkenswaard the 32nd Guards Brigade was allotted a subsidiary route through Helmond as far as Grave, where the lead would be taken by whichever brigade arrived first. Our main worry concerned the initial break-out, as an armoured division depends largely on momentum for its success and usually relies on the infantry to make the original hole so that it can get a flying start. In this case the advance had been too rapid and sufficient infantry was not available, so we must perforce make the hole ourselves. The difficulties were fully realised and finally we were given seven squadrons of Typhoon rocket bombers on call, with a squadron-leader in person up near the front to call his flock out on to our targets. So often ground to air co-operation failed lamentably in practice, due to faults on both sides; but on this occasion it was to work perfectly, because all eyes were on the break-out and because the squadron-leader himself controlled his own aircraft from the ground.

At midnight the news came that the operation was definitely to take place as arranged; the airborne landings would start at one o'clock in the afternoon and we were to advance an hour and a half later. Early in the morning Divisional Headquarters moved to the factory on the canal bank from which Lieutenant Cresswell had originally observed the by now famous bridge. Shortly before mid-day the Irish Group, which was to lead, started drawing up nose to tail just short of the bridge. It was unfortunate that air conditions made such a late start inevitable, as everybody realised that a tough battle would have to be fought to get through the crust surrounding the bridgehead. Though the 11th Armoured Division had tried by feints to the East to mislead the Germans as to the direction of our attack, they would have had to be very foolish to be deceived and had continued to reinforce the troops blocking the main road to Eindhoven. About ten miles to the North this road crossed the River Dommel and it was not clear from air photographs whether this bridge was intact. The Household Cavalry were told to inspect it and to discover at the same time the depth of the enemy defences. Lieutenant A. R. J. Buchanan-Jardine undertook the task and decided to make a dash for it with two scout-cars straight up the road; there was indeed no other possible route. The two scout-cars raced through the German lines and were on the far side before the defenders recovered from their surprise. Near the bridge a tank was blocking the road; a position of observation was taken up in a wood by the side and the bridge was seen to be intact, as vehicles crossed it. Local Dutchmen now told Lieutenant Buchanan-Jardine that the woods to his rear were full of Germans and he concluded that the moment had arrived for him to return as he had come. The two scout-cars therefore sped once more past anti-tank guns, bazookas and infantry, all of whom were fortunately too slow in opening fire. They both regained the bridgehead safely, Lieutenant Buchanan-Jardine earning the Military Cross for his spectacular dash. The news he brought back of the extent of the German defences was not exactly encouraging, but this was only to be expected; the air operations were essential and up the main road it had to be.

At a quarter to one the fighters appeared—swarms of them diving furiously every time a German gun opened up; and then, over to the West and flying very low in a solemn train, came the airborne fleet, a seemingly endless procession. At a quarter-past two the air was rent by the opening strains of the barrage. There were no half measures about this, eleven field and six medium regiments being allotted to us together with the heavy mortars of two divisions, and the missiles screamed over us unceasingly, the fountains of their bursts clearly visible to the leading troops straight up the road beyond the start line. At two-thirty-five the Irish led off, No. 3 Squadron in the lead, supported by No. 1 Company. They moved slowly up the road at eight miles an hour, the plan being for the barrage to roll forward ahead of them at the same speed. The dust was so great and the noise so terrific that for some time they could not tell whether they were too near or too far or even in the barrage, but at first everything went smoothly and it was not long before the leading tanks had crossed the Dutch border. "Advance going well—leading squadron has got through" came over the wireless; but then, quite suddenly, the news was flashed back that a tank had been hit, followed by similar reports of eight other tanks in scarcely as many seconds. The head of the column had driven clean through an anti-tank screen, the members of which had held their fire until the barrage had passed well over their heads, after which they had come to life again. The last three tanks of the leading squadron and the first six of No. 1 Squadron behind it had been hit with the result that No. 3 Squadron, less three tanks, was intact in front but between it and the remainder of the group was a nasty gap of half a mile littered with burning hulks. Even if it had been possible for the other tanks to get by, the same fate awaited them. Marshy country with pine trees and numerous ditches on either side of a causeway road did not afford them any opportunity for deployment.

Obviously the Typhoons provided the only answer and nobly they responded to the appeal; this was where their detailed knowledge of our plan really came in. They knew just where our own tanks and men were and shot up everything else in all directions; many targets were engaged with rockets within a hundred yards of our own troops, but nevertheless no casualties as a result were reported. Meanwhile all the tanks kept up a continuous fire also from all weapons and for nearly half an hour complete bedlam appeared to reign. The turning point in the battle came when Sergeant Cowan, commanding a seventeen-pounder Sherman, spotted a German self-propelled anti-tank gun and scored a hit with his first shot. The crew at once trotted in to surrender and, after persuading the crew of a neighbouring gun to surrender also, willingly pointed out to us the positions occupied by all their comrades. What a truly extraordinary people the Germans are! Then the Typhoons were called off and a sweeping attack was carried out by the two leading groups to capture or kill any Germans remaining alive in the woods on either side of the road. They were ably assisted in this task by the two battalions of the 50th Division, the 2nd Devons and the 1st Dorsets, who had been given the job of clearing our flanks until we had broken through the enemy screen. Quite a few Germans were found crouching at the bottom of their slit trenches among the trees; most of them were frightened to death by the overpowering attack of the Typhoons and were heartily relieved at becoming prisoners, tears literally pouring down many of their miserable faces. Little time was available for dealing with them and they were therefore simply ordered to double back down the centre-line. Many gladly covered the whole distance to the 5th Guards Brigade Headquarters in Olympic style.

The barrage now started again and the advance continued; from then on it was child's play and nothing more than the odd shot was encountered before the crucial bridge just South of Valkenswaard was reached at half-past seven. Fortunately this was not severely damaged and the town was quickly occupied and all approaches blocked. The Germans who remained were in a state of great confusion and were all eventually rounded up; that they were not alone in their confusion was shown when later on in the evening a Dutchman from the Post Office arrived at Group Headquarters to say that the German commander at Eindhoven had rung up to tell the garrison that reinforcements were on the way and that they must hang on at all costs. He was told to say in answer that the reinforcements must hurry as they were eagerly awaited; none the less there was still no sign of them when the advance continued at first light.

Spirits were high in the division that morning. It is true that the enemy positions had been stronger than anticipated and the quality of the troops higher, but this only made the achievement of the Irish Group the more notable. Identifications established that two battalions of the 6th Parachute Regiment and two battalions of the 9th S.S. Division had been engaged, the presence of the S.S. battalions coming as a complete surprise. They had been supported by a large number of guns and mortars and, while they had succeeded in extricating a few of these and some opposition could therefore still be expected, the full programme for the initial day had been accomplished and junction with the American paratroops was well in sight. News of the latters' progress was meanwhile very vague but eventually a message was passed back by Captain G. M. Balding, who was leading a Household Cavalry patrol and had established contact, asking for a telephone call to be put through to Zon 244. This was done and an American major answered the call and informed us that the bridge there had been blown up when their troops were only two hundred yards from it. He was able to give the exact width of the gap and said that their own sappers were preparing the approaches.

It was at Valkenswaard that the centre-line split. The Irish were to continue due North on the main axis through Eindhoven, while the 32nd Guards Brigade Group, with the Welsh leading, was to turn East towards Leende, Geldrop and Helmond. At six o'clock the next morning, September 18th, the Irish resumed the advance, but they soon met considerable opposition; the German infantry were once more making full use of the wooded country which lined each side of the road and were supported by Panthers and anti-tank guns. At Aalst they were held up completely and the Grenadier Group was ordered to follow the Household Cavalry, who were already engaged in trying to by-pass Eindhoven to the West in order to make contact with the Americans. Before long Major F. E. B. Wignall reported that his squadron of armoured cars had gone clean through and joined up with the paratroops, but, splendid news as this was, it did not necessarily mean that the tanks could follow. It was a disappointing day for the Grenadiers; no enemy were seen but, every time that the advance seemed to be progressing, a canal or a stream would intervene with a frail wooden bridge that invariably broke after a couple of tanks had crossed. They were recalled to the main axis when Eindhoven was finally reached.

The news from the Household Cavalry now spurred the Irish on to fresh endeavours. Aalst fell, but they were held up again a little further on by several anti-tank guns and concrete strong-points forming the Southern defences of Eindhoven, and centred on yet another bridge. A staged attack, with its attendant delay, seemed unavoidable. Lieutenant D. Tabor, commanding the forward troop of armoured cars, dismounted and managed to get on foot to a position almost behind the enemy defences, from where he could see them withdrawing, a movement which could not be detected from in front. Major G. E. Fisher-Rowe had meanwhile looped to the West with No. 1 Company, through Gestel, and soon reported that the way seemed clear and that the only obstruction to movement was the crowd. On hearing Lieutenant Tabor's report the column on the main road also quickly moved on, passing a line of at least six eighty-eight-millimetre guns whose crews had fled. The welcome was just like

Brussels, with everywhere orange banners and flags, fruit and flowers. By this time the U.S. 101st Airborne Division was in complete possession of the town and of the road leading to the Wilhelmina Canal; so the Irish pushed their way through as best they could and dashed on to Zon, which they reached just as darkness fell. There they found the American regimental commander in the village school. It was the division's first acquaintance with American parachutists and their looks were as impressive as their enthusiasm was infectious. Yes, certainly the bridge was gone but the tanks had to stop for the night anyhow. The job of throwing a new bridge across was just what the sappers were pining for, and they had everything prepared, thanks to the information received from the Americans over the telephone.

The Welsh Group had found progress similarly difficult on the secondary axis. After considerable fighting Leende and Heeze were clear by dusk, but Geldrop appeared strongly held. Patrols at first light subsequently confirmed this and, as civilian reports received during the night stated that Helmond, the next town on this route, was the main enemy stronghold of the whole area, the General decided that the whole division should now use the main centre-line, as this was by then known to be held by the Americans right through to Grave. The two Brigade Headquarters had moved to Eindhoven and Valkenswaard respectively and Divisional Headquarters just South of the latter town, while supply units had all been brought as far forward as possible to ensure the minimum delay. The move of Divisional Headquarters was singularly fortunate, as shortly after its departure a really heavy bombing attack was made on the Escaut bridge and factory area. The bridge was untouched and the numerous anti-personnel bombs did little damage in the absence of our troops.

The bridging had been well up in the column and Lieutenant-Colonel C. P. Jones, commanding the Royal Engineers, aimed at having his task completed by first light, at six o'clock. The bridge was in fact ready almost exactly on schedule, a very fine achievement on the part of the 14th Field Squadron, and ten minutes later the first tank crossed. This time the Grenadiers led and very quick progress was made as the airborne troops had cleared the route and secured the bridges. All these were held by them and they cheered wildly as our tanks sped past, arousing a corresponding spirit of elation among our men. By seven o'clock the leading troops were already through Veghel and by half-past eight they had crossed the River Maas at Grave, using the first of the three great bridges which separated us not only from our ultimate objective but also from the 1st British Airborne Division at Arnhem. The Grave bridge consists of nine spans with a total length of about two hundred and fifty yards; it is raised high above the low-lying country on either side and its capture intact by a brigade of the 82nd U.S. Airborne Division, which landed astride the river, represented a very fine performance. A halt was made here, as a liaison officer arrived to say that Lieutenant-General Browning, the Airborne Corps Commander, wished to see the commanding officers of the two leading battalions at his Headquarters, which was in the forest on the high ground some five miles South of Nijmegen and only three from the German border. It must have been a happy moment for him when he saw our troops approaching, as the airborne forces had by now been marooned on their own for two days; particularly so in the event as he had himself commanded one of the Grenadier battalions only a few years previously. He told them that the bridge spanning the canal on the main road about three miles South-West of Nijmegen had been damaged and would not take tanks, but that a suitable diversion to the East existed through Overasselt and Heumen. The column moved on along this after a short halt and by mid-day the whole Grenadier Group was concentrated round the monastery of Marienboom, just South of Nijmegen, while Household Cavalry patrols had reached the River Waal.

By now, Brigadier Gwatkin, General Adair and General Horrocks had all reached Airborne Corps Headquarters in succession, and a conference was held in order to formulate a plan. Up till this moment our information concerning the progress of the airborne formations had been distinctly indefinite, as the liaison officers had been unable to establish wireless communication with Main

Headquarters in the manner hoped. We now learned that the 82nd U.S. Airborne Division held only a part of Nijmegen and had not been able to approach the bridges owing to its very considerable other commitments; these had included not only the holding of the Grave bridge after its initial capture but also the seizure of the high wooded ground to the South-East of Nijmegen and the holding of dropping zones for the succeeding "lifts"; moreover they were not fully up to strength as these latter had been delayed owing to bad weather. Although excellent progress had been made it yet remained a fact that only one of the three great obstacles had been crossed and, while the two remaining bridges were still reported intact, it was surely only a matter of time before the Germans would order them to be blown up. The 1st British Airborne Division was meanwhile on the far side of both; little was known of its situation other than that the original landings had been successful, but the subsequent droppings had equally been delayed by the weather and it was clearly imperative to open the route through to them at the earliest possible moment.

The country that lay ahead was if possible more forbidding from the point of view of armour even than that through which we had come. The town of Nijmegen lies on the South bank of the Waal, which is the true Rhine, for the river divides near the Dutch border, and the lesser river, the Neder Rijn, flows South of Arnhem and formed the third obstacle to our advance. The road and railway bridges of Nijmegen lie to the North-East and North-West of the town respectively and form the only crossings over the river for some twenty miles. The huge modern road bridge has a total length of two thousand feet with a centre span of eight hundred feet and four smaller spans supported on four massive stone buttresses; it is built on high ground and dwarfs the town and even the Rhine itself. The more humble railway bridge suffers by comparison in grandeur if not in length but was reckoned capable of taking one-way traffic. Both bridges afford fine view-points over the low-lying country to the North, which stretches uninterruptedly to Arnhem; so marshy is this that the main roads are built on embankments, making it impossible for tanks to deploy off them at any point. Such was the prospect before us and it was to be expected that the Germans would fight with fanatical desperation in so vitally important a defence.

The plan was quickly made on the basis of information supplied by the Americans and by members of the Dutch resistance movement. The approaches to both bridges were difficult and favoured the defence, but we were told that they were not as yet strongly held. Accordingly a mixed force of tanks and infantry was to pass through the American positions on the outskirts of the town and attempt to rush the bridges before reinforcements arrived. Major-General J. Gavin, the commander of the 82nd U.S. Airborne Division, placed the 2nd Bn. 505th Parachute Regiment under command of the 5th Guards Brigade and this battalion, with No. 3 Squadron–No. 2 Company Group of the Grenadiers, was to form the attacking force. A company of paratroops, a troop of tanks and a platoon of our infantry were directed on the railway bridge while the remainder were to head straight for the road bridge. A third force had the Post Office as its objective, as a report had come in that the wiring for the demolition charges in the bridge was there. The building was occupied almost without opposition, but no wiring was found. Lieutenant-Colonel Goulburn thereupon established his Headquarters there.

The column directed on the road bridge moved off as soon as details with the paratroops had been arranged, at about four o'clock. It moved up the main road into the town guided by Dutch resistance men travelling in the leading tanks and progress was at first swift. However it gradually slowed down until a complete hold-up was imposed on reaching a large roundabout some three hundred yards short of the bridge; this formed a naturally strong position dominated on the South-West by an old fort, while houses and even a bandstand had been carefully transformed into strong-points with loopholes, slit trenches and a deep, if waterless, moat on the South-West side. As the foremost tank emerged into this open space it was heavily engaged by several anti-tank guns; there were also at least two self-propelled guns in the area and a great number of infantry with automatic weapons.

At least one anti-tank gun was destroyed but the leading tank was meanwhile set on fire and the troop leader, Lieutenant J. A. Moller, killed. The next two tanks were also hit and badly damaged and it was seen that a frontal attack could not succeed. Accordingly the only motor platoon still uncommitted was sent on a movement round the right flank in the hope of forcing the position. At the same time Lieutenant M. Dawson found a view-point in a house from which he could overlook the German positions and, after bringing up all available automatic weapons, opened up on the enemy in front. A considerable number were killed and wounded but the fire was returned by an eighty-eight-millimetre gun; this scored a direct hit on the house, which had then to be evacuated. The enemy shelling was intense the whole time and, as it was now getting dark and it was evident that no immediate progress could be made, the force took up dispositions for the night and the outflanking platoon, which had not been able to get very far, was recalled.

The column making for the railway bridge had been similarly held up in sight of the approaches and no further advance could be made owing to heavy shell and machine-gun fire. The railway line proved to be an obstacle to all vehicles and, as the infantry contingent was not strong enough to storm the enemy positions without tank support, Captain J. W. Neville, who was in command, finally ordered a withdrawal and concentrated for the night around the main cross-roads North of the railway station. His force was by this time in the unenviable position of being entirely cut off except by wireless, as the Germans had infiltrated back into the streets by which it had come. His conduct of these operations earned him subsequently the award of the Military Cross.

It was obvious, as a result of the evening's fighting, that the Germans had made good use of the two days' delay to strengthen the defences and in particular, as was subsequently discovered, to bring up some S.S. troops through Arnhem. Determined as the attacks had been, there had been no stage at which either force looked like being able to rush the bridges or even seriously to disturb the forces protecting them. Moreover it was doubtful if the road bridge could have been held even in the event of capture unless the old fort dominating it had also been cleared of the enemy. Consequently General Adair made a plan with General Gavin by which the systematic clearing of the town would start at dawn the following morning, preparatory to a major attack on the bridges fully supported by artillery later in the day; the risk of the Germans blowing them up in the meantime was fully appreciated, but there was no alternative. It was however decided to make an assault crossing of the river West of Nijmegen at the same time; once across the troops concerned were to wheel right in order to attack the road bridge from the North. There was no question of any further fighting troops reaching the area for at least twenty-four hours and all contingencies must somehow be guarded against by the two divisions; the 5th Guards Brigade therefore assumed responsibility, with the one American battalion still under command, for clearing Nijmegen prior to seizing the bridges. This freed the 50th U.S. Parachute Regiment to undertake the assault crossing, supported by two squadrons of the 2nd Bn. Irish Guards. The 32nd Guards Brigade, which had concentrated by nightfall between Grave and the Waal–Maas Canal, was to provide the Coldstream Group for the reinforcement of the 82nd U.S. Airborne Division on the right flank. Determined enemy attacks supported by a few tanks had necessitated limited withdrawals here, and some concern was felt lest a German build-up might be taking place in the Reichswald behind. With excellent communications of all kinds to the Ruhr and to Cologne, both within fifty miles, supplies and reinforcements could easily be brought up and, if once they could regain possession of this high ground, any further advance to the North would be rendered impossible. The Welsh Group took over the defence of the Grave area and formed the only possible reserve. The Household Cavalry, in addition to supplying one squadron to support the 82nd U.S. Airborne Division, had to patrol and reconnoitre to the West between the Maas and the Rhine, and to both flanks of the centre-line South of the Maas.

At eight o'clock on the morning of September 20th, the Grenadier Group started on the laborious task of clearing the town. Helped by the American paratroop battalion the advance proceeded slowly but steadily from house to house, in the face of fierce resistance. The operation involved three phases, the first two of which went smoothly and were designed to provide a basis for the final attack upon the old fort and high ground that dominated the approaches to the road bridge. By early afternoon Lieutenant-Colonel Goulburn decided that he could safely launch the final assault on this bridge, though progress towards the other had been slower owing to the maze of narrow streets in the old part of the town. The King's Company, with a platoon of No. 2 Company, a section of machine-guns and two tanks, was to clear the houses on the left and work its way forward to the embankment near the bridge. No. 4 Company, in the centre, was to capture the old fort and the park round it and was then to make for the bridge. The Americans, on the right, were to clear the open ground East of the roundabout and then also to advance on the bridge. All attacks were to go in simultaneously at half-past three.

Shortly before this the Americans' assault crossing of the river to the West was launched. The place chosen entailed a crossing of some six hundred yards and on the far side lay a considerable expanse of marshland enclosed by a high dyke and overlooked by an old moated earth fortification. Thirty-two assault boats were lent to them of a type more suitable for the quieter rivers of England. No others were available; however, the men who were to use them seemed to view them without any qualms, although the current was running at three knots. Lieutenant-Colonel Jones, who always seemed prepared for every contingency, also produced for them two rafts to get anti-tank guns across, together with teams to build and to operate them. It was altogether a hazardous undertaking in daylight, as the enemy had excellent observation from the dyke over the whole operation. In order to prevent aimed fire during the launching and crossing, the limited available artillery support, provided by the Leicestershire Yeomanry at very short notice, was augmented by intense fire from the Irish Guards tanks, which also attempted a smoke-screen. Owing to the weather, however, the latter was not altogether effective and on approaching the far bank the assaulting troops were met with heavy fire. Although casualties in the first wave numbered about three men in each boat, they pressed on in the most courageous manner. A foothold was obtained and a small bridgehead held until the arrival of the following waves, some of whom swam the river after their boats were sunk. The ferrying of anti-tank guns and other equipment behind the assaulting force was successfully carried out by the 615th Field Squadron and by six o'clock the troops started to move East towards the Northern end of the Nijmegen bridges.

Good progress had meanwhile also been made by the Grenadiers in Nijmegen itself. The King's Company had managed to get into the Valkhof, an old fortress on the river's edge in which modern defences had been incorporated, by climbing the embankment and cutting a hole through the barbed wire on top. The Germans had not expected an attack from this quarter and two platoons were able to deploy inside before they awoke to their danger. For a few minutes after this the fighting was fast and furious, but our men managed to close with the enemy in their dug-outs and killed or captured most of them. Both leading platoons suffered casualties from small-arms weapons at close range and the company commander, Captain the Hon. V. P. Gibbs, was killed, leaving Lieutenant Dawson in command. Troops in support also incurred severe losses at this time, Captain A. Tasker of the Leicestershire Yeomanry and Lieutenant J. N. Fielden of the 2nd Bn. Grenadier Guards being amongst those killed, but very soon the company was established in the German positions on the Eastern edge of the Valkhof and from there were able to dominate the bridge and to fire on the Germans dug in on the embankment South of it. The reserve platoon was now sent forward and positioned itself only fifty yards from the bridge, capturing a number of prisoners; but the field of fire here was very limited and it was ordered back to the Valkhof, from where all approaches to the bridge could better be covered. The machine-guns were by this time conveniently sited on the roof of the Post Office just behind and firing hard in support but the two tanks had not been so lucky; one was hit by a bazooka and the other found it quite impossible to get into the Valkhof area.

No. 4 Company, under Captain H. F. Stanley, was met with withering fire on its first attempt to attack the fort on the far side of the roundabout but subsequently succeeded in getting across the exposed piece of ground under cover of smoke. The men then worked their way through gardens and along a high wall bordering the park until they were within thirty yards of the fort. One platoon then charged the fort and dealt successfully with the Germans inside while the other systematically cleared the houses West of the park. As soon as the fort was securely held the Americans were able to advance on the right and by half-past six both they and No. 4 Company were established on the embankment leading to the bridge, where they were joined by patrols from the King's Company who had been following their progress. A patrol of No. 4 Company now moved to the edge of the bridge itself and, despite the death of its leader, Lieutenant P. B. M. Greenall, established itself there after capturing quite a few prisoners.

It was now close on seven o'clock and a report was received by the Grenadiers that the American flag could be seen on the far side of the bridge. Communications were not too good and it subsequently turned out to have referred to the railway bridge, but it served as a signal to attempt rush tactics. A short while previously a troop of tanks of No. 1 Squadron had been ordered to move forward over the bridge, but it was still too light and they had been met by heavy anti-tank gun-fire and forced to withdraw. Now it was a little less than half-light and the troop, commanded by Sergeant Robinson, and led by Sergeant Pacey (both of whom won the Military Medal for their courageous act), moved forward again firing all the time. To the astonishment of all onlookers and listeners on the wireless the four tanks drove swiftly on to the bridge and gradually disappeared into the gloom. They were quickly followed in a fifth tank by Captain Lord

Carrington, second-in-command of the squadron, and by the reconnaissance officer of the 14th Field Squadron, Lieutenant A. G. C. Jones, in a scout-car; he had the monumental task of locating and neutralising the charges, about which valuable information had been received from the Dutch patriots. These two also disappeared and still the bridge did not blow up.

It was one of the tensest moments of the campaign. The bridge was lit by the flames of the burning houses of Nijmegen, which made it assume even vaster proportions, and at any moment some unseen hand might yet wreck all hopes of reaching the hard-pressed airborne division at Arnhem. Tracer bullets could be seen weaving fantastic patterns as they crossed and re-crossed the bridge; Germans were firing from every possible vantage-point including the topmost girders whence, as they were hit, they fell to their beloved river far below. Even the wireless operator of the leading tank killed at least one German with his pistol out of the port-hole while the tank commander, Sergeant Pacey, fired his Bren gun from the front. This tank continued its dash straight across the bridge and steered through one of the two narrow gaps in the concrete wall built right across the Northern approaches, coming to a stop a short distance beyond. It was quickly joined by Sergeant Robinson but the other two tanks were less fortunate. They were hit at the far end of the bridge either by anti-tank guns or bazookas, though the driver of one of them, Sergeant Knight, when he found that it had not caught fire, quickly leaped in again and drove on after the others. As Lord Carrington arrived some strange troops appeared and started to attack the tanks with gelignite, but they turned out to be some of the Americans who had made the assault crossing; recognition was quickly effected and the isolated little force disposed itself to the best advantage pending the arrival of reinforcements.

The first of these turned up almost immediately in the form of Captain P. Shervington's troop of seventeen-pounder self-propelled guns of Q Battery of the 21st Anti-Tank Regiment. This was followed about three-quarters of an hour later by No. 2 Company of the 3rd Bn. Irish Guards, and soon afterwards by

No. 1 Company of the same battalion. They had to get out of their vehicles South of the bridge and move across on foot, and only as the leading platoon reached it was the last German on top picked off by the American paratroops, hanging from a girder like a squirrel. Many were still left underneath the roadway and continued to fire at the sappers who were hurriedly setting to work to remove the ample supply of demolition charges; some eighty more of less fanatical disposition were taken prisoners from their places of hiding in the demolition chambers. Throughout the hours of darkness sporadic fighting continued on both banks, and it was a nerve-racking and uncomfortable night for all members of the small force holding the bridgehead; but, although many civilians came in with rumours of impending counter-attacks, none ever developed and by the morning conditions were comparatively quiet.

Long before this Lieutenant Jones had succeeded in seeking out the charges and in rendering them harmless. Although the chambers in the main buttresses were empty, great care had been taken to lay them under the second span from the Northern end. They ran the full width of the bridge, they were connected up and were amply sufficient to destroy the span. Several prisoners stated that they had expected the bridge to be blown up two days previously and the true reason for the failure ever to do so may never be known. Although the total force holding Nijmegen was over two thousand men they were a heterogeneous assortment, strengthened by a fairly large proportion of S.S. troops from Arnhem sent to toughen the morale of the remainder. They were organised in groups, but each group seems to have known little of its neighbours and in particular there appears to have been no guiding hand from above. A willingness to take responsibility on his own initiative has never been a notable characteristic of the German soldier, and it may well have been this lack of central control that caused the bridge to be left intact.

Early in the morning the smaller Grenadier force attacking the damaged railway bridge had also succeeded in reaching the Northern end. They had improved their positions and cleared the area up to the bridge by dint of hard fighting on the previous day, but the tanks could not get up on to the embankment and the infantry alone could make no further progress owing to the exposed position, until the American paratroops reached the far end. Once this occurred the defenders were isolated, though a great many fought as bitterly as those on the road bridge. Four hundred and seventeen dead were counted in addition to a large number of wounded, who were made prisoner.

So between them the Guardsmen and the American paratroops captured the first two and, with the sole later addition of the one at Remagen, the only intact bridges ever seized over the Rhine in the course of the campaign. Moreover the capture had been made in the face of desperate resistance by a very determined enemy. In the words of the official Army Group account, it was "a magnificent achievement brought about by the actions, so brilliantly co-ordinated and executed, of the Guards Armoured and the 82nd U.S. Airborne Divisions". As an epic example of allied co-operation under the most difficult conditions, it augured well for the future.

Chapter Seven

THE "ISLAND"

WHILE THE limelight on these memorable days was naturally fixed on the actions of the Grenadier and Irish Groups in Nijmegen it should not be thought that the remainder of the division was idle. Almost the only fighting troops who for the moment saw no action were those of the Welsh Group guarding the Grave bridge, and this was pure chance, as a desperate enemy attempt to recapture and destroy it might have been made at any moment. The wide commitments of the division as a whole can perhaps best be illustrated by the answer given by Brigadier H. C. Phipps, the C.R.A., when ordered to get the 84th Medium Regiment into action immediately on arrival, with one battery facing East and one West. "Certainly," came his reply, but he added for reasons of caution a reminder that one field regiment was already facing North and the other one South.

The Coldstream Group, although not involved in any major action, had a busy time supporting the 82nd U.S. Airborne Division against numerous German counter-attacks. Its activities during the three days spent in this role consisted of successive moves from one end of the high ground to the other, according to which part of the perimeter was being attacked at the time. The heaviest attack was that which came in early on the afternoon of September 20th, and consisted of a central assault South of Groesbeek, together with converging ones aiming North-West through Mook and South-West through Beek. The central one was a fiasco from the start, but the other two resulted in some stiff fighting in which the Coldstream tanks were involved. At first the Americans thought that they would have difficulty in holding the Mook attack, but on arrival to support them the Coldstream found that they had got matters sufficiently under control only to need the assistance of a troop of tanks. Lieutenant

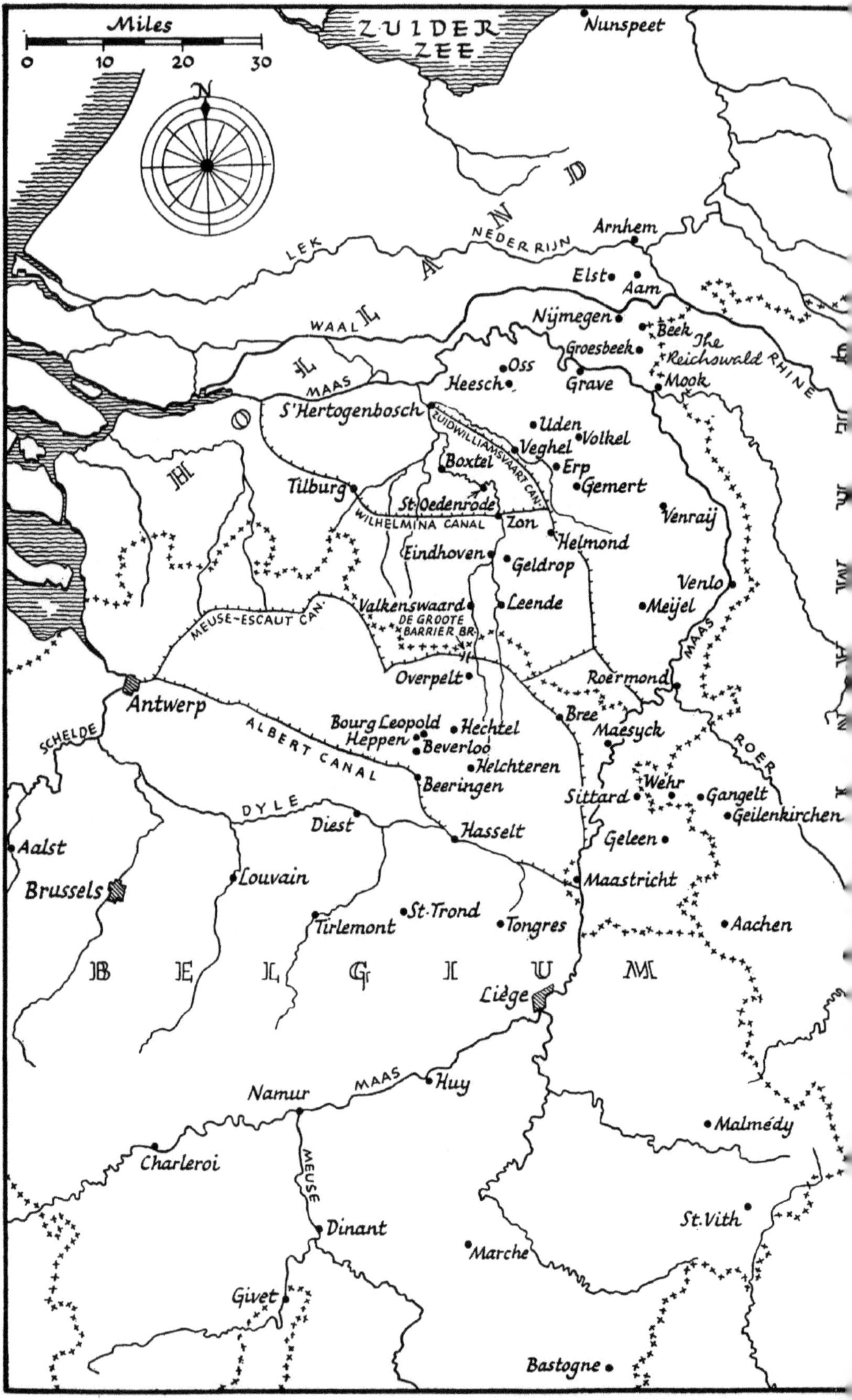
Miles
0
10
20
30
N
ZUIDER ZEE
Nunspeet
HOLLAND
LEK
NEDER RIJN
Arnhem
Elst
Aam
WAAL
Nijmegen
Beek
The Reichswald
RHINE
Groesbeek
Oss
Heesch
Grave
Mook
MAAS
S'Hertogenbosch
ZUIDWILLIAMSVAART CAN.
Uden
Veghel
Volkel
Boxtel
Erp
Gemert
Tilburg
St. Oedenrode
Venraij
WILHELMINA CANAL
Zon
Helmond
Eindhoven
Geldrop
Venlo
Valkenswaard
Leende
Meijel
MEUSE-ESCAUT CAN.
DE GROOTE BARRIER BR.
Overpelt
Roermond
Antwerp
Bree
Bourg Leopold
Heppen
Hechtel
Beverloo
Maesyck
SCHELDE
ALBERT CANAL
Helchteren
ROER
Beeringen
Wehr
Sittard
Gangelt
Geilenkirchen
DYLE
Diest
Hasselt
Geleen
Aalst
Louvain
Maastricht
Brussels
St. Trond
Tirlemont
Tongres
Aachen
BELGIUM
Liège
MAAS
Huy
Namur
Malmédy
Charleroi
MEUSE
St. Vith
Dinant
Marche
Givet
Bastogne

J. H. T. Sutton's troop from No. 3 Squadron was provided; it did considerable execution and, though one tank was blown up on a mine, the crew escaped. No. 1 Squadron supported the Americans in the Beek attack and Lieutenant I. L. Jardine's troop became the first British tanks to operate in Germany when they crossed the frontier in the course of operations on September 21st. The honour, however, to be the first British troops to fight on German soil belongs to the men of Captain R. Williams' troop of Q Battery of the 21st Anti-Tank Regiment. At two o'clock on the previous afternoon Brigadier Gwatkin, who was anxious about the right flank of the Nijmegen attack, sent them to make contact with the commander of an American battalion near Wyler Meer. On the way there they crossed into German territory and encountered thirty-five Germans, who promptly surrendered to them.

Furthest stretched of all, as might be expected, were the Household Cavalry, whose patrols were dispersed to the four winds, some of them as much as thirty miles apart. In one place, cut off entirely from us, they were directing our artillery on to targets passed on to them by the isolated paratroops at Arnhem. In another they had discovered a ferry across the Waal in perfect working order but on the North bank; they were in telephonic communication with the Dutch on the far side who might be persuaded to bring it across; might they use it? They had to be told that they were already far enough afield. Further down the river they observed a steamer flying the German flag and towing four barges; they were manœuvring into a favourable position to engage. Shortly afterwards came the further message that the steamer had been hit and damaged and three of the barges sunk. "Congratulations on brilliant naval action; splice mainbrace" was the answer sent back by Divisional Headquarters.

Possibly the most curious operation of all at this time was the capture of the village of Oss by a small improvised force under Captain P. A. C. O'Donovan, commander of the General's troop of Cromwell tanks. Both this troop and the defence platoon of Divisional Headquarters seldom got the opportunity for an action for which they were always eager, as their roles were primarily protective, but on this occasion luck came their way. When the column was momentarily halted on the way up to Nijmegen on September 19th, with Divisional Headquarters about six miles short of Grave, an American despatch-rider drove up and asked for immediate help, saying that a small party of American soldiers were in trouble some three miles to the West. Belief in this sort of story had been rather blunted by too many false alarms but Captain O'Donovan was sent off to investigate with two of his tanks and a section of the defence platoon under Lieutenant C. Du Cros. They tore off down a fine concrete road that ran at right angles to the centre-line and soon reached the centre of Oss, which appeared quite deserted. Suddenly a voice shouted from a bedroom window that there were enemy in the church, where investigation produced two Germans green with fright. At their appearance a horde of civilians filled the square as if from nowhere, all shouting and getting in the way in every conceivable manner; many of them proceeded also to get drunk with incredible rapidity. Their information was conflicting, but they seemed to agree that there were many Germans still about and very soon a workable order of march was achieved. The tanks led, firing at any house reported to hold Germans; the defence platoon three-ton lorry came next and collected the prisoners, and the town fire brigade was produced to follow and to put out the smaller fires made by the guns of the tanks. The rear was brought up by a charming Franciscan friar on a lady's bicycle who alternately ordered the drunks home with all the authority of his Church and gave comfort to the wounded and dying. There was little organised resistance, and after five hours they found that they had over a hundred prisoners. The fact that many of them were bakers was to prove a great asset, only surpassed by the possession of Oss itself, during the next two weeks; for the village proved to be a colossal dump containing food enough to feed a whole army for many weeks, and this was of extreme value when later the lines of communication were cut. Valuable however as it might be, it was too far away to make it possible during the first few days to spare a force to guard and maintain communications with it; so each morning, until better arrangements could be made, a protective convoy was organised and sent off in search of supplies. A methodical Dutchman was in charge of the dump; he insisted upon a signature for all drawings and on examining his book it could be seen that, while XXX Corps was drawing regularly in the mornings, the Germans at S'Hertogenbosch were equally doing so in the evenings.

This was a period too when our anti-aircraft gunners had almost more opportunity for action than at any other in the campaign. The enemy air effort was often on a considerable scale and the 94th Light Anti-Aircraft Regiment took full advantage of the chance offered them. On the afternoon of September 19th a short sharp battle with fifteen aircraft near Malden resulted in two of them being shot down by A Troop in full view of our men. Early on the following morning B and D Troops fought six Focke-Wolfs which attacked the 32nd Guards Brigade column while it was halted on Grave bridge; they provided an exemplary display of snap-action, for their guns were not laid out in normal deployment but were in the column on the road, which at the time was blocked by three lines of traffic. One aircraft immediately crashed while another was seen to fall further away.

It is now time to revert our attention to the Nijmegen bridges, the capture of which had opened once more the prospect of being able to carry out our final primary object—the crossing of the last water obstacle, the Neder Rijn, and the subsequent linking up with our hard-pressed troops in the Arnhem area. At first knowledge of conditions there had been most scanty as wireless communications had been both intermittent and faint, but the adjutant of the Sappers of the 1st Airborne Division succeeded in crossing the Neder Rijn on the evening of September 20th and infiltrated through the enemy lines during the night to our positions in the bridgehead. He brought the news that two brigades were firmly established in the Oosterbeek area to the West of Arnhem but that the third brigade, which had been given the task of capturing the main road bridge in Arnhem, had had a very difficult time. After landing on the high ground North of the town it had succeeded in capturing the Northern end of the bridge and in removing the demolition charges there. But the enemy had brought up troops very quickly and after very fierce fighting our men had lost the bridge itself, though they were holding out in houses from which they could cover the bridge with fire. They were confident that the Northern end was all right, but there might be demolition charges at the Southern end and unfortunately it was also uncertain whether they would be able to hold out till we could reach them. One of the other brigades had tried to fight their way through the town to their aid but had suffered very heavy casualties. The whole division was very short of supplies as the dropping had been only partially successful; the weather had been very bad and the flak had been intense, causing severe losses to the Stirlings and their brave crews, who were forced to fly at a very low level for the purpose.

This information was disquieting enough to provide an additional spur, had any been needed, to our determination to push through at once to Arnhem if humanly possible. The Irish Group was ordered to take over the lead from the Grenadiers and at mid-day on September 21st the advance began, No. 1 Squadron in front on its own followed by two squadron-company groups. It was fully realised that conditions would be very difficult if the opposition proved at all serious, owing to the hopeless unsuitability of the ground for armour, as previously explained. Ammunition too was short owing to the rapid advance and only a medium battery was available in support; a field regiment could be expected later, but the guns were unable to deploy until the advance had begun. Worst of all, the air support that had proved so invaluable in the original break-out would be largely lacking, as there were as yet no advance landing-grounds. One tentacle was however allotted with a limited number of Typhoons on call.

Captain Langton led off with No. 1 Squadron and had gone about two miles when suddenly all three tanks of the leading troop were knocked out on rounding a bend. Captain Langton himself, who was following immediately behind, just pulled up in time in the shelter of a little orchard surrounding a farmhouse. The infantry of the group following quickly tumbled off the tanks and took up fire positions in the ditches on each side of the road; they came under intense mortar and shell-fire and started to suffer heavy casualties. Meanwhile Lieutenant A. L. Samuelson, commanding the leading troop, had crawled back down a ditch and reported that heavy fire was coming from the right and that there seemed to be a number of infantry in the orchards on either side of the road. Lieutenant-Colonel G. A. M. Vandeleur, who had now come up in his scout-car, attempted to go forward to discover the source of the trouble but experienced some difficulty in turning when fired upon and had a lucky escape. It was painfully obvious that advance along this axis was for the moment out of the question, and deployment of the armour to either side was impracticable owing to the numerous deep ditches which ran not only on either side of the road but also at right angles. He ordered the tanks to remain where they were, while infantry reconnaissance parties were sent to either flank to discover if the enemy position could be turned or an alternative route of advance found. The artillery was meanwhile brought down on all the suspected enemy areas but was not nearly enough to loosen the opposition effectively. The occasion was an ideal one for air support, which alone might have made the Irish Guards' task possible, but unfortunately the contact car allotted to them failed to get into touch with the Typhoons owing to faulty wireless communication. The only other contact car available within the division was promptly summoned but proved equally useless.

The Welsh group, which had been transferred to the 5th Guards Brigade in place of the exhausted Grenadiers, was now brought up an alternative road to the East and was soon also engaged in hard fighting; but though the efforts continued till dark progress was slow owing to the exposed nature of the country and to the good siting of the German defences. The Irish were within striking distance of Bemmel station, seemingly the centre of the resistance, when night fell, but General Horrocks came to the conclusion that the junction with the airborne forces could not in the circumstances be carried out by armour. The 43rd Division was therefore ordered to take over the assignment on the following day and the Irish and Welsh Groups were meanwhile to concentrate in tight pivot positions for the night.

At five o'clock that evening about two-thirds of the Polish Parachute Brigade had been dropped in the area North-West of Elst. The weather was still far from favourable and this factor, combined with heavy enemy flak, caused most of the drop to take place nearer to Elst, and consequently to the German positions, than had been intended. A number of casualties resulted and there was delay in concentrating them in the area South of the Neder Rijn from where they were to cross to reinforce the airborne division. If a junction could speedily be effected with them all might yet be well.

The Household Cavalry saw their chance and took it. With customary dash Captain A. V. Young of C Squadron took advantage of an early morning mist to slip clean through the German lines on side roads to the West and by daylight had joined up with the Poles, an achievement for which he subsequently obtained the Military Cross. He found with them the G.S.O. I of the 1st Airborne Division, who reported that his troops were short of food, ammunition and medical supplies, and that they could not hold out for more than a further twenty-four hours. On hearing this the squadron leader, Major P. Herbert, sent forward a second troop under Lieutenant R. J. Wrottesley, which also got through successfully. During the course of the day these two troops continued to send back a stream of valuable information, at one period again directing the Corps artillery on to targets passed on to them by the isolated paratroops at Arnhem. Major Herbert attempted to follow with the remainder of his squadron and the mist was still thick as he passed through the outposts of the 43rd Division, but soon afterwards it began to clear and the leading car went up in flames. The road lay along an embankment and as the surrounding country became visible a village three hundred yards ahead was seen to be full of Germans, while in the fields below were several enemy tanks. The armoured cars put down smoke and quickly reversed out of sight under heavy fire; no further losses were sustained, probably because the German tank gunners found difficulty in elevating their guns sufficiently to fire with accuracy at them on the high embankment. While the 129th Brigade of the 43rd Division was attacking up the main axis, General Horrocks decided to direct the 214th Brigade along the route taken by the Household Cavalry. It seemed as though this road could not be so strongly held and the brigade was allotted some tanks of the 8th Armoured Brigade to assist them in escorting the amphibious vehicles carrying the ammunition, supplies and medical stores so sorely needed by the airborne division. Nevertheless a staged attack proved necessary before the enemy defences could be breached, after which a mobile column was pushed through which succeeded in linking up with the Poles before nightfall. Unfortunately the banks of the river proved too steep and in addition were under close-range fire from the opposite shore, but some supplies were got across by rafting during the course of the night.

It was as well that this alternative route was used, as the 129th Brigade found progress very slow owing to the continued strong resistance and the difficulty of deployment. So determined in fact was the opposition that, in spite of a converging assault by the 214th Brigade from the West on the subsequent day, it was not till three days later that the position was properly cleared up with the occupation of Elst. During these three days the 5th Guards Brigade had the task of protecting the right flank of the 43rd Division as far as the Waal, while keeping an armoured regimental group in reserve for counter-attack if necessary. This task included the capture of the small town of Bemmel and this was attacked by the Welsh Guards on September 24th; but once again the surrounding country was unsuitable for armoured movement and ideal for defence, of which the Germans were not slow to take advantage. Infantry was supplied in the shape of the 69th Brigade of the 50th Division, which was put under command and captured the place after hard fighting the next day. This was the beginning of the fighting on the "Island", as the swampy land North of the Waal came to be called, a particularly dreary and unpleasant episode of which almost every element of the division was destined to have a taste during the course of the next three weeks. For the present however it remained the concern of the 5th Guards Brigade, as the 32nd Guards Brigade was ordered to turn its attention quite suddenly to something very different on the afternoon of September 22nd.

This was something as unpleasant as it was unexpected and consisted of the cutting of our supply line between Veghel and Uden, about midway to Eindhoven. The American paratroops were insufficient in members to guard more than the nodal points and it had been hoped that VIII and XII Corps, moving up on the right and left respectively, would make sufficiently rapid progress to remove the risk of any danger by the time the enemy had recovered from their surprise so far as to take offensive action of any kind. The resistance however had proved very stiff indeed on both flanks and so far both corps were only just about abreast of Eindhoven. After an attack on Zon the previous afternoon, which was beaten off, a force of lorried infantry with a few tanks and guns had placed themselves firmly across our centre-line, effectively cutting off the only means of land communication with the outside world. It was essential that the axis should be opened again with all possible speed; it was an ideal task for armour for which there was so little use on the "Island", and therefore the 32nd Guards Brigade was the obvious choice. Brigadier Johnson was told to move at once and authorised to take over command of all corps troops in the area immediately on arrival.

The Grenadier Group, which was enjoying a well-earned rest in Nijmegen, was ordered to lead off; so quickly did it do so that, although the cut had only taken place at about one o'clock, it was already at Uden by tea-time. The town presented a strange sight. A company of American paratroops had set up their headquarters in a school; Royal Army Service Corps columns or pieces of columns were parked around the streets; staff officers and their cars crowded the pavements; the scene was a motley of commanders separated from their units and units from their commanders. The interruption of all journeys had thrown everything into confusion but the Americans said that there was no sign of the town being attacked; moreover their colleagues at Veghel reported in similar terms, although the German force astride the road was in considerable strength.

A troop of tanks and a platoon of infantry were sent off down the road to investigate. On reaching a level-crossing about two miles out one of the tanks was hit by a bazooka, whereupon the force halted and took up defensive positions; but it was recalled later as it was by now quite dark and its mission of locating the enemy accomplished. An elaborate plan was now made to clear the opposition the following morning. The operation was preceded by a heavy concentration from the 130th Battery of the Leicestershire Yeomanry together with a platoon of the Northumberland Fusiliers' heavy mortars and all those of the Grenadiers. This proved so discouraging to the Germans that they melted away and the only opposition met with took the form of a few stray shots as they withdrew Eastwards. At three o'clock contact was established with the 44th Royal Tank Regiment, a squadron of which was working with the Americans at Veghel, and the road was again clear; two squadron-company groups were disposed across it in order to ensure that it remained so.

The Coldstream Group, less Captain the Hon. D. M. G. J. Willoughby's company and a troop of tanks, which had been despatched to guard the now even more important food dump at Oss, had followed immediately in the wake of the Grenadiers. Its orders were to clear Volkel and its airfield, afterwards swinging South and West to Boekel and Erp with the object of finally disposing of all threats to the axis from the East. No. 1 Company–No. 3 Squadron Group, under Major Lord Long and Major the Hon. H. R. Allsopp, was told to attack Volkel while No. 1 Squadron was to follow through and round to secure the far side. The assault, following an artillery barrage, quickly reached the outskirts, but here serious opposition was met. The leading tank was knocked out at close range; then in quick succession Lord Long was killed and Lieutenant A. B. Whitehorn, the only remaining officer in his company, was wounded. Company-Sergeant-Major Farnhill took over command and so distinguished himself in the ensuing fighting, that he was awarded the Distinguished Conduct Medal. But the battle was hard and it was some time before the village was clear and the tanks positioned at the far side. Casualties were unfortunately heavy and provided a classic example of the awful cost in lives that even a comparatively unimportant engagement can sometimes exact.

It was expected that further stiff fighting would be necessary to capture Boekel and Erp the following day, but reconnaissance parties sent in the early hours of the morning found both these villages empty; civilians said that the enemy had withdrawn to the South-East during the night. One platoon was sent by the 5th Bn. Coldstream Guards to occupy Boekel as an outpost position pending the arrival of the 231st Brigade of the 50th Division up the re-opened axis to take over there and at Volkel. These troops got through all right and duly relieved both the Coldstream and the Grenadiers, but the axis had only been open for just over twenty-four hours when it was cut again at about half-past four on the afternoon of September 24th. This time it was South of Veghel and the attack came in from the West by elements of the 6th Parachute Regiment, which had been by-passed in the original drive for Nijmegen. Tanks and a few self-propelled guns were again employed with the infantry and, despite a spirited battle fought by one scout-car and the crews of several three-ton lorries under the personal command of Brigadier Glyn Hughes, the appearance of the armour settled the issue. Brigadier Hughes was now Deputy Director of Medical Services at Corps Headquarters and had earned particular affection when he had held the equivalent post in the division throughout most of its period of training. His interest in and knowledge of tactics were quite unusual in one of his profession, and he must have revelled in this unexpected opportunity of exercising command in the field. The duties of members of the supply services were especially arduous at this time and this little action provided a good example of how their fortitude can be every bit as high as that of the fighting troops. Many of our drivers had been heavily bombed in Eindhoven on the night of September 19th when we lost nineteen petrol and seven ammunition lorries, and there existed the constant threat of attack from the flank. Few supply columns can have driven more miles with so little rest and under such harassing conditions as did ours during the advance through Belgium and Holland.

We were told not to concern ourselves with this new cut. While it was probably reasonably easy to clear the road momentarily it was another matter to prevent renewed infiltration, unless a fairly wide sector to the West were also held. The 101st U.S. Airborne Division was to fight off the pressure as best it could until the area could be properly cleared by the 7th Armoured Division advancing up the left flank. In any case an almost equally good supply route would now be available at any moment further East, through Helmond and Gemert. We were already disposed quite far enough to the South and, as the pressure of the 7th Armoured Division was carried further North, so was it anticipated that attempts to cut through would be carried out nearer the Maas. None of our troops were in this area, other than the isolated garrison at Oss, and consequently we were ordered to place one regimental group in the area where the centre-line met the main road from S'Hertogenbosch and turned right for Grave. The Coldstream Group duly moved there on September 25th, the majority being stationed astride the main road West of the junction, while the whole of No. 2 Squadron was despatched to Oss to join the company and troop already there. This was just as well, as that evening an attack by enemy infantry developed in some strength, though with little co-ordination. It is a large village and it was not possible to do much more than guard the actual approaches to the food dumps; this they did however with great distinction and the attack was driven off, though not before some Germans had got into a house next to one of their posts and had had to be blasted out by a six-pounder at close range. Many casualties were inflicted and a considerable number of prisoners taken, while our own losses were three killed and four wounded.

On the same afternoon a patrol of the reconnaissance troop of the 2nd Bn. Grenadier Guards was despatched to explore the road running North-West from Uden through Nistelrode to Heesch, a large village on the main road from S'Hertogenbosch to Grave and only a bare two miles short of Oss. Nistelrode was clear and the leading tank was only some thirty yards from the main cross-roads in Heesch when it was hit by an anti-tank gun and fire was brought to bear on the patrol from all directions. As a result of this a stronger patrol of the King's Company–No. 2 Squadron Group was sent out; it reached Heesch just as light was failing and, after also suffering the loss of one tank, was ordered back to Nistelrode for the night, where it was joined the following morning by the majority of the group.

A carefully planned attack was staged that afternoon, preceded by a barrage of the Leicestershire Yeomanry's guns and all available mortars. Behind the barrage came the King's Company–No. 2 Squadron Group on the right of the road with No. 4 Company–No. 1 Squadron Group on the left; the tanks moved slowly forward with the infantry deployed between them; and as they advanced they fired almost uninterruptedly with small arms and with their main armament of high-explosive shells. The noise was shattering and the expenditure of ammunition enormous, but it paid handsome dividends because hardly any fire came back and the bewildered Germans emerged from ditches, hedgerows and cellars to surrender in large numbers. Both groups reached their objectives with practically no casualties; not a single tank was knocked out and only two men were killed and four wounded. One hundred and seventy Germans were taken prisoner and a fair number were killed and wounded. While the prisoners were being rounded up Lieutenant R. Luff, commander of the tank of No. 2 Squadron which had been knocked out the previous evening, appeared from a barn with a member of his crew. They had spent the last twenty-four hours hiding in the middle of the enemy outposts and reported upon the shattering effect on the Germans of our barrage, which they themselves admitted frankly to have been highly unpleasant.

By darkness both groups were consolidated round the cross-roads so as to block all possible approaches. The greater part of the village was entirely clear, but it was very straggling and there were still Germans in the Western outskirts and in the woods beyond. Lieutenant-Colonel Goulburn decided to clear this area the following morning by making a wide sweep from the North. No. 1 Squadron–No. 4 Company Group undertook this, moving as fast as possible with a troop of tanks supporting each platoon, while two platoons of No. 3 Company, which had been brought up from Nistelrode for the purpose, cleared the area behind them and looked after any prisoners taken. There was a considerable number of Germans about, but they were evidently taken by surprise and could only offer belated and half-hearted opposition. The leading troops suffered practically no casualties, but the two platoons following were not so lucky as both were caught by mortar-fire when moving across open country. A platoon of the King's Company ran into an ambush a little later while moving up to co-operate in this action and also lost a number of men, but by the end of the day the whole area was firmly in our hands and sixty-eight more prisoners had been taken. The enemy might have been thought by now to have had enough, but shortly after midnight a heavy artillery and mortar concentration fell on the centre of the village and it soon transpired that this was the prelude to an attack when infantry were heard moving in from the West. Major R. Hoare, who commanded the 130th Battery of the Leicestershire Yeomanry in support, had registered another cross-roads at the Western end of the village very accurately. When the Germans were heard coming in he fired a concentration on it with excellent result; all available automatic weapons also opened up and the attack was completely broken up before it ever came to close quarters. Fourteen prisoners were taken who provided some useful information.

Statements made by previous prisoners had indicated that recent enemy activity to the West of us had been the result of efforts on the part of the troops there to get back to Germany. This was now confirmed, and we learned from an officer that all that remained of the 712th Infantry Division was involved in the attempt. This division had been resting and refitting on the islands North of the Scheldt estuary, after taking a brief and comparatively inexpensive part in the Battle of France, until it was suddenly ordered on September 21st to return to Germany at once by the quickest available route. This undoubtedly lay through Grave and the curious part was that this officer had only heard that allied airborne troops had landed near Nijmegen and Arnhem; he had no knowledge of any landing near Grave, nor did he know that any of our land forces were within miles until our capture of Heesch. Even after that he and his fellows remained so confident that they had expected to be able to retake the village quite easily by a surprise night attack, thus enabling the remainder of the division to pass through Grave the following morning.

But by that morning, September 28th, they seem to have appreciated at last the realities of the situation; no further activity occurred and on the next day a considerable stretch of ground to the West and South-West was occupied without opposition. On September 30th, the reconnaissance troop and a platoon of the Coldstream Group cleared the village of Geffen and joined up with the 7th Armoured Division moving up from the South.

Our communications were now at last more than secure, but meanwhile our final objective had had to be renounced. Four days earlier, during the night of September 25th–26th, the 1st Airborne Division had been brought South across the Neder Rijn. The decision had been taken with infinite regret, but its bridgehead was no longer tenable owing to casualties and shortage of ammunition and supplies. Any necessary reinforcements could only be provided on a limited scale by night with assault boats; moreover the area, without Arnhem, was not suitable for development as a Corps bridgehead owing to difficulties of expansion and of building and maintaining a bridge on that particular stretch of river. A heavy barrage was put down from across the river to cover the withdrawal of the airborne troops and of a battalion of the 43rd Division, the 4th Dorsets, which had crossed the previous night in order to hold the flanks while the operations were in progress. These continued till six o'clock in the morning, when intense enemy fire made further crossings impossible; but by that time well over two thousand men, the great majority of those remaining, had been evacuated.

The loss of so many courageous and highly trained men without their objective being achieved was tragic, but there is every reason to suppose that the operation would have been completely successful if the weather had been more favourable. The arrival of the Polish Parachute Brigade and of the additional regiment of the 82nd U.S. Airborne Division on September 19th, as planned, might have provided in time the essential extra infantry for the tasks at Nijmegen and Arnhem. Furthermore, better weather conditions would have permitted adequate air supply and the normal scale of air support to the ground troops. As it was, the effort was far from in vain; the plan as originally conceived was nine-tenths successful and the possession of the Grave bridge and of Nijmegen were to be of vital importance in the later operations.

Even after the withdrawal of the airborne division the Germans showed how nervous they still were of the threat implicit in our possession of the Nijmegen bridges by repeated attempts to destroy them. Several bombing attacks were made. A particularly determined one was carried out by jet-propelled aircraft diving out of the sun at dawn on September 28th; these obtained a very near miss at each bridge, dislodging one section of the frail railway bridge from its seating and causing slight damage to the more robust road bridge. Following this, on the subsequent night, sudden explosions occurred at both bridges; one span of the railway bridge was destroyed while a ninety-foot gap was blown in the surface of the road bridge, reducing it to single-line traffic but doing no damage to the structure. The cause of these explosions was at first a mystery and gave rise to considerable speculation, but before long it became known that they were the work of amphibious saboteurs. Of the twelve men who carried out the attack ten were captured, one was killed, and the remaining one was never found. They had been trained in Venice, which they had left on September 15th, arriving at Arnhem a few days later. There they were briefed and divided into two parties; one consisting of eight men was to tackle the road bridge and the other of four men was to deal with the more fragile railway bridge. They were equipped with three charges, each manned by four men and consisting of two torpedoes twelve feet in length and two and a half feet wide lashed together. They wore tight-fitting rubber suits, with flappers on their feet to assist swimming and steering, and they were able to submerge if they wished by means of a mask with an air container.

They were launched from their own lines some five miles above the town around midnight and reached their respective bridges without being detected. The torpedoes were armed by being stood vertically on end and it was in this position, attached to the buttresses, that they should have been fired. The railway bridge party succeeded in doing this but the current was too strong for the road bridge party to be able to do so, and they had to lay theirs horizontally alongside the buttresses and arm them with emergency igniters. The men then swam off downstream, intending to land at Ochten, a few miles below and in their own hands. However, whether through exhaustion or faulty map reading, which must both be deemed excusable when submerged in a cold river on a dark night, they emerged too soon and were captured by some astonished loyal Dutch. Only one of the charges beneath the road bridge exploded; the other remained, watched with considerable anxiety by those above, till a very brave and skilled naval officer succeeded in ensuring that it should remain silent. The bridge was open to two-way traffic by the evening and the gap was soon afterwards closed by short spans of a Bailey bridge.

While the 32nd Guards Brigade was dealing with the threat to our communications, the 5th Guards Brigade had remained on the "Island", where it had been placed temporarily under command of the 43rd Division. The Irish Group was put into reserve to

Lieutenant General Sir Olive Leese Bt DSO, photographed as Commander Eighth Army, who was appointed as the first GOC of the Division and had the responsibility of forging the Division through a rigorous training programme. (*RHQ, Coldstream Guards*)

Major General Allan Adair DSO MC, late Grenadier Guards, who succeeded Leese as GOC of the Division and commanded it in action from Normandy to the end of the war in Europe. Adair was an effective and popular commander. He succeeded to the baronetcy in 1949 to become Sir Allan Adair Bt. (*RHQ, Grenadier Guards*)

Lieutenant Colonel (later Brigadier) J.O.E. Vandeleur DSO and Bar, Commanding Officer 3rd Irish Guards and commander of the Irish Group, whose dash to seize the bridge over the Meuse-Escaut canal at Lommel led to its being dubbed 'Joe's Bridge'. The bridge played an important role in the subsequent Arnhem operation. In the film 'A Bridge Too Far' Vandeleur was played by Michael Caine. (*RHQ, Irish Guards*)

General Sir Alan Brooke who, as Commander Home Forces in 1941, ordered the creation of Guards Armoured Division. Brooke became Chief of the Imperial General Staff in December 1941 and was later promoted to field marshal. (*NARA*)

During training in England, soldiers of 2nd Irish Guards carry out a river crossing in assault boats. (*RHQ, Irish Guards*)

Field Marshal Lord Cavan, Colonel of the Irish Guards, inspects the Covenanter tanks which had been issued to the Regiment. Note that the censor has obscured markings on tanks and uniforms that might provide information to the enemy. (*RHQ, Irish Guards*)

Not every training exercise went smoothly. This tank has crashed and overturned before catching fire 'somewhere in England'. (*RHQ, Irish Guards*)

Much training was carried out in Covenanter tanks, one of the Cruiser series that was never used operationally due to its shortcomings. Here a 2nd (Armoured) Bn Welsh Guards' Covenanter crosses a scissors bridge. In the turret is Major Jim Windsor-Lewis, who later commanded the Battalion. (*RHQ, Welsh Guards*)

Captain Sidney Emmanuel's Covenanter fords a river. (*RHQ, Welsh Guards*)

The artist Rex Whistler, who served in 2nd Welsh Guards, is seen applying his skills to the Battalion's signage. Lieutenant John Rex Whistler was killed in Normandy, aged 39, on 18 July 1944. (*RHQ, Welsh Guards*)

As final preparations for Operation OVERLORD were being made, troops preparing to embark for France were visited by members of the Royal Family. On 17 May 1944 HRH Princess Elizabeth inspected 2nd (Armoured) Bn Grenadier Guards. HRH had recently been appointed Colonel of the Grenadiers. The attention given to uniforms and boots is clear from this image. (*RHQ, Grenadier Guards*)

Lieutenant (later Captain) John Gorman, 2nd (Armoured) Bn Irish Guards, earned the Military Cross near Cagny on his first day in action during Operation GOODWOOD in July 1944. Gorman ordered his driver to ram a King Tiger, the first encountered in Normandy. The tank was disabled, as were others nearby. (*RHQ, Irish Guards*)

The knocked-out King Tiger with Lieutenant Gorman's 'Ballyragget' alongside it. (*RHQ, Irish Guards*)

Cromwell tanks of 2nd (Armoured) Bn Welsh Guards in the Normandy bocage. As the Battalion was the Division's reconnaissance unit it was equipped with the Cromwell, which was much faster than the Shermans of the other battalions. (*RHQ, Welsh Guards*)

Approaching Caen, Guards infantry work closely with Guards tanks. The creation of the regimental groups made armour/infantry co-operation much more effective. (*Taylor Library*)

Moving through the difficult *bocage*, a Sherman Firefly with its long-barrelled 17-pounder gun leads. Only the Fireflies, of which there was one in every troop, could meet the German Tigers and Panthers on equal terms. (*Taylor Library*)

Enthusiastic French civilians line the roads in Beauvais on 31 August 1944 to watch Guards Armoured Division pass through. The Sherman about to take the corner was from 1st (Armoured) Bn Coldstream Guards. (*RHQ, Coldstream Guards*)

The passage of a small town or village could be difficult as may be seen here in Villers Brettoneux, also on 31 August. Someone has placed a French soldier's Adrian helmet on the glacis plate of the leading Sherman of 2nd (Armoured) Bn Grenadier Guards. (*RHQ, Grenadier Guards*)

Shermans of 2nd (Armoured) Bn Grenadier Guards near Arras on 1 September. Guards Armoured Division was carrying out a blitzkrieg advance in co-operation with 7th and 11th Armoured Divisions that would take them deep into Belgium over the next few days. (*RHQ, Grenadier Guards*)

Scenes of destruction and confusion met the Guards' tanks on their advance. As the Allied armies fought their way out of Normandy through the Falaise Gap, they were witnesses to many scenes such as this. (*RHQ, Grenadier Guards*)

Evidence of the difficulties of the *bocage* is the Culin-cutter on the front of the 2nd (Armoured) Bn Grenadier Guards' Sherman on the left. Improvised by a US armoured unit NCO, Sergeant Curtis Culin, such cutters enabled tanks to cut a way through the high banks and hedges of the bocage. Tanks equipped with these devices were known as Rhinos. (*RHQ, Grenadier Guards*)

The spoils of war: a Panzer V Panther knocked out and captured by 2nd (Armoured) Bn Welsh Guards. (*RHQ, Welsh Guards*)

Guards Armoured Division enters liberated Brussels on 4 September to a rapturous reception. The first Guards tanks reached the city the day before. It is impossible to identify the unit to which this Sherman, swamped by grateful citizens of Brussels, belonged but it may have been 2nd (Armoured) Bn Grenadier Guards. (*RHQ, Grenadier Guards*)

The GOC, Major General Adair, is cheered by citizens of the Belgian capital. The tank, a Cromwell, was from Divisional Headquarters rather than 2nd (Armoured) Bn Welsh Guards. (*Taylor Library*)

Crossing the road bridge at Nijmegen. Tanks of Guards Armoured Division and infantry of the US 82nd Airborne Division took this bridge after a difficult battle that put the entire plan behind schedule.

On Nijmegen Bridge during Operation MARKET GARDEN. The bridge was the target for the US 82nd Airborne Division in MARKET, the airborne element of the operation, with the British XXX Corps carrying out Operation GARDEN. This involved the corps, led by Guards Armoured Division, fighting its way along Highway 69, which linked the major drop/landing zones at Eindhoven and Nijmegen, both taken by US airborne troops, and Arnhem, where British and Polish airborne troops were dropped. (*Taylor Library*)

A Sherman Firefly leads a column near Nijmegen with infantry in close support. (*Taylor Library*)

A Sherman of 2nd (Armoured) Bn Grenadier Guards carrying paratroopers of the US 82nd Airborne Division with whom the Grenadiers formed a strong alliance. (*RHQ, Grenadier Guards*)

Cromwells of 2nd (Armoured) Bn Welsh Guards on Highway 69. The road was two-lane single-carriageway, with much of it raised above the surrounding countryside. In many places the ground alongside was soft and unsuitable for tanks, forcing the armour to use the main road and making the tanks easy targets for German anti-tank guns. Thus it became known as 'Hell's Highway'. (*RHQ, Welsh Guards*)

In late-December 1944 and January 1945 the Division formed part of the Allied defence of Belgium after the German counter-attack that became known as the Battle of the Bulge. The armoured units were based at St Trond to be ready to operate in a counter-attack role. On Christmas Day they were ordered to Namur to protect the line of the Meuse. The weather conditions may be appreciated from this image of two Grenadier Shermans at St Trond. (*RHQ, Grenadier Guards*)

Montgomery's 21st Army Group crossed the Rhine in Operation PLUNDER in late March 1945, Guards Armoured Division crossing by this bridge at Rees, led by the Grenadier Group, on Good Friday morning, 30 March. (*Taylor Library*)

The advance into Germany took the Division from Rees via the Dutch towns of Groenlo and Enschede and thence to Bremen and Hamburg. A Sherman is seen crossing an intact bridge near Enschede. (*Taylor Library*)

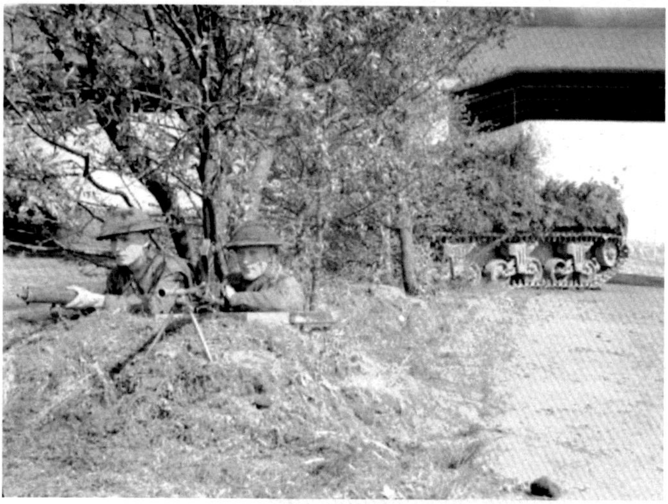

A well-camouflaged Sherman Firefly of 2nd (Armoured) Bn Irish Guards with two guardsmen of 3rd Irish Guards. One of the infantrymen has a Bren light machine gun while the other holds a PIAT anti-tank weapon. Infantry worked closely with the tanks, each providing support for the other. Tanks operating without infantry were vulnerable to attack by enemy infantry with hand-held anti-weapons. (*RHQ, Irish Guards*)

Dutch civilians welcome Guards Armoured Division in Enschede. They had endured almost five years of German occupation. (*Taylor Library*)

Captain Ian Oswald Liddell, 5th Bn Coldstream Guards. On 3 April 1945 the Coldstream Group was ordered to seize a bridge over the Ems river near Lingen. The bridge was well defended and prepared for demolition but Liddell sprinted towards it, mounted the roadblock before it and neutralized the demolition charges, which included six large bombs. He did this under fire from automatic weapons and then stood up to wave his men forward. For his actions, he was commended for the Victoria Cross, the award of which was announced in the *London Gazette* of 21 April. By then Captain Liddell had been killed in action. (*RHQ, Welsh Guards*)

On the day Ian Liddell's Victoria Cross was announced, Guardsman Edward Charlton, Irish Guards, earned the last VC of the European war. Near Wistedt a German counter-attack was launched on an Irish Group troop/platoon position. Guardsman Charlton's Sherman was hit and set on fire but he climbed on to the blazing tank to remove the turret-mounted Browning machine gun with which he then engaged the attackers. Although wounded badly, he propped the heavy weapon on a gate and continued to load and fire with one arm until, wounded again, he collapsed and was overrun. He had gained enough time for his comrades to retrieve the situation. Charlton's posthumous VC was awarded on the basis of evidence from a German officer who was taken prisoner. (*RHQ, Irish Guards*)

Shermans of 1st (Armoured) Bn Coldstream Guards on the advance into Germany in April. (*RHQ, Coldstream Guards*)

Hostilities over, a Cromwell of either Divisional Headquarters or 2nd (Armoured) Bn Welsh Guards drives through Scheeßel, near Rotenburg. (*RHQ, Welsh Guards*)

At Rotenburg on 9 June 1945 Guards Armoured Division held a parade to mark its final day as an armoured formation. The parade was attended by Field Marshal Montgomery, commander of 21st Army Group, Lieutenant General Sir Miles Dempsey, Commander of Second Army, the commanders of I and XXX Corps and the Major General Commanding the Brigade of Guards, Lieutenant General Sir Charles Loyd. Montgomery, whose escort was a troop of Household Cavalry, took the salute. As the tanks drove off the parade ground the Guards bade farewell to armour. (*RHQ, Welsh Guards*)

rest and refit at a large *schloss* and farm near Oosterhout; but, after the capture of Bemmel on September 25th, the Welsh Group was given a position to hold at a village called Aam, two kilometres East of Elst, which was held by the 43rd Division. The German resistance to the North was continuing to be very stubborn and their counter-attacks were frequent and vicious, but during the tenure of the Welsh Guards these were restricted to the sectors on either flank and they lived in comparative peace and quiet. On September 28th the 3rd Bn. Irish Guards was ordered to relieve them. This it did, taking with it No. 2 Squadron of the 2nd Bn. Irish Guards and retaining a troop of seventeen-pounder guns of the 21st Anti-Tank Regiment; these were sited in the forward company area to cover the autobahn, along which any armoured counter-attack designed to recapture the Nijmegen bridges must come.

The day of the take-over and the following day remained comparatively quiet, but on September 30th there was a marked increase of shelling and a large enemy patrol bumped into the forward company during the night. In the course of the next morning it became obvious that something serious was afoot. At eleven o'clock shelling became intense and a violent attack was launched against No. 2 Company, under Major M. V. Dudley, coinciding with an attack on the 50th Division on our right. Two Panthers appeared and hit one of our seventeen-pounder guns, wounding the commander and crew, though one of them was accounted for shortly afterwards by another of our guns. Thereafter attacks developed along the whole front and shelling increased still further. Several direct hits were made on Battalion Headquarters. The rear-link wireless half-track was destroyed and the building set on fire; the battery commander, Major F. C. W. Timmins, and all his staff were killed and casualties started to pour in at an unpleasant rate; the Regimental Aid Post got two direct hits and had to be moved. To add to other embarrassments crowds of refugees came in for protection and cover. They pleaded for evacuation in transport but this was out of the question as the roads were under constant fire; they were crowded into cellars and evacuated across country during lulls in the shelling.

Just before dark a particularly violent attack, supported again by tanks, succeeded in over-running one of our forward posts and in capturing an anti-tank gun; but a counter-attack, assisted by a bold manœuvre on the part of a troop of tanks under Lieutenant D. Daly, restored the position. Another group of Germans occupied some farm buildings just in front of our lines. These had however been registered by our gunners, in addition to being under the direct observation of two troops of tanks; the combined action taken resulted in no further movement being seen from that quarter. Day ended with all positions held firmly, but yet another attack was made on the forward company at dawn the next morning. Panther tanks had driven up during the night—their engines were extraordinarily silent—and closely supported an assault made by infantry armed with flame-throwers. One tank was destroyed with a Piat by a platoon commander, Lieutenant C. W. D. Harvey-Kelly, another by a tank, and a third by an anti-tank gun. But flame-throwers are very formidable weapons and finally the forward posts were over-run. None the less the German effort seemed by now to have been fully spent and during the rest of the day they contented themselves with shelling our positions; even this decreased a good deal after their gun lines had been heavily bombed and rocketed by our aircraft.

A special word of praise is due to the support given by the West Somerset Yeomanry during this action. When Major Timmins was killed, Lieutenant-Colonel B. Wilson, the regimental commander, came up to take his place and direct the guns in person. All their shoots were executed with pin-point accuracy and to them must go the credit for breaking up most of the attacks before they became threatening. Their forward observation officers showed great gallantry in manning their positions, particularly Captain D. G. Thorne, who continued to direct the fire of his guns despite the fact that his tank had become ditched in full view and within easy range of a Panther and that he himself had received a wound in the head as a result of which he subsequently lost an eye. For this action he was awarded the Military Cross.

Subsequent information showed that, although the enemy line was held by makeshift battle groups of very mixed material, the attacks were made by panzer grenadiers of the 9th and 116th Panzer Divisions. This explained the presence of the Panthers and of the flame-throwers, though none of these were carried on the vehicles, as might have been expected. The concentration of guns in support was also quite unusual at the time; it was estimated that about one hundred and fifty had been engaged altogether, of which about half were North, and half South, of the Neder Rijn. It had been an exhausting battle and had cost the Irish Group one hundred and seventy casualties, so the General decided to relieve them by bringing up the Coldstream Group, which had been virtually out of action for ten days. Furthermore during that period the 5th Bn. Coldstream had been reinforced by a draft of one hundred and twenty, including Major M. E. Adeane and Major J. de H. Hamilton, both of whom had been in the battalion at the start of the campaign and had been wounded in Normandy. The former now became Lieutenant-Colonel Hill's second-in-command. At the same time the 5th Guards Brigade withdrew to a rest area between Grave and Nijmegen, where the Grenadier Group was once more reunited with it, and handed over command of our troops on the "Island" to the 32nd Guards Brigade, which was put under the 50th Division. The Welsh Group returned to the 32nd Guards Brigade and remained established in a lay-back position at Ressen, though two companies had been sent up to Aam that day to reinforce the Irish and remained on under the Coldstream.

Although a renewed attack was constantly expected, enemy activity during the four days spent by the Coldstream at Aam was restricted to periodic bouts of heavy shelling. This rendered an underground life essential, which was far from pleasant in the mud and wet, but prudence gained its reward in surprisingly few casualties. Some good patrolling was done at night and resulted notably in four prisoners, all panzer grenadiers, being taken in the early hours of October 3rd. Information obtained from them about an impending attack on our neighbours at Elst proved very valuable, as it enabled them to break it up with shell-fire before it fully materialised.

Only one squadron of Coldstream tanks was committed in support of our own infantry at Aam and the other two were made available to assist the 50th Division on the right. The 231st Brigade of this division attacked on October 4th in order to straighten out the line and these two squadrons were consequently involved in some heavy fighting. No. 3 Squadron, on the left with the 7th Bn. Dorsets, met strong opposition and lost one tank, the gunner, Lance-Corporal Catling, being killed while engaged in trying to extricate it after being hit. Their objective, the village of Heuvel, was finally captured, but some casualties resulted, including Lieutenant J. H. Baddeley, who was wounded in the chest by a mortar while doing a reconnaissance on foot. On the right No. 2 Squadron's attack with the Hampshires went like clockwork and about eighty prisoners were taken, though the shelling was heavy and the infantry lost about sixty men. According to one of our officers the artillery and mortar-fire was as intense on this occasion as it was in the days of the Caen battles; some very heavy guns were used, a few craters being large enough to hold a carrier. The operation was wholly successful and curiously enough no counter-attack was ever made. The two squadrons withdrew with a counter-attack role for the next two days till, on October 6th, the whole brigade left the "Island". The 53rd Division took over the commitments and Guards Armoured Division was once more reunited in the reserve area South of Nijmegen.

Chapter Eight

NIJMEGEN AND SITTARD

ALTHOUGH, in the opinion of Field-Marshal Montgomery, Operation "Market Garden" had been ninety per cent successful, certain factors now made it obvious that the Second Army could not at once proceed with its original plan of attacking so as to threaten the Western face of the Ruhr. In the first place, for administrative reasons, the port of Antwerp had to be opened at the earliest possible moment and it was increasingly apparent that our thrust towards Arnhem had not forced the Germans in any way to lessen their hold on the Scheldt Estuary. In the second place the Germans continued to engage our forces on the "Island" and it was therefore necessary to garrison this vital sector with at least two divisions, as it was the key to our future strategy in the North. And thirdly the enemy on our Eastern flank and West of the Maas was stronger than we had originally anticipated. We simply had not got the resources to cope with all this and carry out the re-grouping necessary for another immediate offensive. Thus, first things coming first, the Field-Marshal's next operation was to open the great port of Antwerp and this task became the primary objective of the First Canadian Army, which now had I Corps under its command, nor was it until November 28th that the first convoy was safely berthed at Antwerp and that port opened for the maintenance of both American and British armies.

Meanwhile for over a month the division remained near Nijmegen. During this time both units and staffs were principally concerned in resting and refitting and in training for further operations. Neither the country nor the climate were particularly appetising, especially at that time of year, and memories of mud and floods and generally foul conditions will not easily be forgotten; we learned too that the British climate is far from enjoying a monopoly of fog. None the less, there were compensations. The rest itself, though galling in many ways, was most welcome and necessary after the hectic battles and advances of the summer. Shooting enthusiasts found quite a number of partridges and these, with plentiful supplies of mushrooms from the meadows bordering the Maas, made a welcome change from army rations and the German food captured at Oss. The Dutch inhabitants were very friendly and hospitable, and despite the language difficulty a large number welcomed us to their houses and made us feel at home. There was a number of fine football grounds and we found that they played remarkably well; many matches were played with Dutch teams during these weeks. Dances were held; cinemas and concerts were given in great variety; and a divisional club was instituted just South of Grave, where entertainment, refreshment and baths could be obtained both by officers and men. Best of all, forty-eight hours' leave to Brussels and Antwerp started. It was at this time too that the "Eye Club" for officers was opened, at the Hôtel d'Anspach in Brussels, which was to give such excellent service till after the end of the campaign. At first, owing to difficulties of accommodation, such leave was available for officers only, but within a fortnight it was extended to include all ranks.

On October 12th a Divisional Parade was held, when the King visited the area and inspected the troops from every unit at the divisional club at Grave. His Majesty talked to a number of officers and men on parade, and met all senior officers in the club afterwards.

At the end of the month the Major-General Commanding Brigade of Guards, Lieutenant-General Sir Charles Loyd, toured the division and discussed, among other matters, the various changes necessary in technique, equipment and appointments. Casualties both within and without the division entailed many changes among commanders and staff at this time. Lieutenant-Colonel E. H. Goulburn gave up command of the 1st Bn. Grenadier Guards on being appointed commander of the 8th Brigade in the 3rd Division. He had commanded the battalion for two and a half years, during all the period of its most intensive training and throughout the campaign so far, and his departure was deeply felt. He was succeeded by Lieutenant-Colonel Lord Tryon, whose tenure was however very short, as a week later he was transferred to the command of the 4th Bn. Grenadier Guards in the 6th Guards Brigade, owing to his experience with tanks. He in turn handed over to Major L. S. Starkey, who had been second-in-command for over two years.

The 1st Bn. Welsh Guards also experienced a change in command when Lieutenant-Colonel C. H. R. Heber-Percy, having recovered from the wound which he had received in Normandy, returned to take over from Lieutenant-Colonel J. F. Gresham. Within the battalion, too, X Company Scots Guards had to say farewell to Major P. Steuart-Fotheringham, who had commanded it throughout its independent existence since the disbanding of the 4th Bn. Scots Guards in September 1943; he was succeeded by his second-in-command, Captain E. J. Hope. The 3rd Bn. Irish Guards obtained a new second-in-command in Major B. O. P. Eugster when Major D. H. FitzGerald was transferred to the staff of XXX Corps.

Headquarters XXX Corps also deprived us, by transfer to corps level, which led shortly afterwards to his promotion as a brigadier, of a highly popular figure in Lieutenant-Colonel Jones, who had commanded the divisional engineers since the early spring of 1943. It was he who was responsible for so training them that they were second to none in the whole of the 21st Army Group and, had he left us for any other sphere of activity, his loss would have been hard to accept. In the circumstances, though, it was agreeable to know that we had an old and trusted friend in a key position above us, and we had every reason to congratulate ourselves on his successor, Major J. N. Thomas, commander of the 14th Field Squadron. Major Thomas had been with the division virtually since its foundation, and no officer better fitted for this vital post could have been found.

Major P. F. C. Winnington relinquished the appointment of D.A.A. and Q.M.G. at Headquarters, the 5th Guards Brigade, on being appointed second-in-command of the 2nd Bn. Grenadier Guards, and was succeeded by Captain T. F. Blackwell, Coldstream Guards, who up till then had been G.S.O. III.

On November 1st General Horrocks held an investiture at Divisional Headquarters. This was by no means our first acquaintance with General Horrocks as a considerable number of officers had attended his conference before the Escaut break-out and a fortnight before, on two successive mornings, he had addressed large and representative gatherings from the division. He had given an analysed account of operations so far, stressing in particular the outstanding part we had played in the advances to Brussels and to Nijmegen. He drew attention to the fact that our lines of communication were very stretched, and that no major operation eastwards could now be taken until the great port of Antwerp was open for allied shipping. The first essential was for the Canadians to clear the Scheldt estuary, in order to allow supplies and reinforcements to come through Antwerp. The liberation of all the ground on either side of our peninsula up to the Maas would also be necessary before XXX Corps could resume its intended drive into Germany.

Meanwhile, although few of us were called upon to carry them out, we all nevertheless had our operational roles. XXX Corps had taken over responsibility for the front facing the Reichswald, between the rivers Maas and Waal, on the return home of Airborne Corps Headquarters; the line was held by the 43rd Division and the 82nd U.S. Airborne Division with the 8th Armoured Brigade in support, while the Guards Armoured Division formed the counter-attack reserve. At first our counter-attack role was limited to an Easterly or South-Easterly direction, the latter South of Grave, but on October 17th, on the departure of XII Corps from the "Island" to take part in the operations to clear the Scheldt Estuary, our possible activities were extended to the North and West also. But despite the scope of our potential tasks it was always improbable that we should be called upon in respect of any of them and in fact the whole corps front remained comparatively quiet throughout the period.

Certain of the units, however, had special tasks of their own which involved them in greater activity than the rest of the division. The 3rd Bn. Irish Guards certainly had the most interesting and unusual of these tasks in having entrusted to them the responsibility for the close protection of the bridges in Nijmegen against attack from land, water or air. This was far from being a sinecure, as may be imagined from the attacks on them already recounted. For the purpose two anti-aircraft troops, a battery of three-inch mortars and a troop of searchlights, together with special detachments of sappers and supply troops, were allotted to them. The battalion always had two companies on duty at a time and they had to be very alert, as every floating object must be engaged with small-arms fire and the searchlights had to be supplemented with mortar flares to ensure more efficient illumination. In addition, on foggy nights a rifle platoon went out in tugs and moored itself just short of the naval boom which had been installed to intercept enemy mines. Throughout there was a certain amount of spasmodic shelling by long-range enemy artillery, particularly near the road bridge, which was still under observation from the Reichswald, although a smoke screen was kept going permanently in order to hide it as much as possible. There were also several bombing attacks which did little harm, but nevertheless occasional casualties were suffered; one jet-propelled bomber dropped a stick just outside Battalion Headquarters, killing Lieutenant P. G. E. Sarsfield Hall. Daily drill parades were held in the streets with the sentry's ear cocked for the arrival of shells; the detention room got a direct hit one day which released the occupants, sending them to hospital instead of to prison. Although the duties were heavy, relaxation was obtained at a night club run under Battalion Headquarters, where the Dutch girls danced with great verve and the band was excellent. The band leader got wounded one day but stuck to his fiddle in spite of it.

There was no need for tank support in this role and the 2nd Bn. Irish Guards was put under command of the 82nd U.S. Airborne Division and billeted in the Southern suburbs of

Nijmegen. The squadrons took turns in being available to support the Americans at short notice, but no enemy attacks developed; there was very little activity and they were free to spend most of their time in training.

The 1st Bn. Grenadier Guards undertook the task of guarding the bridges over the Maas and over the Maas–Waal canal. There were six in all and their existence was vital for the entire supply system of the troops in the Nijmegen area. The guard duties were sufficiently large to prevent the companies on duty from doing much training, but with the exception of three platoons at the Grave bridges the whole battalion was housed in billets and very comfortable. These bridges were guarded for a month but during that time no attempts were made by enemy forces or saboteurs to destroy any of them.

The two field regiments were in action after October 12th in support of the 82nd U.S. Airborne Division but no officers were required for observation with the forward troops, so for a change battery and troop commanders were able to see their commands and to carry out much needed inspections of equipment and some useful training. Guns were calibrated and a good deal of course shooting was carried out; to course shoot at an actual enemy was quite a new experience for many. In addition officers from the battalions were invited to come along and practise correcting artillery fire, which they enjoyed and which served them in good stead later. These latter activities were carried out with single guns, which were moved some distance away from the real gun positions so as to give no chance to the enemy sound rangers. Another interesting fact which should go on record is that on the evening of October 23rd, the second anniversary of the battle of El Alamein, all guns of XXX Corps which could be brought to bear fired a *feu de joie* into Germany at ten o'clock. While finding much to admire in the American paratroops, our gunners were particularly struck with the efficiency of their communications; this was mainly due to the excellence of their equipment, both their wireless sets and their telephone installations being better than our own. The result was that they were spared to a great extent the difficulties of getting through and the tortures of constant repetition from which we often suffered. In saying this it should be made plain that no slur is intended on our own admirable signallers, who struggled manfully and usually without complaints with our inferior material.

The sappers too were not idle. Unfortunately for them, they are too valuable under all circumstances to be ever entirely unemployed. In addition to the usual domestic tasks of the squadrons in support of their brigades, they carried out some watermanship and rafting training on the Maas. They also were responsible for the maintenance of the roads in the divisional area, no light task in that sodden country, where the generally indifferent surfaces soon became quagmires after a few tanks had passed over them.

The Northumberland Fusiliers also provided their share of support for the Americans. The mortar platoon carried out three shoots, firing in the course of them eleven hundred bombs in all. The machine-gunners on the other hand were not employed until on November 4th the platoons attached to the 5th Bn. Coldstream Guards and the 3rd Bn. Irish Guards accompanied these battalions, when they were despatched to take over a portion of the line in the Venlo sector, South of Grave. VIII Corps had met difficult going and strong opposition in its efforts to clear the West bank of the Maas. A good deal of ground had already been gained, but a strong counter-attack had been made at Meijel, in the repelling of which the battalions of the 6th Guards Tank Brigade had greatly distinguished themselves. After this a semi-static phase had ensued and the infantry battalions of the 11th Armoured Division were now very tired after a long period of holding the line. The 8th Bn. the Rifle Brigade and the 3rd Bn. Monmouths therefore came under the 32nd Guards Brigade for a few days' rest while our two battalions took over from them under the 11th Armoured Division. The positions were very unpleasant, in marshy open country in full view of enemy observation; consequently movement during the day was reduced to a minimum. However, the farms had comfortable cellars and most companies were able to rest under cover during the day. The trouble lay in the nights which were very dark at this time and some thirteen hours long, and sentries had to rely on their ears and on a variety of mines, booby-traps and trip flares erected by successive units during their occupation of the positions. The companies were strung out on a wide front with no reserve and the attentions of an active enemy established in close proximity made it necessary to have a fifty per cent stand-to. The opposition came from paratroops, who conducted extensive patrolling and who were supported by comparatively heavy artillery and mortar-fire. Quite a few casualties were occasioned by this, including Captain P. Fanning of the 5th Bn. Coldstream Guards, who was killed by a stray salvo while looking for billets for his carrier platoon. Our two battalions did some excellent patrolling themselves and had established domination of no-man's-land by the time they were relieved a week later.

The Household Cavalry during all this period were detached and put under direct control of VIII Corps in a reconnaissance role on its left flank, holding the line of the Maas from Vierlingsbeek to Cuijk, a distance of twelve miles. In view of the great length to be covered the 3rd Reconnaissance Regiment was placed under their command. It was likely to be a quiet sector, although the Germans had two small bridgeheads on our bank, one near Boxmeer and the other near Gennep; neither had been liquidated, as the ground in which they were situated was dominated from the enemy bank, and there were too few men available to hold them even if they should be won. The country was entirely flat; near the Maas the fields were small and surrounded by high fences, but further back from the river they became much larger and were not enclosed. Their main function was to provide instant warning of any enemy counter-attack from this quarter aimed at the Grave bridge, in which case we were to move into action immediately. Nothing of the kind in fact occurred, though they provided a great deal of valuable information on many occasions. Lieutenant-Colonel Abel-Smith's plan by day was to man a series of observation posts which overlooked most of the enemy bank, and to patrol with armoured cars between them; by night a series of strong-points were held along a railway line which ran parallel to the river and about two miles away from it, while listening patrols stationed themselves on the river bank and fighting patrols reconnoitred the villages in between. At first light an air O.P. searched the river for signs of boats or bridging material brought up during the night. Almost every night German patrols were operating in the sector and it was found exceedingly difficult to intercept them. The Household Cavalry were employed holding this river line from October 1st until November 12th, when they reverted to normal command and moved to the area of Asche in Belgium to rest.

Early in November orders came for the division to move South on November 12th to the Maastricht sector. The First Canadian Army, after having completed the clearing of the estuary country, was to take over the whole front from the sea to Nijmegen and the Second Army was to extend its front to the South. XXX Corps, on being freed from responsibility for the Nijmegen region, was to relieve the northernmost troops of the Ninth U.S. Army, which was about to resume the offensive. The 43rd Division was to go in next to the Americans in front of Geilenkirchen, while we were to hold the stretch of country from there to the Maas.

We duly moved on the appointed day, in those inevitable early hours of the morning which seem inseparable from any large-scale military movement. The drive was long and dreary, back along the all-too-familiar road through Eindhoven, Valkenswaard and Hechtel, and the traffic congestion was worse than usual. The whole British Army seemed to be on the move in all possible directions and in fact a very large portion of it was. But at least we neither anticipated nor experienced any interference from the enemy and on the whole most of us were pleased to go. We felt that it was time for a change of atmosphere and that neither climate nor scenery could well be more depressing than those of Nijmegen.

On arrival we discovered that conditions on this front had up till now been extremely quiet; this was sufficiently evidenced by the fact that the town of Sittard, which formed the nucleus of the position, was still functioning normally in every way, although only some four thousand yards from the enemy front line. The 113th U.S. Cavalry Group, which handed over to us, had done a certain amount of patrolling which had resulted in a fairly good knowledge of the enemy's forward dispositions, but little was known of his reserves and he on his part had shown small desire to be aggressive. Activity had been restricted to occasional patrols and small artillery concentrations on opportunity targets ever since the line was established, and for that matter it should be emphasised that nothing in the nature of what is normally understood by the word "line" existed on this sector; it merely happened to be the place where the Americans had ceased to advance. The troops on both sides had been too thin to man a proper defensive line; they were only sufficient to hold the villages as strong-points and to cover the country in between them with patrols.

Our principal function initially was to strengthen the left flank of the Ninth U.S. Army during its forthcoming attack. The 43rd Division was to participate to a limited extent in this attack, but our role for the present was likely to be confined to static defence. Since this was essentially an infantry concern, the larger and more vulnerable part of the sector was put under the 32nd Guards Brigade, which established its headquarters in the Southern outskirts of Sittard. Three of the regimental groups were placed under its command; the Grenadiers held Gangelt on the flank of the 43rd Division, the Coldstream held Wehr on their left, and the Welsh were positioned directly in front of Sittard. The 5th Guards Brigade held the stretch of country in front of the Maas until the line crossed that river just North of Maesyck. In addition to the Irish Group, the 744th U.S. Light Tank Battalion and the 17th Squadron of the 113th U.S. Cavalry Group were placed under Brigadier Gwatkin's command. The Americans kindly allowed them to remain for a couple of weeks until arrangements could be made for their replacement by the 8th Hussars, the 1st Bn. the Rifle Brigade and a composite battalion made up from the Royal Army Service Corps and from the Royal Electrical and Mechanical Engineers.

The greater part of the fighting troops of the division was quartered on German soil for the first time. Unexpectedly most of the civilian inhabitants were found still to be in residence and, although some of them claimed to be Dutch, they were all treated with equal suspicion. Billets were occupied in their homes but, when telephone lines were laid, orders were given that wireless procedure should be used on them. At first some of the inhabitants were even working in the fields in front of our forward positions but we could scarcely allow this, and within two or three days they were all evacuated with the greater part of their livestock; though enough of the latter eluded the net to ensure a more than usually varied diet for our men during the ensuing month. On the whole the evacuation was carried out in a humane fashion and at least with more consideration, as afterwards transpired, than by the Germans themselves in the villages opposite, where several civilians were shot for not obeying orders promptly enough. Once all the buildings were empty the billeting problem was easily solved, a matter of no little importance as only a small proportion of the men were needed to man the forward positions and the climate of a Dutch November is not the most genial known.

The five weeks spent by the division here represented the longest space of time that it was ever to spend consistently on one sector, and on the whole many worse choices might have been made. The country, while not exactly hilly, was not quite as flat as it was further North and abounded in game to an even greater extent. Once out of the front line and in Holland, the towns and villages were clean and tidy as always with the Dutch, and the inhabitants were always willing and anxious to do anything to make our stay among them more agreeable. For those who had the opportunity to get so far Maastricht was an especially fine old town, built on a good site and possessing a large number of magnificent buildings, fortunately wholly untouched by the war. Altogether it was hard to realise, as was the case, that we were in the heart of the Dutch coal-mining district, and moreover that the mines were mostly still in active production. Divisional Headquarters, at Geleen, was in fact within a mile of what allegedly was the largest coal-mine in Europe and yet there was no trace of the dirt and grime that seem inseparable from our coal-mining districts. On enquiring we were told that the smoke was mostly consumed internally by means of modern methods and that the absence of slag-heaps was accounted for by packing the waste material back into the exhausted seams below. No matter how it was achieved, the result was undeniably successful and made us wonder why we could not do as well at home.

During the whole period at Sittard activity was limited to patrolling and desultory shelling; tedious though it was at the time, the experience gained both by the infantry and the gunners was to prove exceedingly valuable later on. The Germans opposite were of mediocre quality and, though perhaps rather more numerous than ourselves, far less well furnished with supporting arms and ammunition. Like us they held widely separated strong-points sited for all-round defence and entirely surrounded by mines and booby-traps. This rendered the capture of prisoners a matter of great difficulty but enabled us very rapidly to form a reasonably accurate picture of the defence line. We found that the Americans had mapped this out very well and moreover that it changed very little during our stay, except that the smaller positions were sometimes occupied and sometimes not. Once the positions were located we confined ourselves to ensuring by patrolling that the line was still held and to attempts to capture an occasional prisoner. The latter task took some time and even when finally the Irish, the Grenadiers and the Coldstream all succeeded their prizes had little to tell us of interest, though subsequently this was found to be but natural. The Germans retaliated in kind and one night the Grenadiers lost two men who were engaged on a mere contact patrol well within our own lines; their fate was not known till five months later, when they were liberated from a camp in Germany. Three Germans also crept into a Welsh Guards company billet one evening, to the consternation of two guardsmen who were engaged in cooking chips, but, by dint of superior cunning and their fists, the only weapons available at that moment, they drove them off, though one was wounded in the skirmish.

Casualties during this time were fortunately very slight, though the 5th Coldstream Guards lost Lieutenant D. H. Fletcher and a guardsman when they struck an enemy minefield while on patrol; and the 3rd Bn. Irish Guards suffered an unfortunate hit from a shell on Battalion Headquarters which killed Lieutenant R. O'Kelly and Sergeant Matthews, who had led their Intelligence section admirably from the beginning of the campaign. Altogether danger from shelling was about the only risk that had normally to be faced at this time, and even this was both infrequent and localised. The only places that suffered moderately severely were Gangelt and Sittard. The latter town, quite untouched hitherto, was treated to such particular attention at the end of November that it was thought wiser to move out the majority of the troops quartered there. It is likely that this shelling formed part of the cover-plan for the Ardennes offensive due to start before long, but at the time it seemed that it might be the prelude to some form of counter-attack in an attempt to draw off some of the pressure being exerted by the Americans on our right.

An attack on Geilenkirchen on November 19th had gone well, carried out by the 43rd Division and the 84th U.S. Infantry Division, loaned to XXX Corps for the purpose. Despite vicious counter-attacks all the objectives were solidly in our hands within two days, a very gratifying result considering that the East bank of the Wurm, on which Geilenkirchen stands, formed part of the original Siegfried Line. This attack had been co-ordinated with a major offensive started two days previously by the Ninth U.S. Army on our right and intended to reach the Roer valley, the only serious obstacle remaining short of Cologne and the Rhine. It took nearly a fortnight of hard fighting to achieve this but by that time, in addition to the six original German divisions holding the thirty-mile front involved, ten further divisions, five of them armoured, had been committed; all had suffered severely, and two or three catastrophically. It was a fine achievement on the part of the American troops, of whom many in the division were able to see something at this time owing to our own comparative inactivity. Their methods might be somewhat different from ours and even seem curious and unorthodox, but there could be no doubt about the excellent results when they were put into practice. Divisions such as the 29th and the 30th Infantry who fought in this battle could have challenged comparison with the finest of our own.

Certain of our units arranged to exchange officers and non-commissioned officers with the Americans at this period; among these were the sappers, one of whose officers, Lieutenant R. B. Beeson, notably distinguished himself. He was visiting a detachment of the 171st Engineer Combat Battalion with the forward troops when the Germans counter-attacked and cut off the position. His conduct was such throughout the action, culminating in volunteering to carry a message across bullet-swept country when the wireless had failed, that he was recommended by the American commanding officer, Colonel Keasey, for an immediate award. He was given a Bronze Star.

The Roer is only a small river and under ordinary circumstances would have proved no very formidable obstacle to a modern army. But unfortunately its water was controlled further South by a series of dams, designed to provide for the needs of the thickly populated industrial area round Aachen. These dams were so constructed that several successive floods could be staged by demolitions, each one sufficient to wipe out any bridges that might be built over the river. The plight of even a considerable force thus marooned without communications on the far side would have been highly unenviable. The First U.S. Army was at present directed on these dams and until it had captured them intact or otherwise a halt must be called. However, it was obviously desirable in the meantime to bring our line level with the river up to the point where it meets the Maas. Apart from the advantage of being able to attack simultaneously across the whole length of the Roer the enemy salient pointing directly at Sittard and Maastricht presented a constant potential threat to the American lines of communication.

Thus was conceived Operation "Shears", and we were cast for the leading role. With this in view the 7th Armoured Division, which had just completed refitting after the Scheldt estuary campaign, was brought down to take over the line; we were to attack through them and the whole division was taken back into reserve positions at Geleen and elsewhere behind the Dutch frontier towards the second week in December. The country over which the operation was to take place was low-lying in many parts and thickly forested in others; these factors coupled with the time of year, rather than the degree of opposition expected from the enemy, led us to make unusually detailed plans, which were studied carefully for days in advance. Units were provided with air photographs, going maps and defence over-prints of the area to be occupied and the advance was to consist of five phases in which the various battle-groups were to leap-frog to their objectives. Special command posts were dug for the various Headquarters in the forward area to provide against possible heavy shelling once our intentions were realised. Gun-pits were dug for the artillery and considerable quantities of ammunition were dumped. The sappers were allotted an assault squadron with two assault bridges and several brushwood fascines and the commander of the assault regiment concerned, Lieutenant-Colonel J. F. D. Savage, came to live at Divisional Headquarters to help with the planning. Also attached was a platoon of mine-locating dogs; these had given a recent demonstration at Geleen, which had aroused considerable interest and in which they had shown distinct ability.

But these elaborate preparations were never put to the test. When the orders were originally given out on December 9th we were told that the operation was planned for three days later, but that it would be postponed unless there was a hard frost meanwhile. Actual weather and ground states were such at the time that the following quotation from Tennyson's "Idylls of the King" was published as an estimate of probable battle conditions:

"Like this last dim, weird battle of the West
A death-like mist slept o'er the sand and sea;
While of the chill to him who breathed it, drew
Down with his blood, till all his heart was cold.
For friend and foe were shadows in the mist,
And friend slew friend, not knowing whom he slew."

On December 10th a squadron of the 2nd Bn. Grenadier Guards carried out a training exercise in which every single tank became bogged, and the following day the operation was duly put off for two days. On the 12th it was again put off to the 16th and the next day, as the rain and fog grew increasingly worse, it was finally cancelled altogether. Small regret was felt in any quarter.

Several changes took place among Commanders and staff during the month spent at Sittard. Lieutenant-Colonel J. O. E. Vandeleur, who had commanded the 3rd Bn. Irish Guards since its formation, was appointed to command the 129th Brigade of the 43rd Division and was succeeded by Lieutenant-Colonel T. W. Gimson. Lieutenant-Colonel W. M. Sale, after almost two years' invaluable work as A.A. and Q.M.G., left Divisional Headquarters in order to take command of the 1st Household Cavalry Regiment; he handed over to Lieutenant-Colonel H. Prideaux, who had been D.A.Q.M.G. for a considerable time during the training period. Two very unwilling officers left for the next course at the staff college in Major the Hon. Miles Fitzalan-Howard, Brigade Major the 5th Guards Brigade, and Major R. M. Pratt, the Northumberland Fusiliers Company Commander. They were succeeded respectively by Major H. S. Young, Irish Guards, and Major B. van der Gucht; the latter officer was already a popular figure in the division as he had been second-in-command of the company until shortly before the invasion. The sappers again suffered a severe loss in the departure to hospital, owing to an accident, of Major P. Greer, commander of the 14th Field

Squadron. His successor, Major W. A. H. May, did not arrive until a full month later and the second-in-command, Captain P. J. Robinson, carried on most capably until then.

On December 1st Field-Marshal Montgomery had held an investiture at Divisional Headquarters. After presenting the decorations, he made a speech in which he praised the work of the division and gave details of the proposed United Kingdom leave scheme, which was to start after Christmas. This had made many of our thoughts turn to the possibility of a period of rest after our labours, and with the cancellation of Operation "Shears" came the news that we were shortly to be taken altogether out of the line. XII Corps arrived to take over the sector in place of XXX Corps, which went back to Belgium to plan for the next phase. We were to follow in a few days to occupy a rest area near Louvain. It sounded too good to be true and indeed in the event it was. For on December 16th Field-Marshal von Rundstedt launched his Ardennes offensive.

Chapter Nine

WINTER IN BELGIUM

ON DECEMBER 16th, the very day of the opening of the Ardennes offensive, detailed orders were issued for the move of the division to Louvain. The 32nd Guards Brigade Group, consisting for the purpose of the Welsh Group and the 2nd Bn. Irish Guards only with ancillary troops, was to move first, in two or three days' time, to be followed just before Christmas by the remainder of the division. But by the 18th it had already become evident that the German counter-offensive was a distinctly ambitious affair, with two main thrusts, each led by two panzer divisions. Several revealing documents had already been captured. One of these gave St. Vith as a primary objective—it was already enveloped but still holding out—with Huy on the Meuse as a final objective, together with the rolling up of the entire Allied line in the Aachen sector to the North-East; another was the now famous Order of the Day signed by von Rundstedt himself and stating that this was the great moment for which the German Army had been waiting. He stressed the point that it was their last opportunity to drive the Anglo-American armies back and that for this "gamble" everything available in the way of men, supplies and equipment must be committed without stint. He also laid it down that full use must be made of captured American material, particularly vehicles and petrol, thus underlining his own lack.

Nevertheless it was as yet an entirely American concern; the 21st Army Group was not involved and we were told to go ahead with our plans as arranged. The 32nd Guards Brigade Group moved in consequence to Bree, where it was to spend two or three days on the way to Louvain, on the morning of December 19th.

But events were moving swiftly and that evening fresh orders came through—the First and Ninth U.S. Armies, those to the North of the German thrust, were being placed under operational control of the 21st Army Group on the following day. XXX Corps was to prepare itself for possible action forthwith. We ourselves were still to proceed to Louvain, but at once, and for "rest area" we were to substitute "concentration area".

December 20th and 21st were days of constant movement and equally constant uncertainty of plans throughout the division. The 32nd Guards Brigade did in fact move to the Louvain area but more to get there out of everybody else's way than for any other reason; by the evening of December 21st all units were in some miraculous way assembled in a reserve position North of Namur, the 5th Guards Brigade having been diverted on their way back from Sittard. While there was every reason to feel confident that the Americans would succeed in halting the German drive short of the Meuse, the stakes were so high that no risks could be taken. Consequently XXX Corps was positioned North of the river across the approaches to Brussels and Antwerp. The 43rd Division was on our left, centred on Hasselt and Tongres, with the object of preventing any crossings between Huy and the Dutch frontier; the 53rd Division, on our right, was ordered to prepare for demolition all bridges over the Sambre between Charleroi and Namur and was stationed in immediate defence of Brussels; our task, in the centre, was to prevent any crossing of the Meuse between Namur and Huy, and to be prepared in general for a counter-attack role. The 5th and 32nd Guards Brigades, which had reverted now to normal groupings, were based at St. Trond and Tirlemont respectively; the Household Cavalry was despatched across the Meuse to carry out special reconnaissance work with a view to ensuring that we were not caught unawares. It was to establish liaison with the Americans and also with the 29th Armoured Brigade, which had orders to prevent at all costs a crossing of the Meuse South of Namur and as far as Givet. This commission our armoured cars carried out with their usual dash and the next day, December 22nd, they penetrated as far as Marche to make certain that it was still held by our Allies, as it firmly was, in view of repeated reports of its capture.

Notwithstanding these orders, units were advised to seek good billets and to prepare to celebrate Christmas in comfort. They were put at six hours' notice and it was generally hoped that none of us would in the event be called upon. Some were lucky, others less so; for on December 23rd unpleasant accounts began to come in of the 29th Armoured Brigade being in contact with German tanks South of Namur. The next morning these accounts were confirmed with the news that five of the tanks had been destroyed and that German elements were in the outskirts of Dinant. The Welsh Group was promptly warned to be ready to proceed to Namur at a moment's notice and late at night on Christmas Eve, when definite orders came, the net was cast wider. The whole of the 32nd Guards Brigade Group was to move South at dawn.

The Brigade Order Group was held in the luxurious sugar refinery offices at Tirlemont at midnight, as Christmas Day was ushered in. Seldom can a more dejected and bewildered group of officers have assembled. Some commanding officers were at a distinct disadvantage owing to the absence of members of their staffs, who had justifiably though unfortunately elected to take advantage of the six hours' notice to go and celebrate Christmas Eve in the local cafés; certain difficulty was also found by some units in persuading everybody that the orders were genuine and not just a poor joke. None the less everything somehow got sorted out as though by a miracle during the night and the column duly left at first light. A sprinkling of snow lay on the ground and it had been freezing hard for several nights. It was bitterly cold as the sun rose a deep orange amid a setting of lowering clouds that told plainly that more snow was not far off. It was just the sort of Christmas Day that one had always longed for as a child but there was a general feeling that this was decidedly not the way to spend it, as grim murmurs of "Merry Christmas" were exchanged with all too little conviction.

The Welsh Group led the way and were already in Namur by eight o'clock; for X Company it was a memorable occasion, since the town was the scene of the first battle honour ever won by the Scots Guards. The Group was directed on to the high ground across the Meuse which overlooked Namur, with orders to hold all the approaches at all costs; although the 29th Armoured Brigade lay ahead it was in contact and one could never be certain that infiltration might not take place. The Coldstream Group was placed in reserve in a counter-attack role in the villages of Cognelée, Danssoulx and Vedrin, about three miles behind Namur, but two companies, each supported by a troop of tanks, went forward to hold the Meuse bridges in the town. These bridges, which were now handed over to the 615th Field Squadron by the sappers of the 11th Armoured Division, were vital links in the American communication system and, as they were prepared for demolition, the danger of sabotage to them was very great. Captured documents had shown that the Germans intended to make great use on this occasion of troops specially trained for sabotage purposes. They were employing paratroops dropped in small groups near vital targets in order to effect their destruction; also men of the "Brandenburg Division" of which so much had been heard in Intelligence circles in the past that most people had come to consider them a myth. However, they were now seen to be very real and to be operating in areas far ahead of the fighting. They were wearing American uniforms, carrying American arms and travelling in American vehicles. Five had already been apprehended West of the Meuse and presumably many were still at large. They spoke perfect English and one had actually had the effrontery to act as an American military policeman controlling traffic in Liége; he was only caught because he was indiscreet enough to claim to come from Texas when talking to a genuine citizen of that State. They were obviously very slippery gentlemen with whom it would not do to take risks.

Brigade Headquarters established itself just West of the Coldstream Group at Emines and the gunners went into action and started to dig gun-pits in the frozen ground just North of Namur; the 86th Field Regiment had been allotted to the brigade in addition to the West Somerset Yeomanry, so artillery support was well provided for. Although it always seemed unlikely that the Germans would get so far, numerous reconnaissances were carried out to decide on alternative courses of action in the event. Once the unwelcome move had been made there was at least the consolation of a change of scenery after the months spent in the damp and dismal plains. The country round Namur consists of open rolling country with scattered woodlands and smiling valleys reminiscent of some of the more attractive of our own counties.

On December 26th news came that the 6th Airborne Division was being brought out from England and that the 5th Parachute Brigade would take over all positions the next morning. The paratroops were suffering the indignity of coming by land and sea and their Christmas Day must be reckoned to have been a lot more disappointing even than ours. Just before they arrived we experienced our one and only active contact with the Ardennes offensive when the Germans bombed Namur that night. The damage to the town was negligible, but one bomb detonated a large charge buried in the East abutment of the railway bridge, and also some small cutting charges on the upper girders. This blew a twenty-foot gap in the bridge and wounded two guardsmen. They were the sole casualties suffered in the course of this episode and by the evening of December 27th the whole brigade group, after handing over to the paratroops, was once more happily installed in its previous quarters in and around Tirlemont. We were welcomed back by the inhabitants with genuine warmth and in many cases literally with tears of gratitude. They thought that the better news from the Ardennes had more to do with that dawn departure than it actually had.

The 5th Guards Brigade Group had been luckier with regard to its Christmas, since it remained in the St. Trond area with a general counter-attack role only. Brigade Headquarters was not however so fortunate in its own accommodation. Thinking that they would only stay for a night or two, the staff had taken rather austere lodgings in a monastery at Velm; eventually they were forced to share these cramped and inadequate quarters with the monks for several weeks. They therefore might not themselves have objected to a move, but in fact only two units did move at all, the 3rd Bn. Irish Guards and the 14th Field Squadron. With Q Battery of the 21st Anti-Tank Regiment in support, they were despatched on December 27th to take over from the 43rd Division and guard all bridges over the Meuse from Namur up to the Dutch frontier. This task only lasted for three days, at the end of which they returned after handing over responsibility to the Americans.

For by the end of the year the tide had once more turned and the initiative was passing increasingly from the Germans. They had calculated on meeting second-rate American troops only and had never anticipated the magnificent resistance put up in the St. Vith area. Fighting had continued here for nearly a week after it was surrounded and, as the area lay astride the natural supply routes to feed the German advance, this had been highly inconvenient. Moreover the penetration, deep though it was, remained strictly canalised throughout and all attempts to break through the flanking pivots had proved unavailing. These flanking pivots of Malmedy and Bastogne were held respectively by the 82nd and 101st U.S. Airborne Divisions and their fighting during this time has since become an epic. Having come to know something of them both in the course of the Arnhem operation we had immediately felt a new confidence the moment we heard that the defence of these two key localities had been entrusted to them. A further plan which had gone wrong was that of maintaining the momentum through supplies of captured petrol; this was upset by the American custom of laying pipe-lines right up to their forward positions, with the result that there was very little to fall into enemy hands.

Finally the good luck regarding the weather with which they were blessed during the early stages had deserted them. Flying conditions, which had been hopeless for days previously, became very much better around Christmas and devastating attacks were carried out both on their fighting troops and on their supply columns. The latter were particularly vulnerable in that they were limited to the use of the two or three main roads which provided the only entrances to the salient. The Germans showed their resentment of these attentions by putting up their own strongest effort in the air for a very long time at dawn on New Year's Day. In all some eight hundred aircraft took part, and some indication of the pains taken to secure enough experienced pilots is shown by transfers having been made from stations as remote as Prague and Vienna only two or three days before the attack. Few bombs were dropped, the activity for the most part taking the form of machine-gunning of airfields with a view to disrupting our own air effort. The attack was well planned and security excellent. The raids were most effective at Brussels and Eindhoven and a large number of our aircraft were put out of action; but the German losses of aircraft were higher and those of pilots incomparably so. The only serious attack in our area was made on the American airfield at St. Trond. Q Troop of the 94th Light Anti-Aircraft Regiment, which was attached to the Leicestershire Yeomanry, added to its laurels by breaking this up effectively. One enemy aircraft was destroyed and crashed in the gun area, and two more were hit. This brought the proved regimental score since arrival on the continent to forty destroyed and twelve confirmed as damaged, no mean feat considering the generally small scale of enemy air activity. The 2nd Bn. Grenadier Guards also had the satisfaction of shooting down a German fighter and it crash-landed not far away; the pilot was unhurt and was captured after an exciting chase across three fields by a Sherman tank, cheered on by scores of enthusiastic guardsmen.

Although we remained at six hours' notice in reserve in a counter-attack role for some days longer, all serious threat was past after New Year's Day. It had become merely a question of time before the salient created by the enemy with so much cost and labour would be ironed out. An Allied counter-offensive with this end in view started on January 3rd in which XXX Corps participated, using the available infantry divisions. By January 14th matters had gone so far that British troops were no longer needed and Corps Headquarters returned to Boxtel, in Southern Holland, to resume its planning for the next offensive, the future

Operation "Veritable". The only result of their gamble that the Germans could claim with justice was that, by thus disrupting our own offensive plans, they had staved off the opening bout of the final reckoning in the West by a few weeks. This had been achieved however at the cost of a large part of the one remaining force, the Sixth S.S. Panzer Army, which stood a chance of putting up a good fight. It was recorded at the time that the Ardennes offensive was unlikely to be considered to have been a paying proposition by future historians, and that verdict can now assuredly be confirmed.

Most of the men in the division remained in the same billets until the beginning of February 1945. These billets were almost uniformly warm and comfortable and moreover the local inhabitants often adopted their guests virtually as members of their own families. Their kindness was almost overwhelming and made the period more than a pleasant interlude; it acted as a rest and a tonic to brace us for the stern battles still to come. More friendships were made here than anywhere else during the campaign and not a few marriages took place subsequently, as a result. Apart from the friendly welcome given to us by the Belgians, we were extraordinarily fortunate to spend these weeks under such conditions in view of the unusually severe spell of weather that engulfed the whole of North-Western Europe at the time. The entire countryside lay under a blanket of snow; the cold was intense, and the roads became coated with ice, making the shortest journey quite an adventure. However unpleasant the occasional days of training might be, we all had warm houses to which to return at night, for which we had reason to feel doubly grateful when we thought of our comrades actively fighting on the bitterly exposed hills of the Ardennes.

The leave allocations too became quite generous now that men could be spared. Forty-eight hours' leave in Brussels, not more than two hours' distance by lorry from any part of the divisional area, was always popular; the prices were reasonable and the shops well stocked, the entertainments were many and varied and the joys of liberation had not yet completely subsided. Best of all, eight days' leave at home started on January 1st. The lucky ones were selected by drawing the names out of a hat, all those who had been abroad since the landing in Normandy being given the chance of going before those who had arrived later. Parties left every day, entraining at Bourg Léopold for Calais, where they embarked for Dover and found special trains ready to convey them direct to practically all parts of the country. The delays on the way were sometimes long and tedious, but on the whole the scheme worked very well and above all, no matter what delays occurred, every man was assured his full complement of eight days in the British Isles.

Apart from a series of road checks designed to make things difficult for the special German saboteurs, our only serious occupation during this period was training. It was an occupation not made any easier or more pleasant by the vile weather, but nevertheless a great many of the lessons which had been learnt in battle could now be practised usefully at leisure and in safety. No divisional or brigade exercises were carried out, and training was almost entirely on a squadron-company and troop-platoon basis. It should be recalled that the close and constant working together of armoured and infantry units and sub-units had only developed as a result of experience during the campaign. It had only been practised in England at all during the last few weeks of training on the Wolds and even then it had not been anticipated that the relationship would be nearly so intimate as in fact it became. Each group in consequence first held discussions on the various tactical subjects required, and these discussions were followed by practical demonstrations and in some cases by field-firing exercises. The Grenadier Group carried out such an exercise very successfully in the form of an attack on a deserted village on an old German field-firing range near Helchteren. The Coldstream Group carried out an equally successful signals exercise from the point of view of communications. But it was less successful from that of transport; the snow was so deep that roads were indistinguishable and a column of vehicles turned down a railway line by mistake and came face to face with a train. Fortunately the driver proved to be very co-operative, in true Belgian fashion, and helped to push a bogged half-track out of the snow.

Both field regiments carried out course shooting on the Lommel ranges, near Bourg Léopold, which had just been opened and which were the only ones of their kind in the British sector. In addition the Leicestershire Yeomanry instructed the 2nd Bn. Irish Guards in shooting their tanks in an artillery role, a lesson which was to prove most helpful in the future. The 94th Light Anti-Aircraft Regiment also went to Lommel and concentrated in particular on learning the new, though still secondary, role of ground shooting for Bofors guns. The sappers practised construction of light improvised bridges and in any case were kept very fully occupied in maintaining the roads throughout the divisional area.

Possibly the most interesting task fell to the lot of the Northumberland Fusiliers. At the end of December the General had asked Major van der Gucht whether he thought it was possible to form a flame-throwing platoon within the company; the latter had stated that he thought that it was. In consequence, armed with the necessary authority from Army Headquarters to hold surplus men, he went off to select from the reinforcements at Bourg Léopold what was destined to be the first complete platoon of "Wasps", as they came to be called, in the British Army. It consisted of six flame-throwing carriers, a Jeep with a wireless set for the commander, two fifteen-hundredweight trucks, a three-ton lorry for fuel and a motor-cyclist. The platoon was trained by a War Office team and by the end of January was ready to go into battle with the remainder of the company.

An important addition to the division appeared towards the end of January in the 2nd Bn. Scots Guards. Glad as we all were to welcome them, our feelings were tinged with sadness when we learned that they were eventually destined to relieve the 1st Bn. Welsh Guards. This battalion had fought magnificently throughout the campaign and moreover was the only original infantry unit of the division; but the necessary reinforcements to sustain it during the hard fighting that was still expected were not likely to be forthcoming and to this argument there was no answer. Both battalions were to be comprised in the division during the next operation in order to give the Scots Guards time to assimilate the latest fighting technique. While they had won great battle honours both in the desert and in Italy they had spent the last seven months in re-forming at Stobs Camp, in Scotland. While half the men were veterans of many battles the remainder, forming the body of the rifle companies, had never fought; in fact most of them eight months previously had been members of the ground staff of the Royal Air Force. In spite of the seasoning of experience the new job was a mystery to them all. Working as part of a battle group in armoured warfare meant little or nothing and, despite rigorous training for this work in other respects, they had never been within a hundred yards of a tank while in Scotland. Consequently it was thought advisable for them to have the opportunity of studying the methods used by the division while they were still surplus to establishment.

Chapter Ten

THE REICHSWALD BATTLE

TOWARDS THE end of January 1945 rumours began to hint that the division would soon be involved in active operations once more. On February 1st the first of a series of conferences was held at Divisional Headquarters to explain the plan of the forthcoming offensive. This and the succeeding conferences at brigade and unit levels were of a highly secretive nature, security at the time being of particular urgency in view of the number of agents known to be operating behind our lines. It was not difficult to guess, however, that something important was afoot, if only because all the field guns left in advance, with all unit signs carefully painted over.

The chosen few learned that the intention was to clear the enemy entirely from the territory between the Maas and the Rhine. The initial assault was to be made by the First Canadian Army, reinforced by XXX Corps, and was to consist of an attack from the general line Mook–Nijmegen with the object of breaking through in a Southerly direction. We were the only armoured division involved and our role only came into existence after the break-through had been achieved; then we were to advance through and seize a commanding ridge of high ground North of Sonsbeck, and from there to push forward a strong mobile column with the object of capturing the Rhine bridge at Wesel if, by any miracle, it should still be intact. This last task was allotted to the Welsh Group because of the speed of their Cromwell tanks.

It was hoped that this attack, known as Operation "Veritable", would draw off the German reserves and thus enable the First and Ninth U.S. Armies to break out from their hard-won positions along the Roer and swing North-East to meet us on the Rhine and opposite the vital Ruhr. The American part was called

Operation "Grenade", and its timing depended on the degree of success achieved by our attack and also to some extent on the fate of the Roer dams.

The initial attack was timed for half-past ten on the morning of February 8th, and the division moved up during the preceding forty-eight hours to a reserve position in and around Tilburg. Although the journey is not normally a matter of much more than three hours it took most units anything up to twenty-four and occasionally even more to reach their destinations. The routes had often to be circuitous, owing to the amount of troops moving, and the condition of the roads as a result of the sudden thaw after weeks of intense frost was quite appalling. Some of these, notably the main road from Tirlemont to Diest, became literally impassable after the passage of a few tanks and indeed remained so for weeks afterwards. It was a foretaste of what was to come but somehow, often by dint of building up the roads again in a purely temporary fashion, everybody was suitably installed by the evening of the 8th. As it turned out, we could have spared ourselves the effort of so prompt an arrival.

The initial attack went well and exactly as planned. Although the weather interfered considerably with the air programme, the artillery support was excellent and all objectives ordered for the first day had been attained by midnight. Both our field regiments played their part, starting at five o'clock in the morning with the preliminary bombardment and continuing from ten till two o'clock with an immense smoke-screen to cover the advance of the five attacking infantry divisions. They reported that the noise was enough to wake the dead, with a thousand guns of all calibres firing from a comparatively small area. The effect at the receiving end must have been highly unpleasant and indeed opposition was distinctly patchy except on the right, where reserves were most readily available. On the following day progress continued steadily, though again more slowly on the right, and by the evening we had reached the outskirts of Cleve. But on February 10th the weather, which had been bad throughout, began to become a serious handicap, and a point was reached when only consolidation could be effected until supplies and support weapons could be got up to the infantry. All troops, except those on the extreme right, were dependent on the main Nijmegen–Cleve road as their only supply route; both the Rhine and the Maas had risen above the recognised danger mark and before long there were some two feet of water over this road for a length of five miles. Alternative routes had to be found, but they were indifferent and also over saturated ground. Meanwhile also the Germans at last blew up the Roer dams, thus inevitably postponing the American attack for some days. The battle must clearly continue to be a slow infantry one for a while and there could be no question for the moment of our being employed in the originally intended role.

Orders were consequently sent for the 32nd Guards Brigade to move up to Nijmegen on February 11th with a view to being prepared to act directly under XXX Corps as an infantry brigade group; therefore, in addition to its three infantry battalions, the 2nd Bn. Welsh Guards, the West Somerset Yeomanry and Y Battery of the 21st Anti-Tank Regiment moved also. It was not necessary for its other normal component, the 615th Field Squadron, to move, as all the divisional sappers were already hard at work.

The 51st (Highland) Division had fought its way through the South-West edge of the Reichswald Forest and had cleared the main road beside the Maas almost as far as Gennep during the first two days. XXX Corps Troops Royal Engineers had started repairing the endless series of craters and blown culverts of which this road by now consisted, but they were urgently needed elsewhere and consequently our sappers were called in to help. A brigade of the Highland Division was to make an assault crossing of the flooded River Niers during the night of February 10th and then to capture Gennep. This was successfully accomplished and the following morning, while the 615th Field Squadron continued to open the road, the 14th Field Squadron began to tackle the job of replacing the destroyed bridge over the river at Gennep. Sporadic shelling was directed at the site throughout the day; at first it was inaccurate but towards the afternoon it began to cause trouble, culminating in an unlucky hit among the equipment at about four o'clock which killed Sergeant Dixon and wounded two officers and four sappers. Further work was then ordered off till after dark by the brigade commander, who arrived shortly afterwards, but by daylight the next day the bridge was open to traffic. Major W. May, commander of the 14th Field Squadron, displayed great courage and resolution on this, his first, operation with us; it contributed largely to the award of the Military Cross which he received not long afterwards.

By the following day, February 13th, the Reichswald had been completely cleared but no troops were across the River Niers except at Gennep. The 32nd Guards Brigade was now put under command of the 51st (Highland) Division and moved through Gennep in order to attack Eastwards towards Goch; this attack was to converge with others destined to be made Southwards across the river. Enemy opposition had increased as reinforcements arrived and already nine divisions had been identified, including the only two available armoured ones, the 15th Panzer Grenadier and the 116th Panzer; the first was not unexpected but the arrival of the latter had only been made possible by the flooding of the Roer. The armour was, however, being employed further East on the sector for which we had been originally destined, and the opposition at Gennep had so far consisted of infantry strengthened with paratroops.

The brigade objective was the village of Hommersum and the plan was for the 5th Bn. Coldstream Guards and the 1st Bn. Welsh Guards to seize initially the wooded ground South-East of Gennep, after which the 3rd Bn. Irish Guards, supported by a squadron of tanks, was to pass through and capture the actual village. The operation started at half-past three on the afternoon of February 14th and was very successful; all objectives were captured at the cost of very small losses to ourselves, most of these suffered by the Welsh, who came across many mines in the woods. Seventy-eight prisoners were taken and, although a large number of them were paratroops, they did not show much inclination to fight and their morale was generally poor. Hommersum lies just the far side of the Dutch border, and it was the first German locality to be captured by troops of the division.

Although this action was carried through in model fashion and against such slight opposition, the Germans soon showed their objections. A strong fighting patrol engaged our troops during the night and the next afternoon a small but determined attack was put in on the village from the South; this was both preceded and succeeded by very heavy shelling both from artillery and from mortars. Altogether there was a good deal of shelling during this period but fortunately casualties were slight as the buildings nearly all possessed excellent cellars and the remaining troops were well dug in; since the soil was a peaty sand this was quickly done and the bombs dug deeply into it, causing little damage. On the whole those which were inclined to cause the most trouble were the few directed on the rear areas, which were not altogether spared attention. One such landed on the officers' mess of the 128th Field Ambulance in a house in Gennep next door to brigade headquarters, wounding among others the commanding officer, Lieutenant-Colonel M. Scott.

The next attack took place on the afternoon of February 16th and was directed on Müll, a collection of farmsteads to the South-East of Hommersum. It was the first of a series designed to beat in the defences of the town of Goch and was made by the 5th Bn. Coldstream Guards. Complete success was achieved and one hundred and thirty-five prisoners taken, but a good many casualties resulted from the shell-fire; losses were particularly severe at battalion headquarters and included the larger part of the pioneer platoon, who were caught in the open by an unlucky burst of mortar bombs. Also wounded was Major T. Graham who, as commander of the 373rd Battery, West Somerset Yeomanry, had supported them regularly and devotedly throughout the campaign. Apart from casualties the action was peculiarly difficult and unpleasant owing to the conditions. The rain had been more excessive than usual and movement for vehicles was well-nigh impossible; the tracks quickly became morasses and of the squadron of Welsh Guards tanks that was in support only two of the nineteen that started were able to reach the final objective with the infantry. The recovery tank became bogged in its turn and the squadron commander, Major N. L. T. Fisher, finally walked the last six hundred yards and directed the rest of the action on foot, though wounded.

At first the Coldstream position was distinctly exposed, but in the evening a battalion of Highlanders captured Hassum station, to the North, together with a hundred prisoners, and early next morning the 1st Bn. Welsh Guards attacked the actual village of Hassum. It had been heavily bombed that day, a heavy barrage was to fall in it beforehand, the new artificial moonlight was to be provided and altogether it was expected to be far the more serious affair of the two. Yet it turned out to be a walk-over; the village was found to be deserted and the battalion consolidated without a single casualty. It transpired subsequently that it had been evacuated about the time that the Coldstream attack had gone in and only nine wretched individuals were hounded out of the ruins and made prisoner. Nevertheless one of them proved to be of great interest in belonging to the 8th Parachute Division and consequently in providing the first proof of the long-expected arrival of elements of this formation from Roermond.

Though both these attacks were so successful, the subsequent shelling was again very severe and resulted in several casualties to both forward battalions in the course of the next few days. Lieutenant R. J. S. Howard of X Company and his orderly were both severely wounded when a small shell landed in their slit trench; the Welsh Guards also suffered a serious loss in the wounding of Major W. D. D. Evans, M.C., who had commanded his company brilliantly since the Normandy days. The Coldstream too had their share and suffered even more than the others from the weather conditions. Rain continued incessantly and the tracks up to their position became impassable except to Weasels. All supplies for the drenched and mud-caked men had to be brought up in these vehicles and at one time it even seemed doubtful how their relief could be effected.

On February 21st, as the final attack on Goch by other divisions was proceeding, the 3rd Bn. Irish Guards attacked the village of Vrij and a bridge to the North of it, with the object of opening up a main road which would get behind the German defences from the South-West. The day started badly when the sappers reported that the only two possible centre-lines were impassable to tanks. Supported nevertheless by a troop of self-propelled guns and the usual barrage from the artillery and mortars, the two leading companies, No. 1 Company on the left and No. 4 Company on the right, moved off at one o'clock and for some time the advance proceeded pretty well. As they approached their final objectives, however, opposition became very stiff indeed; not only were they subjected to heavy small-arms fire from three sides but shell- and mortar-fire became intense and casualties started to mount up. The wireless carriers blew up on mines or became bogged in the sea of mud and battalion headquarters lost all touch with Nos. 1 and 3 Companies on the left centre-line, where thick country made it impossible also for them to see what was going on.

The two leading companies meanwhile were both held up some distance from their final objectives. The Germans opposite No. 1 Company proved to be numerous and determined, and were well dug in around the small copses and houses in the area. Further progress proved impossible and Major G. E. Fisher-Rowe, the company commander, was killed while extricating his leading platoon. Some time before this Major D. M. Kennedy, M.C., had swung off with No. 3 Company to the left of No. 1 Company and attacked his own particular objective, a castle, which overlooked a road bridge over a small stream just South of Hassum. A German officer, who was captured two days later by a battalion of the 51st Division, told the story of this attack, of which he had been an eye-witness; he had been particularly struck by the bravery and determination with which it was pressed home. Major Kennedy and eleven non-commissioned officers and guardsmen with him were shot down within twenty yards of the castle, as they were trying to storm into the place through a breach in the walls caused by our artillery fire. The survivors of this company, a weak platoon, were extricated later by No. 2 Company from the positions which they had dug round a farm close by, under cover of a smoke screen.

While Nos. 1 and 3 Companies were doing their best to cope with a very unpleasant situation, No. 4 Company was having similar difficulties. It was being shot at by a variety of weapons from all sides, including even the rear, and had to retire some three hundred yards, where the men could dig in in a less exposed situation. They brought fifteen prisoners back with them, who provided information which explained the severe reception that the battalion had received. They were part of a fresh regiment which had been put into the line the day before to reinforce the troops which were confronting the 32nd Guards Brigade.

Throughout the afternoon a troop from the 615th Field Squadron had been doing magnificent work, often under intense fire, trying to clear the right centre-line of mines. In an hour and a half they had already lifted over fifty, but there were obviously many more unlifted and by four o'clock an impasse had been reached. The battalion had suffered very severe casualties, with two company commanders killed, all the platoon commanders of the three rifle companies concerned wounded and over a hundred other ranks killed and wounded. Both centre-lines were still blocked and further progress of vehicles along them was out of the question. This made supply problems insoluble and, when the facts were established and sent back, Brigadier Johnson ordered the battalion to retire behind its original start-line under cover of smoke. This was effected quite smoothly but the losses left a bitter taste. Leadership had been excellent and the men had fought superbly; it had just been one of those unlucky days for which nobody could be blamed but which occasionally come in war, often when least expected.

Major D. Yorke, commanding the 439th Battery, West Somerset Yeomanry, in support of the Irish Guards, distinguished himself also and received the Military Cross for his part in this action. During the periods of heavy enemy mortar- and shell-fire, when all who possibly could were sheltering, he stood calmly in the open, spotting the positions of the German weapons and directing the fire of his own guns on to them. The successful extrication of the battalion was largely due to the covering fire plan arranged by him in the face of extreme difficulties of observation and communications.

The 2nd Bn. Scots Guards had been brought up to take over the Irish positions in Hommersum the previous day and remained with the 32nd Guards Brigade to be inoculated gently with the unpleasant conditions of a European battlefield in winter. This enabled the 3rd Bn. Irish Guards to go back immediately to Nijmegen to rest and refit. The 5th Bn. Coldstream Guards was transferred to the 5th Guards Brigade on February 23rd, which entailed them going straight into the line again South of Goch as will be recounted later. Thus during the next week a much reduced brigade, consisting only of the Welsh Group and the 2nd Bn. Scots Guards, was gradually pinched out. For the last three days of this period command of it was taken over by the 52nd (Lowland) Division, which had been brought in to strengthen the right flank of the advance down the Maas.

Early in the morning of February 23rd the Ninth U.S. Army at length was able to make the assault crossing of the Roer. Despite its still swollen state and vile weather conditions six main bridges and several minor infantry ones had been erected by the following morning and within three days a bridgehead large enough to form a base for large-scale operations was established. To conform with these a new operation was now planned by the First Canadian Army, designed to break through the enemy defences between Udem and Calcar and exploit forward to meet the advancing Americans. II Canadian Corps, which had been responsible for the left sector since February 15th, was to make direct for Xanten; XXX Corps was to swing round on the right through Kevelaer and Geldern and make for the Wesel crossing. The Guards Armoured Division as a whole was to be kept in reserve during the initial stages, but the 5th Guards Brigade was allotted a sector of the front to hold just East of Goch through which the initial attack was to be made.

The battalions, which had up till now remained at Tilburg, moved up and concentrated in Nijmegen on February 21st. Two days later they moved forward again, a particularly uncomfortable process for the tanks. The only sure means of getting them up to the field of battle lay in directing them along the railway track between Gennep and Goch; each sleeper caused a shuddering jar throughout each tank, but they got through with the loss of only a very few bogged on the wayside.

Positions were taken up during the night. The sector allotted to the brigade was very narrow and only two infantry battalions were required. The 1st Bn. Grenadier Guards took over the village of Halvenboom and the 5th Bn. Coldstream Guards that of Buchholt, about a mile and a half further South. The 2nd Bn. Grenadier Guards was in support, with one squadron with each of the infantry battalions. The Irish Group and the 1st Bn. Coldstream Guards were in reserve and had no specific tasks. The 4th Bn. Grenadier Guards of the 6th Guards Tank Brigade was on the immediate right in support of the 8th Infantry Brigade, the only occasion during the campaign when it fought directly alongside. The positions of the forward companies in particular were highly unpleasant; not only was the country as featureless and sodden as usual but all movement by day was well-nigh impossible owing to siting on a forward slope in full view of enemy observation. Luckily most of the invariably shattered houses had strong cellars which still survived and owing to these few casualties were suffered. None the less the shelling was constant and the tedium was only compensated for by the infinitely larger number of missiles ceaselessly bombarding the enemy.

Throughout February 25th our guns kept up an almost continuous barrage on all known enemy positions and at four o'clock the next morning the first wave of the attacking infantry went through. In addition to artillery fire of all calibres our mortars joined in and our tanks also gave them covering fire in the initial stages. All troops were warned to lie low at first, as it was thought that the enemy guns would retaliate, but remarkably few shells came back and our men had a dress-circle view of the operation.

It was carried out on our sector by the 3rd Canadian Division and the 11th Armoured Division and went well from the beginning. By eleven o'clock Keppeln had been captured and, despite two stiff counter-attacks by the 116th Panzer Division in the afternoon, by nightfall Calcar also was in our hands, together with the whole of the important ridge of high ground to the South of it; Udem was then attacked by armour with the aid of artificial moonlight and fell within two hours. It was a highly successful day, over two thousand prisoners were taken and the 5th Guards Brigade was left high though far from dry by the receding flood of war.

On the following day opposition stiffened. The initial force of the attack was spent, a large number of paratroops were brought up to strengthen the defence, and notably in the Hochwald area on the Canadian front we were facing a large ridge of thickly wooded country where armoured operations were out of the question. Nevertheless progress continued to be made and slowly but surely the enemy hold loosened. This was especially the case on the front facing XXX Corps, where Kervenheim fell on March 1st and Weeze and Kevelaer the next day. On the morning of March 3rd we established contact at Berendonk, just North of Geldern, with American troops advancing from the South.

The advance of the Ninth U.S. Army had been very rapid. On February 27th the enemy main line of defences had been broken through on a three corps front and within two days München-Gladbach, Neuss, Roermond and Venlo were captured. Once the extent of this onslaught was realised the Germans decided, as became clear subsequently from captured documents, to hold a line through the Hochwald, Sonsbeck, Issum, Kempen and Krefeld to cover eventual withdrawal over the Rhine. Apart from the fact that sufficient troops were no longer available to hold so long a line effectively, the decision was taken too late and the Americans were already through it in several places along the Southern and Central sectors before it could be manned. The plan had perforce to be jettisoned and a much less ambitious one adopted of holding a small bridgehead centred on Wesel and pivoting on the Hochwald position. As soon as this unwelcome decision was reached the Germans once more gave proof of their ability to make a rapid and complete escape, finding time none the less to make an abundance of craters and to leave innumerable mines and booby-traps to delay our advance.

At last orders came on March 2nd for the 32nd Guards Brigade to leave the 52nd Division and for the Guards Armoured Division to prepare to fight as such in the customary regimental groups, with the 2nd Bn. Scots Guards under direct divisional command. Our task was to exploit the advance of the 3rd Division to the East from Kevelaer, with the object of pushing the remaining Germans still West of the Rhine across that river at Wesel. The Grenadier Group, leading the advance of the 5th Guards Brigade, passed the starting-point at Goch at half-past one on the morning of March 4th. The night was very dark and the roads were often blocked with rubble and with other transport, but by seven o'clock the leading troops had passed through Wetten and were in contact with the 3rd Division Reconnaissance Regiment. The weather was of the gloomiest with alternate hail and snow, and the news they gave was far from encouraging.

The immediate task of the 5th Guards Brigade was to pass through the leading positions of the 3rd Division beyond Kapellen, which lay some two miles East of Wetten, and to secure the high and largely wooded ground which ran East from there to Bonninghardt, a feature which dominated the flat country beyond as far as Wesel. But armour cannot always follow where infantry has led, and so it proved on this occasion. The Germans in this area had been withdrawing slowly and systematically, and an enormous crater had been blown in the road where it crossed a small but impassable stream. Reconnaissance further on foot showed that the bridge across the River Nenneper into Kapellen was also destroyed and that a hundred-foot Bailey bridge would be needed to span it. The 14th Field Squadron therefore perforce settled down to fill the crater and then to build the bridge. Meanwhile every possible effort was made to find alternative ways round, but the Grenadiers were baulked by more cratered roads and anti-tank ditches in all directions.

There was no chance of the bridge being completed before the evening; Brigadier Gwatkin therefore ordered the Irish Group, which had not got further than Kevelaer, to try to get through to Kapellen by an alternative route through Winnekendonk. This road was reported to be passable only to tracks; but for them it presented no great difficulties and at four o'clock the head of the column reached Kapellen. The light was already failing and it was vital to get a footing on the high ground before dark, if humanly possible; two blazing Churchill tanks of the 6th Guards Brigade at the far end of the village showed that opposition was only too clearly to be expected. A plan was quickly made and, supported by the guns of the Leicestershire Yeomanry which had followed behind, No. 3 Squadron–No. 2 Company Group quickly advanced and occupied Hamb, a small village barely a mile away and immediately below the ridge. No enemy had yet been seen and while the infantry paused to consolidate Lieutenant G. N. R. Whitfield, who was commanding the leading troop of tanks, pushed on towards the high ground to the North. Just before he reached a farmhouse where he intended to wait for the following infantry a small anti-tank gun suddenly opened up. Four tanks were hit, including his own, but none of the projectiles actually penetrated their armour and only one had to be abandoned. The remaining tanks deployed in a field. It was by now quite dark and, in the absence of infantry, the armour on the high ground had obviously to wait for the dawn.

The whole Irish Group consolidated round Hamb. During the evening shelling and mortaring of the village became very heavy and was also pretty accurate. From a study of the map it was quite apparent that reinforcement of the tiny force on the high ground before daylight was essential if Hamb was to remain tenable, quite apart from the need to facilitate a further advance. No. 2 Company was therefore told to send a platoon to seize a small feature, assisted by three of Lieutenant Whitfield's tanks which had withdrawn slightly during the night. This party led off at six o'clock and met no trouble in the initial stages except that two of the tanks somehow got bogged and also went off the air. Lieutenant Whitfield thereupon continued alone with Lieutenant R. H. S. O'Grady and his platoon across an open field some two hundred yards from the objective. Almost at once the opposition made itself felt, with about three machine-guns on the left and five on the right; several casualties occurred among the infantry and two sections were pinned to the ground. Lieutenant O'Grady led his remaining section into a slight hollow and managed to advance towards a farmhouse covered by Lieutenant Whitfield, who had silenced most of the machine-guns by firing everything he had. As the tank and the nine men of the platoon who were left reached the farmhouse, a German with a bazooka opened fire from behind it. He missed with his first shot, obtained only a glancing hit on the tank with his second and then decided to leave, urged on by a grenade thrown by Lieutenant O'Grady. Two more Germans were flushed from the top room of the farmhouse and the small party then cleared the copse which crowned the feature.

By this time it was broad daylight, which revealed all to the Germans. No. 2 Company–No. 3 Squadron Group set off to reinforce the small party but were pinned down on their start-line by heavy fire from all directions. They were under direct observation by machine-guns and also self-propelled artillery, which kept moving about on the edge of some woods a thousand yards to the left. Of eight tanks that set off six were hit, but the remaining two got through and their assistance was more than welcome; although surrounded by Germans at very close quarters on all sides the party held on grimly in the knowledge that the enemy were now denied uninterrupted observation of Hamb. Twenty-seven prisoners were taken before the Germans were finally driven back by the Grenadiers working round the left flank. This latter operation was helped enormously by the Irishmen's gallant action, for which Lieutenant Whitfield and Lieutenant O'Grady were both awarded the Military Cross.

Once the Irish Group had got through to Kapellen the Grenadiers had been told to reverse and follow round behind them; this they did, and harboured towards midnight in a very boggy field about a mile West of Kapellen. Early the next morning, March 5th, the advance continued. Two battalions of the 185th Brigade had secured the South-Western part of the Winkelscher Busch to the North but were unable to progress; the Irish Group, as we have seen, was held up in front of Hamb to the East. The Grenadiers were ordered to strike North-East between them and No. 3 Squadron–No. 2 Company Group led out in the direction of an important road-junction on the high ground. They were fired at by mortars and machine-guns but reached it and cleared the woods around, taking twenty-four prisoners and knocking out two self-propelled guns at a thousand yards' range. But the country was now covered with dense woods ideal for defence; heavy shelling and a quantity of small-arms fire made it necessary to make a more precise plan before moving on.

Prisoners already captured had reported that they had been ordered to retire when hard pressed to the Metxekath area, where instructions would await them. Metxekath was a small hamlet where the majority of the roads traversing the woods converged and lay nearly two miles further East than the most advanced point yet reached by the Grenadiers. Its capture seemed imperative if the woods were to be secured, but in view of the thick country more infantry would be required. The 5th Bn. Coldstream Guards was therefore again transferred to the 5th Guards Brigade and was ordered to pass through the Grenadiers and carry out the final stage of the attack.

The action opened at half-past two, supported by a creeping barrage from the Leicestershire Yeomanry strengthened by three medium batteries. The Grenadiers first cleared the woods for about a mile further East and as far as the nearest troops of the 185th Brigade to the West. They found few enemy but a number of mines and met with a good deal of mortar and machine-gun fire, which killed Lieutenant D. E. Pike and four guardsmen. Within three hours they were firmly in possession of all their objectives and the Coldstream were launched. It was not an easy battle for them through thick fir woods until the clearing in which the hamlet lay was reached; its difficulty increased when the vehicles comprising the command post ran into a patch of mines. Metxekath itself proved to be exceptionally strongly defended with well-sited anti-tank guns fully supported by infantry. The defenders fought valiantly hand to hand before they were finally overrun and at least one of them shot himself sooner than be captured. Lieutenant M. W. Wall, who led an assault platoon, was awarded the Military Cross and Lance-Sergeant J. Lindsey, one of the forward section leaders, the Military Medal. The total number of prisoners taken during the afternoon was one hundred and fifty-one, and by darkness the whole area was completely clear.

Patrols sent out during the ensuing night made no contact, but there could be little question but that the remaining high ground to the East, including the village of Bonninghardt, would not be given up without a struggle. The 32nd Guards Brigade accordingly took over and issued orders for the attack to continue in the morning. At eleven o'clock the task of clearing the remainder of the wooded area was to start; the 2nd Bn. Scots Guards, in its first action of the campaign, was assigned the Northern half and the 1st Bn. Welsh Guards, in what was to prove its last action, the Southern half; each battalion was allotted a squadron of the 2nd Bn. Welsh Guards in support. If this operation went well the 1st Bn. Welsh Guards was to continue and attempt to seize Bonninghardt itself, our original objective.

The operation did go well and with the contribution of considerable help from the artillery the woods were fairly clear by mid-day. The infantry found that, if they kept sufficiently close behind the barrage, most of the Germans were surprisingly willing to surrender. This was particularly welcome, as the tanks were unable to penetrate into just the denser parts of the woods which lent themselves most readily to defence; many of the German positions were in fact quite invisible in the thick trees and their occupants could only be detected as they climbed out to surrender. Even so the affair was not exactly a picnic and occasional groups fought fiercely. All the leading companies suffered casualties; the 2nd Bn. Scots Guards suffered an especially regretted loss when Company-Sergeant-Major Lumsden was killed in a comparatively simple attack on a small isolated wood after the main operation was complete.

As soon as consolidation had been effected Lieutenant-Colonel Heber-Percy ordered his battalion to carry out the second attack, which was duly launched at about five o'clock. For this two squadrons of tanks were allotted, No. 3 Squadron supporting No. 3 Company in the lead on the right and the Light Reconnaissance Squadron X Company on the left. The ground was very open until the confines of the village were reached and despite heavy shelling in support casualties were fairly heavy. A great part of the fire came from the open left flank and the tanks soon dealt with this effectively with smoke; not however before Sergeant T. J. Waters of the mortar platoon had been killed and Captain A. N. B. Ritchie, commanding X Company, wounded. Good team-work between tanks and infantry meanwhile put the forward companies on their objectives by nightfall, and, as darkness fell, hand-to-hand fighting in the village developed; it was well into the night before all the defenders had been dug out of their various hiding-places and we could claim full possession.

Resistance in the village was much keener than it had been in the woods, a fact easily explained when prisoners evidenced that the defenders of the latter were Wehrmacht troops while those of the former were paratroops who fought with blind fanaticism. These were members of the 22nd Parachute Regiment, and it was particularly gratifying that the commanders of both its remaining battalions, Captain Wittstock and Captain Heinrichs, were among those captured. Captain Wittstock was a representative of the best type of German officer, not often met with any longer at this stage of the campaign. He approached the interrogator with the remark: "Have I the honour to be with the First Guards Panzer Division?" When told that he was, he stated that he was satisfied and added that he was very impressed with the good treatment he had received at the hands of his captors. His own men spoke very highly of him. Captain Heinrichs on the other hand was a typical Nazi with all the usual arrogance and conceit. In all the operation produced two hundred and forty-three prisoners, and in addition a large number of Germans were killed. Unfortunately our own losses were not light; in addition to those already mentioned, Captain E. M. Ling, Lieutenant F. N. H. Widdrington, Lieutenant N. P. G. W. Waite and Company-Sergeant-Major N. Davies, all of the 1st Bn. Welsh Guards, were among those wounded.

Capture of the high ground was now complete. Occupation of further territory was likely to prove difficult in that all ground in advance of our present positions was on a forward slope in full view of the whole remaining bridgehead, and upon which heavy guns on the far bank of the Rhine could also be directed. However it had to be done and the 32nd Guards Brigade was ordered to act as a pivot, between the 52nd Division on the right and the 4th Canadian Armoured Division on the left, in the final push to the Wesel bridge. The Canadians had captured Sonsbeck on March 5th but had not yet succeeded in clearing the village of Veen, due North of the woods now held by the 2nd Bn. Scots Guards. In order to free the latter their positions were taken over by the 1st Bn. Grenadier Guards, together with one squadron of tanks, during the afternoon of March 7th. The Grenadiers had no further contact with the enemy, but during the first twenty-four hours lost a number of men from heavy shelling and mortaring, the trees increasing the lethal effect most unpleasantly. This gradually died down after the Canadians established themselves in Veen the following day.

Straight across our front, and about two miles beyond the forward edge of the Bonninghardt feature, ran the main road which followed the left bank of the Rhine. It was reckoned that the defence of the bridgehead must finally collapse once we could succeed in crossing this road. Half-way to it ran the parallel railway-line, connecting, as the road also did, the towns of Rheinberg and Xanten; this railway-line was embanked, as was also another line which ran through Bonninghardt to Wesel and which crossed the first at right angles. Brigadier Johnson ordered the 2nd Bn. Scots Guards, supported by No. 2 Squadron of the 2nd Bn. Welsh Guards, to secure the ground as far as the junction of the two railway-lines on the afternoon of March 7th. If necessary the Coldstream Group was to follow through and accomplish the final task of cutting the road.

A stream ran directly at the base of the ridge and must be crossed as an initial step. From a farmhouse on the Eastern outskirts of Bonninghardt where an observation post had been set up could be seen, surprisingly enough, an intact farm bridge. It lay at the bottom of a gully that offered some protection and it was decided to advance down this gully and attack across the bridge, supported by tanks firing from the top. Captain J. Purser, who was commanding the 615th Field Squadron in the absence of Major Neale on leave, reckoned that the bridge should be strong enough to take tanks, but a scissors-bridge tank was included in the order of march just behind battalion headquarters as a safeguard. Heavy artillery was provided in addition to the West Somerset Yeomanry, who were able to deploy on a large airfield at Bonninghardt, where the admirable air-raid shelters dug by the Germans proved most convenient and comfortable for the command posts.

At half-past four the attack was launched and, after the companies were across the bridge, the tanks started to follow. The arch was strong enough but the surface was just too narrow and soon the tank tracks began to grind the edges and to endanger the structure. Fortunately at this moment the scissors-bridge arrived and was quickly laid; the remaining tanks crossed and traffic continued to flow. As the advance continued and as darkness began to fall the battle developed a positively festive appearance, with the fire of the German tracer bullets from the railway embankments on each side and the blaze of all the houses set on fire by our tanks. Right Flank and G Company pushed on up to the Wesel railway while Left Flank tried to reach the North–South line, but the failing light just prevented the tanks from helping the infantry in establishing themselves effectively on the embankments. As it was they dug themselves in as well as they could in anticipation of an uncomfortable night.

Although the defenders proved to be paratroops, opposition on the ground had been moderate only and our men noted that their fighting quality had deteriorated considerably in the two days since their last encounter. Altogether one hundred and six prisoners were taken, showing that they had been quite thick on the ground and might have put up a better fight. On the other hand the shell- and mortar-fire had been both heavy and accurate and continued so during the night; in particular some self-propelled guns were very ably handled and caused us a great deal of trouble. The scissors-bridge, which provided the only exit from the battlefield after the collapse of the farm bridge, became blocked by a broken-down tank and the squadron of tanks, commanded by Major N. M. Daniel, had no alternative but to form a close harbour for the night. Lieutenant P. A. Carter and Lance-Sergeant H. J. Millard were killed and their tanks destroyed by shelling during the night, while at dawn an even worse disaster occurred when four tanks were knocked out in quick succession. The harbour area had been carefully chosen in one of the few spots screened from observation from in front, but one of the German guns had stolen round to our rear in the village of Alpen, which had unfortunately not yet been occupied by our neighbours, and all too quickly seized the advantage provided by its initiative.

After dark the sappers started to build a Bailey bridge over the stream about half a mile to the North of the other bridge, at a point where one carrying a metalled road had been destroyed. In addition Mechanist Quarter-Master-Sergeant F. Roughton of the 2nd Bn. Welsh Guards worked under fire at the tank stuck on the scissors-bridge during most of the night and finally recovered it, re-opening that route. Both were necessary in the morning, as it became increasingly obvious that a great last effort must be made finally to eliminate the bridgehead.

The 5th Bn. Coldstream Guards, together with No. 1 Squadron of the 1st Bn. Coldstream Guards under Major J. L. Darell, had been moved up the previous day in the hope of following straight behind the Scots Guards. But operations on both flanks were behind schedule and even when morning came we learned that two attacks, one on either side, were due to take place before ours. There was no question of the Coldstream starting before eleven o'clock and in any case not before a strong-point known as Haus Loo, which dominated the right flank, had been captured by our neighbours.

Few attacks were more thoroughly prepared than this one already was and the lack of anything to do made the hours of waiting unusually trying. A huge supporting programme of artillery, mortars and machine-guns was merely waiting for the word to start, and very necessary it was expected to be, as the enemy shelling showed no sign of diminishing. The fire on the bridge sites continued to be particularly severe and among other casualties there during the morning Captain R. Sykes, commanding the 32nd Guards Brigade Signals Squadron, was wounded while on his way up to arrange for better communication with the 2nd Bn. Scots Guards.

Shortly before mid-day orders came for the attack to be launched at half-past two. Haus Loo was after all still held by the enemy and there could be no guarantee that it would fall meanwhile. But if our operation was put off any longer it might be impossible to complete it in daylight and this was essential. It was realised that the Coldstream were being asked to undertake a most difficult task, and if necessary Lieutenant-Colonel Hill might select alternative objectives a little further back; but if they succeeded fully in its accomplishment all the greater honour would be due to them.

Half of the squadron of tanks was with each of the leading companies and the crossing of the stream was awaited with some nervousness, as it will be remembered that the column had first to move down the escarpment in full view of the enemy. The danger was increased by the need for the tanks to slow up as they crossed, causing something of a traffic jam, but fortunately the very heaviness of the shelling had to a large degree obscured the view. The burning houses and the dust—it had turned unusually hot and dry for March—had produced a thick haze that mercifully hid the column. So at least it seemed, because the forming-up area behind the ridge was reached without trouble.

No. 2 Company, under Captain W. J. Straker-Smith and supported by their half-squadron of tanks under Captain A. Watkins, led on the right; No. 1 Company, under Major D. A. Kennard, M.C., on the left, supported by Major Darell with the other half of his squadron. Both groups crossed the embankment punctually to the minute, but the leading tank on the right struck a mine as it reached the railway-line and blocked the track across. No. 2 Company soon reported heavy firing at close range both from the front and from Haus Loo on the right and was told to slow down until Captain Watkins could find another way to bring his tanks up. This he soon did and together they doggedly fought their way forward to the objective, with No. 3 Company following up behind. On the left the advance went more speedily at first; the tanks got across the embankment at once and fanned out, shooting a great many Germans as they sped forward, while the infantry killed or captured the remainder, following close behind. As they reached the main road, however, where there were numerous houses affording good cover, the opposition became very stiff and the shelling even heavier than before. While consolidating Lieutenant M. Lock's tank received a direct hit in the turret; all the crew were badly wounded and he himself, who had done brilliantly in the battle, died shortly afterwards.

It was one of the stiffest battles ever fought by troops of the division, and the steady and resolute way in which the attack was pressed home under particularly adverse conditions was beyond all praise. Very full publicity was given throughout the Press, more perhaps than that devoted to any other single engagement with which we were concerned. The Coldstream felt very proud of themselves, as well they might. There can be little doubt but that their cutting of the only good lateral road left in the bridgehead was responsible for the taking by the Germans of an immediate decision to evacuate, despite Hitler's especial orders to hold out to the last. For early the next morning the noise gradually died down till all was quiet; then suddenly two thunderous explosions told us that the bridges over the Rhine had been blown up. By the evening all resistance in the Wesel bridgehead was at an end.

Operation "Veritable" was responsible for some of the toughest and most sustained fighting in which the division was ever engaged; as an illustration of this, the Leicestershire Yeomanry had fired in little more than a month about three thousand rounds per gun, more than during the whole campaign up till then. The conditions too were certainly the most unpleasant under which we ever fought. For the Germans they must have been infinitely worse, and the fact that the defence was skilfully conducted right to the end once more served to remind us of their martial qualities, even in defeat. It is noteworthy that very little equipment fell into our hands; there were never many tanks on the front and a large haul of them was therefore out of the question, but the artillery was more numerous and more active than at any period since Normandy and yet very few guns were captured, except immediately after the original break-through in the Reichswald. At the same time guns do not quite make up for men, especially when these are paratroops and had been lost on the scale experienced. In the last week alone the division took no less than eight hundred and fifty-six prisoners, of whom four hundred and seventy-three were paratroops.

Opposition had been harder than expected in the second phase owing to the unavoidable delay, through the excessive flooding, over launching the American assault. This had the effect of attracting to our front several formations from further South, some of them of the best quality. But they were the last that the Germans had and the other sectors were weakened to a degree greater than we had realised at the time. The break-throughs achieved by the Ninth, First and Third U.S. Armies in succession, brilliantly executed as they were, were made possible by the drawing off of troops to contain us; the margin had become too narrow and once initial penetration was achieved no reserves were available. When Operation "Veritable" ended the whole West bank of the Rhine was clear as far South as its junction with the Moselle at Coblenz and the First U.S. Army had already established the Remagen bridgehead on the farside. The final phase was about to begin.

Chapter Eleven

FROM THE RHINE TO THE EMS

THE DIVISION moved back during the night of March 11th to the familiar Nijmegen neighbourhood, to rest and refit. The journey was marred by an unhappy accident; the track of a carrier of the Northumberland Fusiliers snapped and the vehicle overturned, killing Sergeant Merry and severely injuring Sergeant Cooper. Both were experienced men who had seen much active service and their loss in this tragic manner was keenly felt.

The preparations which the prospective Rhine crossing entailed must obviously take some little time and a respite of at least ten days was ensured, so it was worth while to take some trouble over the billeting areas. Some units, around Nijmegen, Malden and Cuijk, were fortunate in finding themselves in more or less undamaged and sometimes familiar surroundings, but others were less so. The Grenadier Group was especially unlucky in that the area allotted, North of Gennep, had been the German front line throughout the winter. It was liberally strewn with anti-personnel mines and the houses were windowless, often roofless, and heavily pitted with shrapnel. There was need for much improvisation, but even in their case this ensured that every man was under cover within a couple of days. The weather, too, as though repentant of its late ill-temper, became suddenly more like May than March; the sun shone every day, warm and brilliant, and the crocuses and daffodils came out, sometimes blossoming right among the bomb-craters and almost inducing one to forget the shattering desolation of those sodden battle-fields.

All units settled down to a more normal routine of existence; a little drill and maintenance, some mild training, cinemas and Ensa entertainments, football and hockey matches and mobile baths. Best of all, forty-eight hours' leave started again on a generous scale both to Brussels and to the towns and villages in Holland and Belgium where we had been so hospitably entertained at various times during the winter months. On March 17th the Irish Guards celebrated St. Patrick's Day in customary style with a parade for the presentation of shamrock in the stadium at Nijmegen, followed by special dinners and an all ranks' ball in the evening.

Certain changes took place during this period. Lieutenant-Colonel L. S. Starkey, who had commanded the 1st Bn. Grenadier Guards for the last four months, left to take up an appointment in England and was succeeded by Lieutenant-Colonel P. H. Lort-Phillips, D.S.O., who came direct from the 3rd Bn. Grenadier Guards in Italy. Lieutenant-Colonel D. H. Fitzgerald took over command of the 3rd Bn. Irish Guards from Lieutenant-Colonel T. W. Gimson who, most unwillingly, was recalled to the staff. Major T. F. Blackwell, Coldstream Guards, succeeded Major H. S. Young as Brigade Major, 5th Guards Brigade.

The 21st Anti-Tank Regiment received orders to train the two towed batteries as mobile infantry. Owing to the shortage of enemy tanks, and to the favourable manner generally in which the battle was going, these batteries had lacked targets almost completely of late. Consequently Z and 2 Batteries were both organised on the lines of motor companies, with half-tracks and carriers substituted for some of their original transport. In future they acted more or less as such and the self-propelled batteries as armoured squadrons, to the extent that, in the 5th Guards Brigade, Q and Z Batteries came to be regarded as an extra squadron-company group known as "Busterforce".

The most notable event, however, during this period was the departure of the 1st Bn. Welsh Guards. This battalion and the 1st Bn. Grenadier Guards had been the only two infantry units in the division during the first year of its existence, which made the parting seem even sadder than it would otherwise have been. But the reinforcement position admitted of no alternative and the fact that the moment must sooner or later come had been realised ever since the 2nd Bn. Scots Guards arrived to join us in the New

Year. The battalion had fought superbly throughout the campaign and the breaking of the partnership with the 2nd Bn. Welsh Guards, through which so much had been achieved, was equally painful on both sides. The men of X Company were transferred to the 2nd Bn. Scots Guards and so remained with the division, but unfortunately there was no room for them as a company and they had perforce to be suballotted, much to their disappointment. The company was addressed both by the General and by Brigadier Johnson the day before it was disbanded, when the reasons for this step were explained and the men were complimented on their magnificent record. The battalion held a farewell parade in Nijmegen Stadium on March 18th. The General inspected them and then, before the March Past, thanked them all in glowing terms for their loyal and valuable contribution to the success of the division. Five days later they entrained for England at the station at Nijmegen, where a large and representative throng gathered to give them a rousing cheer when the actual moment of departure came. The railway-line had only just been reopened with a view to the imminent offensive across the Rhine and it was a curious sensation to witness so essentially peace-time a move in that town which had such violent memories for us all.

On March 21st, at a conference at XXX Corps Headquarters at Pfalzdorf, General Horrocks gave out orders for the crossing of the Rhine—Operation "Plunder", as it was somewhat infelicitously christened. The crossing was to be made by the Second Army on the left and by the Ninth U.S. Army on the right, followed a little later by the First Canadian Army and by the First U.S. Army to the North and South respectively. The initial assaults on the British sector were to be carried out by the 51st Division at Rees for XXX Corps and by the 15th Division, strengthened by the 1st Commando Brigade, at Wesel for XII Corps. These assaults were to be launched on the night of March 23rd and the landing of a complete Airborne Corps behind Wesel would take place the following day. We were destined once more to be the armoured spearhead of XXX Corps, but there could be no question of our crossing before March 28th because no bridge capable of carrying tanks would be ready before then, even in the most favourable circumstances.

The only troops of the division to take part in the actual crossing were therefore the gunners, who added their quota to the barrage covering the assault. In addition to our two regular regiments a third, the 86th Field Regiment (the Hertfordshire Yeomanry), had been allotted to us recently for the forthcoming operation and all three participated in their entirety; also four troops of the 94th Light Anti-Aircraft Regiment, who fired their Bofors guns in a ground role. They all moved up on the night of March 22nd and deployed just short of the Rhine under cover of darkness. Work on the gun-pits was allowed to begin at mid-day the following morning and the silence was broken at five o'clock after which the firing continued unabated till nine o'clock, when the assault began.

News that came back across the river during the night was reassuring and the next morning dawned bright and clear. As ten o'clock approached the eyes of all—it must be admitted that many members of the division whose presence in the area was not operationally necessary were by now also there—were turned expectantly upwards. Exactly as they were due, the first wave of Dakotas carrying the 6th British and the 17th U.S. Airborne Divisions came into sight. They flew at a low altitude, in perfect formation, and within a few minutes the empty Dakotas were on their way back. For the next two hours wave followed wave in continual procession, finishing up with the big gliders drawn by the four-engined Halifaxes. It was thrilling to be an eye-witness of the largest scale airborne operation that had ever yet taken place.

Complete success was achieved and before the next morning all objectives had been captured, including five intact bridges over the River Issel. This enabled quick progress to be made by the ground troops on the XII Corps sector but on the XXX Corps sector things went more slowly, if well enough. Rees was defended by paratroops, who put up a very stubborn resistance; the proof of its desperate nature lies in the fact that only six men were finally taken prisoner, all the remaining defenders being killed.

The bridging and raft sites continued under heavy and accurate mortar and artillery fire until the town fell early on March 26th, when bridging was able to start in earnest.

Within twenty-four hours a heavy bridge was already functioning and full armoured support could be provided in order to extend the bridgehead. On the morning of March 28th we were put at two hours' notice to move and proceeded to do so during the evening. The drive continued throughout the night and was as unpleasant as such military moves usually are—progress at snails' pace with the other columns getting in the way, with the inevitable rain to add to the general discomfort. Daylight found the 5th Guards Brigade installed in the Hochwald Forest area and the 32nd Guards Brigade around Udem and Calcar a little further West. Both localities were old battlefields of a month ago with ruined shell-torn houses and wasted landscapes, the latter pitted with craters and concealing an abundance of unexploded mines. We disposed ourselves as best we could.

On March 29th orders were given out envisaging a move early the next morning. After passing through Rees we were to proceed North through the positions of the 51st Division, which by now had captured Anholt and Isselburg. We were directed on Groenlo and Enschede, and finally on Bremen and Hamburg. It was however made quite clear that, though the break-through further South was complete, the enemy on XXX Corps front, consisting very largely of paratroops, were only falling back as forced to do so behind a screen of demolitions and mines. We could expect no such run as that which we had enjoyed before Brussels.

The 5th Guards Brigade was to lead the advance and in the very early hours of Good Friday morning, March 30th, the Grenadier Group started to move towards the river. The night was dark, with occasional squalls of rain, and as the column drew near to the bridge it ran into the belt of artificial moonlight which covered it. Searchlights were dotted all over the countryside with their beams directed over the water at a low angle; where a nearby tree caught the light the newly budding foliage on the branches seemed turned into ice in the frosty glare. The bridge was laid on pontoons and along each side green lights were suspended from the handrails, swinging gently with the motion of the current and the passage of the tanks and vehicles. The town of Rees, as it rose up on the far bank, appeared all the more picturesque and symbolic in its utter destruction. The experience of crossing the Rhine was essentially dramatic and few of us can have failed to be deeply thrilled. It was a moment for which we had waited so long.

By dawn the head of the column had already passed through Anholt and Dinxperlo without any appreciable delay. The route then swung East behind the line held by the 51st Division almost to the town of Bocholt, which was still being hotly contested. Here, at a road junction where it turned North again, the King's Company–No. 2 Squadron Group had its first taste of unpleasantness in the shape of a road block of felled trees and mines. From then on the going was slow thanks to craters and blocks, all covered by fire. Eventually the Dutch frontier was reached where it bulges East into Germany and by mid-day the Grenadiers were in the outskirts of Aalten. Here the opposition was so strong that the group withdrew to a position to the South whence the bridges entering the town could be covered. Although casualties had not been unduly heavy, they included Lieutenants R. B. Joly and J. A. C. Duncan killed and the King's Company commander, Major N. E. W. Baker, M.C., seriously wounded.

While the Field Squadron was engaged on repairing the main axis, Brigadier Gwatkin ordered the Irish Group to attempt to loop to the left and thus take Aalten from the West. They encountered practically no opposition until they reached a canal about half a mile short of the town, where they found the bridge destroyed. The 14th Field Squadron provided another team to work on this but it had by now become obvious that there would be so much engineering work to do, if a proper speed of advance was to be maintained, that additional help was essential. Consequently XXX Corps allotted us a Corps Field Company to back up the squadrons, commanded by Major B. Baines. This company was brought into action at once and was to do invaluable work for us in helping to clear the innumerable obstacles that we encountered during the following weeks.

By the time the Irish had arrived West of Aalten the Grenadiers had captured intact a small bridge leading into the town and patrols had established that the bulk of the enemy had withdrawn. Two squadron groups were therefore ordered to push through on a narrow front and establish themselves on the high ground to the North. This operation was carried out successfully and by nightfall the town, if not clear, was firmly in our grip and we were well poised to continue the advance the next day. Progress, owing to demolitions, had not been sensational, but it was the biggest advance yet made on XXX Corps sector of the bridgehead and had made the important centre of Winterswijk useless as a pivot of defence.

Soon after dawn the next morning, March 31st, the Grenadier Group led on. A squadron of the Household Cavalry was passed through and soon came upon a road-block, backed by two enormous craters; luckily they were not covered by fire and detours were quickly found. Lichtenvoorde was reached by ten o'clock and found not held and, apart from the waving populace, which reinforced the welcome knowledge that we were back in Holland, the column swept on without incident to the outskirts of Groenlo, a picturesque old town surrounded by a moat. Many civilian reports were received on the way of enemy forces lurking in the woods on either side but, whereas most of them were as usual non-existent, there were a few here, forming a thin defensive crust round the town. However they were not over-keen to fight and gave themselves up in small batches, so that the leading group soon reached the bridge leading over the moat. This was impassable and, though another was quickly found intact, the town was such an obvious bottleneck that the two other company-squadron groups were ordered to follow the Household Cavalry along a minor road which they had found, by-passing the town to the East. Several parties of half-hearted Germans surrendered to them on the way and they quickly rejoined the main road some two miles North of Groenlo. The opposition within the town meanwhile melted away and, after a short engagement just to the North, the whole column linked up once more.

They advanced about another five miles without opposition to the outskirts of Eibergen, but here they ran into more serious trouble. A considerable number of infantry was protecting the Southern approaches and the leading tank was knocked out by a self-propelled gun. The leading group deployed, while the King's Company and two troops of No. 2 Squadron were passed through to the East to attempt to seize a bridge over the River Berkel and so relieve the pressure. They were observed and mortar-fire was opened on them, causing several casualties, including Captain the Hon. S. D. Loch, who had to relinquish his shortly held command of the company. As dusk was setting in they were recalled and the whole group harboured just South of the town.

In the meantime, however, the 32nd Guards Brigade had not been idle. They had only got across the Rhine just in time to harbour near Dinxperlo the night of March 30th, but early the next morning they had followed the 5th Guards Brigade through Aalten and then branched North-West at Lichtenvoorde. Following secondary roads the Coldstream Group moved fast and for some time were only delayed a few moments at a road-junction, where the mopping up of an enemy post resulted in the capture of fifty-five prisoners. The first serious opposition was encountered at Borculo, a town a few miles West of Eibergen and also on the River Berkel, which the Household Cavalry reported as fairly strongly held. Thanks however to some more of the admirable reconnaissance work which we had grown to expect as normal on their part, an intact bridge over the river between the two towns was quickly found and our tanks were soon in the outskirts of Neede. Some armoured cars got through the town but the leading troop of the Coldstream was held up at a concrete factory on the outskirts, where the leading tank was destroyed by a bazooka. A way was found round to the left, but when the tanks attempted to exploit it the road collapsed and, as the light was failing, the group harboured just South-West of the town.

But the River Berkel had been crossed and the Eibergen position consequently outflanked. The Germans there must almost certainly have withdrawn during the night and it was important that both brigades should be in a position to continue the advance on parallel routes at first light. The Grenadiers were therefore ordered to seize river crossings before daylight to allow the Irish Group to go through. To make assurance doubly sure three companies made the assault simultaneously, supported by the entire Leicestershire Yeomanry and a troop of the 84th Medium Regiment, which was now attached to the brigade. The rain came down heavily and the enemy must have lost heart, for no opposition was met; moreover, while two of the companies found the bridges utterly destroyed, the third found an unexpected godsend in the shape of an undamaged sluice-gate, capable of bearing the heaviest tank. The day had been notably successful. Some three hundred prisoners had been taken altogether by both brigades, nearly all from the 8th Parachute Division; and everything was perfectly poised for the next day's operations.

The Irish moved off at seven o'clock and all went well for some miles till Haaksbergen was reached, where two self-propelled guns were located in the outskirts, together with a fair number of infantry. Typhoons were called up to help dislodge them, a task which they accomplished so successfully that the Germans promptly withdrew. They then continued without further incident until they reached the vicinity of the large industrial town of Enschede. They planned to by-pass it to the East and seize some high ground to the North, where an airfield was known to be situated; but on reaching the line of the main railway running East they were held up by fire from several self-propelled guns.

At the same time the Coldstream had made for a bridge over the Twente Canal mid-way between Enschede and Hengelo, an almost equally large town a few miles further West. Both towns were reported to be fairly strongly held, but if a wedge could be driven between them resistance might crumble. Neede had been found evacuated in the morning and, though two pockets of resistance were encountered further on, they caused little delay. Over a hundred prisoners were taken and by eleven o'clock they had reached the canal. The embankment was strongly held and the bridge had four huge bombs on it as demolition charges, but our appearance was utterly unexpected. Lieutenant I. L. Jardine, who was at the head of the leading troop, charged the bridge without hesitation. It was an exciting moment; three tanks got across, then the charges went off when our sappers were within a hundred yards. As the tanks crossed, Germans had run to man the four eighty-eight-millimetre guns that were guarding the bridge and knocked out the two leading tanks of the troop behind, seriously wounding Lieutenant the Hon. R. T. Boscawen. They also destroyed two of Lieutenant Jardine's troop, including his own, but somehow he got his own crew, three of whom could not swim, back over the canal. The remaining one, commanded by Lance-Sergeant Lyon, eventually worked its way back, killing a number of Germans in the process. Lieutenant Jardine was subsequently awarded the Military Cross for these exploits.

Preliminary attempts to get round the canal where it ended to the East in Enschede showed that the area contained a good number of enemy. A set attack, made by three companies of the 5th Bn. Coldstream supported by No. 1 Squadron, was necessary, but once it became apparent that our intentions were serious the resistance collapsed. Major J. L. Darell pushed on with his squadron, destroyed two road-blocks and quickly seized an important cross-roads East of Hengelo which effectively cut the main Rotterdam–Bremen Road. Brigadier Johnson then decided to push the Scots-Welsh Group through in an attempt to capture Oldenzaal before dark. They moved through Enschede at six o'clock, where they were fêted by an enthusiastic population, but on emerging from it the two front tanks were knocked out by anti-tank guns firing from the airfield. It was impossible to locate them in the rapidly fading light and they were ordered to harbour where they were and to attack the airfield at first light.

The Irish Group had meanwhile been involved in a stiffish fight with what turned out once more to be paratroops. No. 2 Company–No. 3 Squadron Group passed through to cross the railway but the leading troop quickly lost two tanks. The next troop, commanded by Lieutenant G. N. R. Whitfield, promptly looped to the right and made for the Enschede–Oldenzaal road. As they approached it another self-propelled gun suddenly appeared in front; fortunately it was travelling in the same direction and three hits in quick succession finished its career. The troop and Lieutenant R. H. S. O'Grady's accompanying platoon disposed themselves round the road-junction and accounted for at least one other German vehicle. But it was getting dark and the column had become very split up, both by the attentions of the German self-propelled guns and by the atrocious condition of the roads. Many of the guns were still about and it was thought wiser to withdraw the leading troops and to concentrate the whole group immediately North-East of Enschede astride one of the main roads leading into Germany.

It had been an extremely productive day in prisoners; sixteen officers and six hundred and eighty men passed through the divisional cage during the twenty-four hours. Nor is this by any means the full count, for large numbers were handed over to the highly efficient Dutch resistance organisation. Indication of the numbers thus involved was provided by the discovery in the one village in which Headquarters, 32nd Guards Brigade, happened to pass the night of no less than a hundred and thirty-five men under guard of the local Dutch in the schoolhouse. One of the most gratifying features of this period was the enthusiasm and reliability of the members of the resistance. Not only was their acceptance of the role of guards for prisoners of great help, as in France and Belgium the previous year, but their information was found to be remarkably accurate and valuable, not to mention the telephone facilities which they often managed to provide, stopping only just short of direct communications with Amsterdam and The Hague.

Both the Coldstream and Irish Groups, situated as they were astride the main German escape routes, spent a somewhat eventful night. The Coldstream captured thirty prisoners, six lorries and a large ten-wheeled affair containing a complete senior officers' mess equipment and five hundred wireless sets; the guard on the road derived great enjoyment from the blank astonishment on the faces of the Germans when they were stopped. The Irish had to take matters rather seriously as they were attacked at four o'clock in the morning by a force of at least seventy Germans who, as it subsequently turned out, were trying to infiltrate through them. A factor adding to the confusion was the arrival of some of their transport, which had been held up and which chose this very moment to turn up. After about an hour fifteen Germans had been killed and forty-two captured, but not before one of them had reached the door of battalion headquarters, where he was shot dead. The Irish themselves had three men killed and thirteen wounded, among the latter Lieutenant D. M. Sarsfield.

The 3rd Division was immediately behind us and relieved us of the job of clearing Enschede and Hengelo, while we were ordered to push on with all speed back across the Dutch frontier into Germany. At first light the Scots-Welsh Group attacked the airfield and found it unoccupied, with the three eighty-eight-millimetre guns which had been so troublesome the previous evening abandoned in perfect order. While this operation was proceeding the Irish Group was already moving through Oldenzaal, which they found clear of Germans and only obstructed by masses of cheering Dutch people. Here they turned due East towards Gildehaus and Bentheim and continued to meet with no obstacle until just short of the frontier, where they found the road blocked by two large craters which it was estimated would take five hours to fill. No. 4 Company was pushed on across the frontier to clear the village of Westenberg, which it managed to do successfully, but there were still many Germans scattered on both sides of the road for some way back, with a good deal of shooting going on. So No. 1 Company–No. 2 Squadron Group was sent off to the right, preceded by a troop of light tanks under Captain H. C. H. FitzHerbert, in the hope that an easier approach to Gildehaus might be found that way, since the main road seemed so well defended. Unhappily it appears that this move had been anticipated by the Germans, who had a well-prepared trap waiting. Although the light troop got right round into Gildehaus they were ambushed there, the tanks destroyed and Captain FitzHerbert killed. Lieutenant P. A. Cuffe in the leading troop of Shermans had not got quite so far when he suddenly found himself surrounded by Germans firing bazookas; his tank was hit and he was fatally wounded. His driver managed none the less to drive the tank away and led the troop back towards the rest of the squadron; but a small bridge over a stream collapsed behind it and the remainder of the troop were cut off. On appeal for help a platoon of No. 1 Company under Lieutenant B. B. Russell was sent forward to help them. It got there without difficulty and took up a defensive position round the tanks and reported over the wireless that the situation was in hand; but soon afterwards communication ceased and nothing was known till about an hour later, when one section returned and reported that the remainder of the platoon and the tank crews had all been killed or taken prisoner. One tank had got bogged and, while the other was trying to tow it out, the German paratroops had managed to hit them both with bazookas. With both tanks destroyed and the wireless out of action the isolated platoon was in a difficult position, with the enemy closing in on them in increasing numbers. Lieutenant Russell decided to withdraw but was killed no sooner than he had given orders to that effect. Sergeant Cleaton took over command and fought a valiant rear-guard action during which five other men were killed until the ammunition ran out, when he and most of the platoon were made prisoner. He himself knocked his captor over the head and got away to join the one section which had succeeded in fighting its way back.

No. 4 Company had meanwhile been able to push on doggedly to the outskirts of Gildehaus; and the 14th Field Squadron had knocked down the first house in Germany, connected with the Customs, and used it to fill in the craters. The main road was therefore once more open and No. 1 Squadron delivered a frontal attack on the town, accompanied by a bombardment with Typhoons. What with this and the fire from the tanks the place was soon an inferno, but it stood on high ground and was well defended. Skilfully concealed self-propelled guns and determined infantry inflicted casualties and two tanks were destroyed. As it was growing dark the tanks were withdrawn and the final clearing carried out by Nos. 2 and 4 Companies. The nerve-racking business of street-fighting went on well into the night, with German posts still showing considerable fight; but before daylight all was over and the stage set for the Grenadiers to move on to Bentheim in the morning.

While the 5th Guards Brigade was involved in this bitter fighting, the 32nd Guards Brigade, directed North-East from Oldenzaal on Nordhorn, had found a weaker spot in the frontier line of defence. The bridge over the Almelo–Nordhorn Canal just short of the frontier was duly blown up but reconnaissance by the Household Cavalry soon resulted in the discovery of an intact one a couple of miles to the West which, though in itself not strong enough for tank traffic, was very soon adapted for the purpose by the 615th Field Squadron; meanwhile the armoured cars pushed right on till they were quite close to Nordhorn, where they were held up by one or two self-propelled guns.

There was every reason to think that there were a lot of enemy in Nordhorn, as the majority of military traffic passing through Oldenzaal during the last two days had been reported by civilians to be travelling in that direction; in addition, our aircraft had seen large numbers of German vehicles of all descriptions streaming North along the road there from Bentheim throughout the morning. But it was most important to capture it before nightfall if possible, and as soon as tanks could cross the canal bridge the Scots-Welsh Group pushed on, with No. 2 Squadron under Major N. M. Daniel and Right Flank under Major W. D. M. Raeburn leading. Three successive bridges in Nordhorn must be captured if we were to get through and the only hope lay in speed, trusting that the obvious chaos in which the enemy were would serve us in good stead. On the whole it did and when the moment came everything went remarkably smoothly. The company-squadron group seized the first bridge intact and although a charge was exploded at the second one it was not effective. The third and most important one, over the Ems–Vechte Canal, was blown up sufficiently to be rendered unfit for tanks, but the infantry were able to get across to establish a bridgehead. By nightfall both battalions were concentrated in the town and all resistance had ceased.

By this time the Household Cavalry had found an intact bridge over the canal just North of the town; it was rickety and a few inches narrower than our tanks, but it just might carry them. Lieutenant-Colonel Windsor-Lewis asked for, and promptly got, permission to take the risk of putting the tanks across and of making for Lingen, twelve miles across flat country that did not appear likely to offer any major obstruction. Risk there was, even at this stage of the war. Tanks are very blind at night and peculiarly vulnerable, so that it is usual for them to withdraw during the hours of darkness to harbour, where all-round protection can be organised. This is so even when communications are assured, while on this particular night the only sure thing was that at the best they would be tenuous in the extreme. But at Lingen the River Ems was reached and, a few hundred yards further on, the Dortmund–Ems Canal, together forming by far the strongest defensive position in front of us short of the River Weser. If we could capture intact bridges over both of these they would be prizes of inestimable value; with this possibility in view any risk was worth while.

By nine o'clock the tanks had already started to move across. No. 2 Squadron-Right Flank Group was still leading, followed by No. 3 Squadron-Left Flank Group and No. 1 Squadron-F Company Group; as usual the tanks carried the infantry with the exception of the two leading troops. The two first groups got across all right but as the third was in the process the bridge collapsed. Both commanding officers were left behind with their headquarters, but the force that had crossed was told to advance as ordered under the command of Major W. L. Consett, commander of No. 3 Squadron. This they did, shortly before midnight, in pitch darkness and torrential rain. As they raced at top speed through the inky night they met groups of bewildered Germans driving or walking along the road towards them, utterly unaware of the situation. Tracer bullets spat from the machine-guns as lorries, motor-cycles and carts, many laden with equipment, were swept off the road into the ditches. They had covered more than half the distance when Sergeant Townsend, commanding the leading tank, overtook a captured Sherman recovery vehicle towing two broken-down self-propelled guns. He quickly disposed of all three, but the wrecks blocked the road and moreover a bazooka shot broke his track and immobilised him. A short but sharp argument followed, as there seemed to be quite a few Germans in the vicinity, but the struggle was decidedly uneven and they soon fled. The leading troop commander, Lieutenant A. A. Upfill-Brown, had meanwhile found a diversion through the fields and immediately the column moved on once more.

Soon after three o'clock they were driving down the incline to the River Ems through Schepsdorf, the suburb of Lingen which lies on the Western bank. But either the noise of the engagement must have carried or someone had been able to get a warning telephone message through, because they were met with considerable, if wild, firing from either side of the road. While the leading platoon of Right Flank set to work to clear the houses the other two made for the bridge, which was still intact. In the face of heavy fire from the opposite side they got across, but as the first tank was moving up to follow them the bridge blew up. Despite this, more infantry were sent across in assault boats until two companies, Right and Left Flank, were established on the Eastern bank. But enemy opposition became notably stronger as daylight dawned and both self-propelled guns and mortars were in evidence. It was plain that Lingen was held comparatively strongly and that a staged assault by infantry across the double obstacle would be necessary; consequently, shortly before midday, orders were given for the two companies to be withdrawn and for the whole group to consolidate West of the river.

So the gamble failed to succeed by a narrow margin; nevertheless the results were well worth-while and we had gained a valuable twelve miles. Altogether we were well satisfied, and if further encouragement were needed it came that night with the news that the First U.S. Army had captured Paderborn and had linked up with the Ninth U.S. Army to surround the Ruhr and so cut off the remnants of the Fifth Panzer and Fifteenth Armies, about a hundred thousand men. Such tonic news made us feel that the end really was at last in sight.

At first light the Household Cavalry were out looking for any other bridges that might still be intact, and before long a report came back that they had found one about three miles to the North, leading across to the small town of Altenlingen. It was fully prepared for demolition and moreover was covered by enemy infantry together with eighty-eight-millimetre guns; but so long as it remained standing a chance existed of capturing it and Brigadier Johnson told the Coldstream Group to try its hand at the venture.

The 615th Field Squadron had repaired the bridge at Nordhorn during the night and the whole of the 32nd Guards Brigade was concentrated around Südlohne, just West of Lingen, by the early afternoon. No. 3 Squadron–No. 3 Company Group was deputed to undertake the task, and the operation was to be under the direct command of Lieutenant-Colonel Gooch. The original intention was for the squadron to try to rush the bridge by taking the enemy unawares and for the infantry to follow on to consolidate, but a preliminary reconnaissance showed that this was out of the question and that the original Household Cavalry reports were only too accurate. There was a formidable road-block on the near side, rendering any approach by tanks impossible; there were six large bombs tied to the bridge, a modern concrete one which they would patently shatter entirely; and there were three eighty-eight-millimetre guns well dug-in and sandbagged, some of whose crews could periodically be seen very much alive and alert.

Lieutenant-Colonel Gooch, after a short conference with Major P. H. Hunt and Captain I. O. Liddell, the squadron and company commanders, decided that only in a co-ordinated attack by the whole group, supported by artillery, was there any hope of capturing the bridge intact; the essence of the plan lay in surprise and in highly effective fire support from the tanks. The West Somerset Yeomanry first of all fired round the bridge without registering and then lifted to the woods beyond. At this moment two troops and two tanks of squadron headquarters, which had taken up a position among the trees along a small escarpment which luckily screened them from enemy view, opened fire while, under cover of smoke, No. 2 Troop fired the Typhoon rockets with which it had been specially fitted. Immediately after the terrifying fire of the rockets and still under cover of the machine-guns the infantry went forward, closely supported by one troop of tanks. The Germans had been given no respite, the fire from the tanks still made it almost impossible for them to do anything but lie flat on their faces and they were taken completely by surprise. Captain Liddell ran on ahead, climbed the road-block and within a couple of minutes had cut the wires connecting the charges and beckoned on his company. The tanks had to charge the road-block five times before it gave way, but within five minutes they too were across the bridge and very soon the whole position was consolidated.

So swift and complete was the success that it might be thought that the defenders proved after all to have been very few, but this was far from being the case. Forty-five dead were actually counted and sixty prisoners were taken, as against our own losses of one killed and nine wounded. The prisoners included the commander of the position, a young captain who complained that he had been caught in the wrong dug-out and could not get back to the one which contained the switch; when he did and pressed it nothing happened, which was not surprising as the line had by then been cut. Despite his shameful performance he was a typically arrogant Nazi, and declared that the fight would go on until Germany was victorious. When the remoteness of this possibility was pointed out to him he merely replied that the Führer said so and that the Führer was never wrong.

To quote the words of General Horrocks, the result was the

best praise for a magnificently planned, perfectly timed and bravely executed action. In some ways it was unique and it very properly won the award of the Victoria Cross for Captain Liddell; but, alas, he never knew this, as he was killed later in the month before the news came through. Lieutenant-Colonel Gooch received the Distinguished Service Order and Captain J. V. Barnes, of the West Somerset Yeomanry, the Military Cross.

It was now seven o'clock in the evening and a decision was made to put some infantry of the 3rd Division, which was following immediately behind us, through at once and to get them over the second obstacle, the canal, during the night. There was even just a possibility that a second bridge might be seized, though only a very remote one, and sure enough at ten minutes past eight two loud explosions were heard which put an end to all hope on that score. All the same a bridgehead was made after a crossing in assault boats and a battalion firmly established on the far bank by the morning. A second battalion was then sent across with the object of pushing down towards Lingen, while the Coldstream Group was given the task of clearing Southwards the main road between the river and the canal.

Throughout this time the 5th Guards Brigade had been persisting in its attempts to force its way through on the more Southerly route. The Grenadiers duly passed through the Irish in Gildehaus at seven o'clock in the morning on April 3rd, but the King's Company–No. 2 Squadron Group, who led, ran into trouble as soon as they debouched into the open country beyond. Further progress up the road was out of the question until the woods were clear and the King's Company was given this task. It was carried out successfully, though Captain W. M. Robson was wounded, when they came under fire at point-blank range from one of the self-propelled guns. Once in our hands the woods provided an excellent forming-up place for an attack on Bentheim, an important road-junction built on the side of a hill and forming an ideal defensive position. Also twelve prisoners had been captured who gave valuable information about the enemy dispositions; while the majority of their troops had withdrawn

East to Schüttorf, Bentheim was still held by some four hundred paratroops.

A plan was quickly made for an attack on a two-company front, with the road as the axis of advance. No. 4 Company went on the right, No. 2 Company on the left, each with a troop of tanks under command. Three lines were taken off the map before which the companies were to pause while the Leicestershire Yeomanry fired concentrations, and the final objective was the Western part of Bentheim. The operation started at about three o'clock and on the whole proceeded with clockwork precision, though No. 4 Company came under heavy fire near the town and most of the tanks got bogged. The opposition came mostly from snipers as the majority of the Germans, according to prisoners, withdrew at our approach. This was all the more surprising as the town was found to contain an imposing old castle, quite inaccessible to tanks, whose capture, if resolutely held, might have proved a difficult and expensive matter. All went so well that, as soon as a footing had been obtained and after five minutes' gun-fire, the two companies were ordered to proceed and to clear the main part of the town. This they did as light was failing; Lieutenant K. Bowles' Wasp platoon of flame-throwing carriers supported them and, deprived of any opportunity for action earlier in the day, let its imagination run riot with pictures of skulking paratroops and set fire to several buildings remarkably quickly. By nightfall the town, apart from the Eastern outskirts, was firmly in our hands. It was a glittering and lurid scene as we consolidated. The Wasps and tank guns had done their work well and pin-points of fire dotted every part; smoke and the crackle of burning timber lasted throughout the night and most of the next day.

Early the following morning the King's Company passed through and cleared the Eastern edge of the town before establishing itself, with No. 2 Squadron, on a hillside just beyond. This commanded a wonderful view of the surrounding country-side, where everything now seemed at peace, except when the Leicestershire Yeomanry decided to bombard Schüttorf and so hasten the departure of the retreating enemy. The flat boggy country to the East offered little prospect of a break-through and the group was not sorry to learn that, as the result of the capture of the bridgehead at Lingen, the whole division would now cross the Ems there before once more diverging on to two centre-lines.

The Coldstream had duly cleared the ground between the Ems and the canal during that day. No. 2 Company–No. 2 Squadron Group soon reported that what had appeared on the map to be a sewage-works was in fact a large military barracks almost the size of Pirbright and apparently still occupied. No. 3 Company was ordered to join them and after heavy shelling from the tanks the two infantry companies set to work to clear the barracks. Fifty dead Germans were counted and over a hundred taken prisoner, bringing the total captured by the 32nd Guards Brigade in the past two days to close on three hundred and fifty. The barracks were found to be full of guns, ammunition and stores of all kinds. By the evening they had arrived opposite the Scots Guards at the destroyed bridge carrying the main road. For his fine leadership during this difficult operation Sergeant N. Duckworth of the Coldstream was awarded the Military Medal.

Chapter Twelve

FROM THE EMS TOWARDS BREMEN

April 5th was in general an inactive day throughout the division, though both this and the preceding day produced the now unusual spectacle of enemy air attacks, principally on the gun areas.

The same day, however, saw great strides in the clearing of Lingen and by the evening another brigade of the 3rd Division had gone through to complete the task and so to open up an exit for ourselves. One counter-attack was put in on the bridging-site over the canal, supported by some very accurate shelling; although it was driven off without great difficulty the mere fact of its being made was surprising at this juncture, but the capture of an Alsatian who was willing to talk soon provided the answer. Whereas the 32nd Guards Brigade had not seen a single paratroop since crossing the Dutch frontier, the counter-attack force was found to have consisted of about a hundred and twenty men of the 7th Parachute Division, supported by several eighty-eight-millimetre guns; he also told us that it was only the prelude to a larger scale attack by the whole division. While this proved to be no more than a pious hope, the arrival of these first-class troops in the nick of time boded ill for our chances of another break-through; the same prisoner also gave us the depressing news that they had already mined the main roads leading East from Lingen. Incidentally we had already begun to discover that the roads in Germany were in general not nearly so good as had been expected. It transpired that those marked as main roads on the map were normally very narrow and paved, while those marked as second-class were mere sandy tracks which were almost invariably mined.

So we were none of us too sanguine when orders came for the 32nd Guards Brigade to move through Lingen the next morning and to aim at seizing a crossing over the River Weser, eighty miles away; and in the event our fears were all too well justified. No sooner had the Scots-Welsh Group advanced outside the perimeter held by the 3rd Division than it found a succession of mines and road-blocks, duly covered by self-propelled guns. Progress was slow and it was costly, both in tanks and in men. The third block was particularly strongly defended and necessitated an attack by F Company. This cost the life of Major D. H. A. Kemble, M.C., a man of great personality and courage who had fought throughout the African campaign.

By the early afternoon we had only got just beyond Laxten, a village three miles East of Lingen where the main road forks, the more Southerly one going to Freren and Fürstenau and the more Northerly one to Lengerich. The Scots-Welsh Group was ordered to concentrate on the latter route and the Coldstream Group was brought up to make for Freren. Both routes, however, continued to be stubbornly defended. Lieutenant H. Richmond, who was commanding the leading troop of the 615th Field Squadron, was seriously wounded by a panzerfaust bomb which hit a road-block that he was clearing on the Lengerich road; he had displayed outstanding bravery throughout the day and was awarded the Military Cross. Once past this road-block some progress was made until the front tank was knocked out by an anti-tank gun. The area proved to contain a number of them and a confused game of mutual stalking with No. 2 Squadron ensued; four of the German guns were destroyed in the process, three of which fell to the troop commanded by Lieutenant D. A. Gibbs. But by this time it was getting dark and orders were given to harbour for the night just short of Nordholten, about two-thirds of the way to Lengerich.

The Coldstream Group equally had trouble with a road-block. A bulldozer, which had been blown up on a mine while trying to clear it, was manned by Germans who proceeded to fire on the leading tanks. This impertinence was greatly resented and the bulldozer summarily dealt with; it made a merry bonfire until well into the night. Another squadron-company group was meanwhile despatched through the woods to the South to try and reach that way the villages of Ramsel and Backum, which were the immediate objectives. Opposition on reaching them was tough and came as expected from paratroops, who showed none of the signs of a beaten foe. None the less thirty were killed and forty-three were taken prisoner, and by nightfall we were in firm occupation of the two villages.

Our own casualties that day were unfortunately far from negligible; in addition to those among the forward troops there were losses further back, owing to accurate shelling of concentration areas and of the main road on either side of Lingen. Among others Captain E. R. Hubbard and a signalman were wounded when a high-calibre shell fell in the area of the 32nd Guards Brigade Headquarters shortly before dawn, and the Northumberland Fusiliers lost two men killed and several wounded on the road, the latter including two of their key men, Company-Quartermaster-Sergeant Lee and Orderly Room-Sergeant Butler.

Orders for April 7th were for the Scots-Welsh Group to capture Lengerich and for the Coldstream Group, after seizing the village of Thuine, to push North-East and to join them there; the 5th Guards Brigade was to take over Thuine and then to make for Freren and Fürstenau.

Right Flank and No. 2 Squadron led off at seven o'clock, preceded by a rolling barrage up the road to just west of Lengerich, where they encountered enemy in some numbers round yet another road-block. As the men of one platoon were dismantling it they were fired on by an anti-tank gun and machine-guns at point-blank range. At this moment Sergeant White appeared from the right, well ahead of his section, and charged the anti-tank gun, killing the whole crew. Then, still alone, he attacked a machine-gun across the road, but before he could reach it he was fatally wounded in the chest; however, he continued to engage the post and accounted for many Germans before he died. Because of his great courage the remainder became demoralised and surrendered and the advance could continue.

Not for long, however; more opposition developed, three tanks were destroyed and casualties began to mount up. At one o'clock the commanding officers gave out orders for a full-scale attack on the town by three companies and two squadrons. Two hours later it started, preceded by two Typhoon attacks in addition to a bombardment by artillery and mortars. The defence crumbled as our infantry advanced and finally the town was occupied virtually without fighting; only stragglers were found, who gave themselves up willingly enough.

This may have been partly due to the Typhoons, but the Coldstream Group could also claim some credit. Thuine fell without any trouble at all, which at first seemed surprising as sixty prisoners were captured, all from the élite 15th Panzer Grenadier Division, which was not known to be on our front. The explanation soon followed; the unit in question was happily on its way to a rest area and had only been suddenly told to dig slit trenches a few minutes before our tanks rushed upon them. Their ready surrender under the circumstances could be excused. From Thuine the Coldstream quickly pushed North-East through the thick Forest of Lingen. They liberated a prisoner-of-war camp, where they received a particularly warm welcome from thirty Coldstream and Irish Guardsmen, and very soon reached the road running South from Lengerich to Freren. We knew from prisoners and captured documents that this was the line that the Germans intended to hold, but they had not had either the time or the troops to re-dispose themselves as they wanted. Once through this vital gap a reconnaissance patrol under Lieutenant J. Lee soon found a route to the main road running East from Lengerich, at a spot about three miles beyond. He was followed by a whole squadron of tanks, which from this point had a magnificent shoot at fleeing German transport and collected a number of prisoners in addition to killing about fifty. This action of cutting the chief escape route, taken entirely on the initiative of the two commanding officers, contributed to the decision of the Lengerich garrison to evacuate while the sole remaining exit, to the North, was still available.

The following day, April 8th, the Scots-Welsh Group rested in Lengerich while the Coldstream Group was ordered to make for the next sizable town, Berge, about twelve miles further on. Resistance continued on very much the same scale; our progress was continually held up by road-blocks and rearguards left at nodal points. The first such enemy pocket was found at a road-junction not much more than a mile from where the Coldstream had harboured. This was mopped up without undue difficulty, though trouble was experienced on this sector throughout the remainder of the day, as enemy remained not far to the South with at least one self-propelled gun, which shelled the road periodically with uncomfortable accuracy. One or two small-scale battles also occurred with groups of Germans who tried their luck with a stray burst of machine-gun fire. One such group even went as far as to fire a bazooka at close range and succeeded in immobilising a vehicle of the 32nd Guards Brigade Headquarters. The column was stationary at the time and Sergeant Quarmby, the brigade transport sergeant, was so infuriated that, with the support of Lieutenant J. Sutton in a tank of the protective troop, he went to search some farm buildings from where the shot had appeared to come. He came back triumphantly with one prisoner, complaining bitterly that the remainder had run too fast for him.

Serious trouble was not however met until reaching a wooded ridge a mile and a half from Berge. Three road-blocks in a row were found here and there was every indication that the town was strongly held: but this was only to be expected. It was an important centre of communications; prisoners had told us that there were large numbers of troops there; and the reconnaissance troop, which had been working round to the left, reported lorries and infantry moving in. The commanding officers decided to adopt the same tactics which had succeeded so well at Lengerich; while two squadron-company groups made a direct attack, a third was ordered to make a wide loop, this time to the North, and to cut the main road leading out of Berge to the East.

After two rocket attacks by Typhoons and a large-scale concentration by the heavy mortars of the Northumberland Fusiliers, one attack went in directly from the West and another from the

South. The leading tanks were soon set ablaze by determined paratroops firing bazookas from the windows of the houses. As the smoke from the burning buildings made observation impossible the infantry then went forward, supported by fire from the tanks. They never stopped firing until the clearing was complete, by which time practically every house was on fire and a pall of smoke hung over the whole surroundings. In the meantime the reconnaissance troop had cut the road to the North and No. 3 Squadron, with a troop of the Household Cavalry, had carried out a wide loop through Grafeld and Börstel. On their way they took twenty prisoners and an ammunition dump, and destroyed installations on a dummy airfield. They had hoped to find a route by which to rejoin the centre-line near where it crossed the Hase Canal and possibly to capture an intact bridge over it, but the roads were appalling and the bridges impassable to tanks; many got bogged, but by dint of superhuman efforts a portion of the force succeeded in getting through to a road-junction a mile beyond Berge so that, with the reconnaissance troop, they ensured that any German wanting to escape would have to do so across country. In the end ninety-one prisoners were taken in Berge and over a hundred dead were counted; as against these figures our own loss of only seven men killed afforded sufficient proof of the skili with which the operation was planned and carried out. Among the prisoners was a well-informed despatch-rider who told us that there had originally been two battalions of paratroops in the town and that just before the battle started no less a person than General Erdmann, commander of the 7th Parachute Division, had been there and had ordered them all to fight to the last man. He was in an open captured Jeep and only moved back when he actually sighted our armoured cars approaching; no doubt he had intended deliberately to set an example to his men, by whom he was admittedly greatly admired and respected.

We could not fail in turn to admire the paratroops for their fighting qualities, whatever we might think of them in other respects; they did not recognise defeat and no risks could be taken with them. Lieutenant M. J. Bulkeley and Bombardier

E. Taylor of the West Somerset Yeomanry went to investigate an apparently empty farmhouse at Ohrte quite near the centre-line that day and were killed in a skirmish that ensued with Germans who were concealed there. Also most unfortunately Major H. D. Tweedie and Major R. B. Hodgkinson, seconds-in-command respectively of the 2nd Bn. Scots Guards and the 2nd Bn. Welsh Guards, took a wrong turning when reconnoitring a harbour area for their group in the late afternoon. They had not gone far when they were fired on by bazookas. Major Tweedie and both drivers were killed and the scout-cars wrecked; Major Hodgkinson was wounded but managed to hide in a ditch for an hour while the Germans ransacked the cars, and was found later by a troop of tanks that had gone out to their rescue. Perhaps the most extraordinary case was that of Sub-Conductor Gubb, R.A.S.C., and Guardsman Trickett, who were captured in broad daylight on the morning of April 9th when walking in the woods within four hundred yards of the harbour area of the 32nd Guards Brigade Headquarters. The former eventually escaped a few days later, but not before the guardsman had been killed in an earlier attempt to get away. In fact any man who took the slightest chance when paratroops were known to be within ten miles did so at the imminent risk of his life. The three stories all point the same moral; altogether in fluid conditions of warfare in an enemy country one cannot be too suspicious or too careful.

We must now return to the 5th Guards Brigade, which took over Thuine from the Coldstream Group in the early afternoon of April 7th. The Germans brought down a heavy mortar concentration on the village as the relief by the Irish Group was taking place and an unlucky hit on No. 3 Company Headquarters killed Company-Sergeant-Major Beresford and a guardsman and wounded everybody who was there at the time. Shortly afterwards group tactical headquarters came under shell-fire and Lieutenant-Colonel G. A. M. Vandeleur was wounded, not seriously, but sufficiently to need to be evacuated. Major J. S. O. Haslewood took over command of the 2nd Bn. Irish Guards.

The trouble appeared to come in the main from the villages of Venslage and Lohe, half-way on to Freren and a little to the South; No. 4 Company–No. 2 Squadron Group was therefore sent off to clear them, a mission which was completed successfully before dark. In the meantime No. 2 Company–No. 3 Squadron Group had been ordered to move into the woods to the North, starting by the track taken earlier by the Coldstream and branching off later to cut the Freren–Fürstenau road at Oberdorf, a village a couple of miles beyond the first-named town. They got through all right and, when the main body advanced on Freren after an artillery barrage early the next morning, the opposition was negligible.

No. 1 Company–No. 1 Squadron Group went quickly through; but about a mile beyond Oberdorf the usual opposition was encountered, entrenched in the woods on either side. By the skilful use of infantry and tanks this was overcome at small cost to themselves and with heavy losses to the enemy; but, after another short run and some two miles short of Fürstenau, they found themselves up against a very determined body of Germans holding a feature which the road crossed at this point. In addition the road was badly cratered, so No. 2 Company–No. 3 Squadron Group was again ordered to move round to the North and if possible to seize a road-junction a mile due North of the town. No opposition was met until they had almost reached it but they were then held up by shelling and small-arms fire. They pushed on finally to the objective and established themselves there; but they lost two tanks and several men, and further exploitation was out of the question.

The Irish Group was now fully committed and it would be dark within three hours. Brigadier Gwatkin ordered the Grenadier Group to despatch a force North-East through the woods further to the North with the object of clearing the villages of Dalum and Bippen. Both were on lateral roads between Fürstenau and Berge and were natural rallying points for any Germans driven South by the advance of the 32nd Guards Brigade earlier in the day. No. 2 Company–No. 3 Squadron Group was selected for this task and advanced uneventfully for about four miles until, just after crossing the railway from Fürstenau to Bippen, it was fired upon by a self-propelled gun. As it was almost dark and infantry could be seen and heard moving about on either side, Major Gregory-Hood, who was in command of the force, decided to harbour for the night in a very tight area just West of the railway.

Fürstenau fell to the Irish the next morning, but only after some fairly heavy fighting. No. 4 Company–No. 2 Squadron Group was moved round to the North during the night and carried out the main attack from that direction after a heavy artillery concentration. The company commander, Major M. V. Dudley, was unfortunately killed by a sniper at the beginning of the attack and the company signallers put out of action at the same time. The resultant failure of control complicated matters seriously for a few moments until Major E. Tyler pushed his tanks forward most boldly and restored the situation. By nine o'clock the town was completely in our hands and the Irish could claim four eighty-eight-millimetre guns destroyed and over two hundred prisoners in the twenty-four hours that had been needed to capture it. They had themselves, however, had fairly severe casualties and they were ordered to rest while the Grenadiers took the lead. No. 2 Company–No. 3 Squadron Group was ordered to continue its advance on Dalum and Bippen; the King's Company–No. 2 Squadron Group to follow tracks through the woods with the object of cutting the Schwagstorf–Bippen road at Kleinbokern; the remainder to move through Fürstenau direct on Schwagstorf. Thus three Grenadier columns advanced simultaneously and must be dealt with one by one.

No. 2 Company–No. 3 Squadron Group advanced without any material difficulty into Dalum, which appeared at first to be empty. Suddenly heavy small-arms fire was opened and the leading platoon and troop commanders, Lieutenant J. C. Moller and Lieutenant A. R. B. Ryan, were both killed. The group immediately withdrew to the woods just West of the village and prepared an attack: artillery support was called for, the tanks fired fast and furiously, and little difficulty was experienced in clearing the place and rounding up seventeen prisoners. But pockets of Germans had infiltrated round to the rear; a half-track attempting to take back some wounded was fired on and as the general situation was obscure the force was ordered for the present to establish a strong-point at Dalum.

The King's Company–No. 2 Squadron Group had to move slowly along the very poor woodland tracks and had occasional trouble with small bands of Germans equipped with bazookas. They lost one tank, but by three o'clock Kleinbokern was captured.

The main body, led by No. 4 Company–No. 1 Squadron Group, set on fire a self-propelled gun as it approached Schwagstorf, but very soon afterwards the leading tank was destroyed by a bazooka and heavy small-arms fire was opened. No chances were taken, and the village was systematically cleared after an organised attack. A large number of Germans were killed and sixty-nine taken prisoner; as our own casualties were two wounded the action can be termed peculiarly successful. It may here be mentioned that in this engagement Q and Z Batteries of the 21st Anti-Tank Regiment R.A. made their first appearance fighting in an infantry role and were reported on by the brigade commander as making a most useful contribution.

Ankum, the next town on the road running East from Schwagstorf, was the immediate objective of the 4th Independent Armoured Brigade, which was by now converging on us from the South. So the Grenadiers were ordered to swing North to Bippen before turning East once more to Kettenkamp and Quakenbrück. No. 4 Company–No. 1 Squadron Group was thereupon told to move through Kleinbokern and, provided that the opposition was slight, to seize Bippen before dark. It was now four o'clock and, pausing only to destroy a self-propelled gun on the way, they reached the outskirts without meeting any serious trouble. But here they ran into heavy fire from an anti-tank gun and infantry; as it was nearly dark and they were isolated by some miles they were ordered back and the whole group harboured in the Kleinbokern–Dalum area. It had been a day of very hard fighting for all of them and they were not particularly pleased to be told that evening by the British Broadcasting Corporation that all resistance in Germany had virtually ceased.

The next morning, April 10th, was cold and misty, and No. 4 Company–No. 1 Squadron Group set out again for Bippen at an early hour. The Leicestershire Yeomanry fired a short and sharp concentration, the tanks knocked out a self-propelled gun and the infantry soon were in firm possession. Three eighty-eight-millimetre guns were found, one destroyed by artillery and the other two just abandoned by their crews; most of the enemy had withdrawn East during the night towards Eggermühlen and Kettenkamp. No. 2 Company–No. 3 Squadron Group had been directed across country on the former village and was already engaged in fighting there. The leading troop, on crossing the Bippen–Kettenkamp road, was caught in the open by two self-propelled guns concealed in some woods on rising ground on its Western flank; Lieutenant A. Jones and several of his men were killed and the accompanying infantry also came under heavy fire. At this moment the situation was eased by the arrival of the King's Company–No. 2 Squadron Group, which had come through Bippen and which helped in clearing both the woods and Eggermühlen itself. They were held in some strength and, though a number of Germans were killed and captured, the guns somehow got away.

These operations were completed by one o'clock, and orders were now received to move North and to capture the bridge over a stream just South of Kettenkamp. Prisoners had told us that the village and a large wood to the South-West were held by a battalion of the Gross Deutschland Regiment. No. 2 Company–No. 3 Squadron Group was left in Eggermühlen as a firm base, the King's Company–No. 2 Squadron Group was told to clear the wood, while No. 4 Company–No. 1 Squadron Group, which had been relieved in Bippen by the 21st Anti-Tank Regiment, made a sweep round the wood to the West to seize the stream crossing. The bridge was captured without difficulty, but the group attacking the wood came under heavy fire when still four hundred yards away. The weight of supporting fire from the tanks and artillery was, however, sufficient to enable them to close with the enemy. Even so very fierce fighting continued for a long time; many Germans had to be evicted from their holes at the point of the bayonet and two committed a European form of harakiri by exploding grenades against their stomachs. It was six o'clock before the wood was clear; twenty-eight dead were counted, fifty-nine prisoners taken and an anti-tank gun destroyed.

A patrol went forward into Kettenkamp at dawn the next morning and found the place deserted; but a huge crater at a spot where the road crossed yet another stream barred any immediate advance. But now this was of no direct interest to us, as the 51st Division was coming up to take over from the 5th Guards Brigade, which received orders to move North on to the 32nd Guards Brigade's route before continuing the advance.

The 32nd Guards Brigade had found progress beyond Berge exceedingly difficult. The country was traversed by water obstacles in every direction and the bridges along the few passable roads were all either destroyed or held and prepared for demolition. Admittedly the Scots-Welsh Group, which was again leading, succeeded in finding an alternative bridge over the first canal when that carrying the main road was blown up at its approach; but the road was only a sandy track quite unsuitable as a main route, and moreover two major bridges and four minor ones still remained before firm ground was reached again. The first of the former, over the Hase Canal just short of Menslage, also went up as we attempted to deal with a road-block protecting it, and this time no intact alternative could be found. A two-company bridgehead was therefore established on the North bank, to enable bridging operations over both waterways to go forward during the night. An attempt was made at the same time to infiltrate through and to seize the remaining small bridges so that the armour could make a dash in the morning through to the last and largest bridge, over the River Hase itself. But the patrols which went forward found them firmly held, and indeed reported that the whole Menslage area seemed to be occupied in considerable strength.

As a result of this nothing spectacular could be attempted the following day, April 10th, although both bridges were open by early morning. Before ten o'clock Menslage and the neighbouring village of Herbergen had been captured, two platoon positions having been overcome in the process, but shortly afterwards a loud explosion was heard which proved to be the blowing up of one of the small bridges, together with a large crater on either side of the gap. The combination proved a formidable task for our sappers, and the rest of the day and the ensuing night were occupied in this and in thoroughly clearing the whole area up to the river with a view to an assault crossing next day. It was a disappointing day in the way of territorial progress, but not unsatisfactory in the losses inflicted on the enemy; a hundred and sixty-five prisoners were taken and our troops reckoned that not less than eighty were killed. As our men slept among the smouldering houses of Menslage that night they were startled by the sound of repeated volleys of shots coming from one of the burning houses. But the mystery was soon solved; the house contained a vast number of bottled peas which had exploded with the heat.

It was impossible to get close enough to the main bridge over the Hase to see the true extent of the damage to it owing to a large volume of accurate small-arms fire. The Coldstream Group, on moving up in the early morning of April 11th to force a crossing and to capture the village of Böen on the far bank, lost several men from snipers; Major R. J. Carew-Hunt, commanding the battery in support, was also killed while trying to get a view of the enemy positions. The 5th Bn. Coldstream Guards suffered another grievous blow at the same time when the intelligence truck went up on a mine; this caused the death of Sergeant Todd, a man of great character and courage who had been a source of strength to the battalion throughout the whole campaign.

The prospects seemed depressing in the extreme and plans

for an assault crossing after nightfall were already being formulated when Major J. de H. Hamilton arrived with the news that an escaped French prisoner had reached his company headquarters after crossing, as he claimed, an intact bridge about two miles to the East. No such bridge was marked on the map nor any road leading to the river in the area, but a platoon supported by a troop of tanks was sent off at once to investigate. Sure enough the bridge existed, though only made of wood and not fit for vehicles. It was held and an attempt made to blow it up, but the defence was altogether not very effective and the platoon was quickly across. It seized a tiny village called Bokah just beyond and consolidated there, while the rest of the company moved up behind and secured the area around the bridge.

So far all was well. But Böen, the essential objective since it covered the only possible bridging site, lay a full two miles away through thick fir woods; it was already early afternoon and an attack by so long and precarious a route, over which no transport could follow, might conceivably prove more than a battalion could deal with. On the other hand it offered the only possibility of securing the site before dark and the casualties from an assault crossing could not fail to be extremely heavy. The risk was worth taking and Brigadier Johnson readily gave his sanction. Only a small post was left behind on the main road and by half-past three the whole infantry battalion was assembled at Bokah.

The large woods were fortunately empty and at five o'clock the attack on Böen was launched. The battle was spirited, as the village was stubbornly held and resistance in individual houses continued for a long time. It was eight o'clock before the whole place was clear, by which time a hundred and ninety-two prisoners were in our hands against a total of forty casualties to ourselves; an unusually difficult operation had been completed at a comparatively small cost with seemingly effortless efficiency. For their outstanding leadership on this as on so many previous occasions, Major J. de H. Hamilton and Major the Hon. D. M. G. J. Willoughby, two 5th Bn. Coldstream company commanders, were awarded the Military Cross. Now was the time for the sappers to live up to the example, and they did. The bridge—a hundred and thirty foot double-double Bailey—was the largest that they had yet had to build and was constructed by a composite squadron of one troop from each field squadron and one platoon of the corps field company, all under Major T. Neale's command. Allowing for this, and for the fact that the troops were already very tired, it was estimated that sixteen hours would be required to build it; however, the job was so well organised and the men worked so hard that it was open in just under ten hours, well before daybreak.

The 5th Guards Brigade was now ordered to move through the bridgehead on to Essen, where it would branch North-East to Hemmelte and Emstek, after which it was to cut an important road running South from Oldenburg; the 32nd Guards Brigade would follow as far as Essen and then proceed due East along the main road to Vechta. The Irish Group, which had had a good rest in the rear since Fürstenau, was told to lead and duly passed through the Coldstream positions at about eleven o'clock. Almost immediately, however, it came up against a booby-trapped road-block and the leading tank went up on a mine. A sapper detachment was, as usual, right up in front and proceeded to clear the block. It was unusually complicated and took so long that the officer in charge, Lieutenant R. Campbell, became impatient and went into it to clear a trap himself; the charge promptly exploded and killed him instantly. He was the son of Brigadier Campbell, Chief Engineer of the Second Army, who had specially arranged to have him posted to the division some weeks before. He had rapidly shown that he was an outstanding officer.

The advance continued, with a company clearing the woods on either side; but this first experience proved typical of conditions met with throughout the day, numerous mines and obstacles being encountered, if none of a very serious nature. Progress was so slow that, when in addition the Household Cavalry brought back the news that Essen seemed strongly held, No. 3 Company–No. 1 Squadron Group was despatched Northwards to the village of Herbergen with a view to taking a short cut to

Hemmelte, should the sandy tracks prove passable to tanks. After clearing the woods on the edge of Herbergen stronger opposition was encountered, but an encircling move by Lieutenant P. Fawcett's platoon enabled the remainder of the company to push straight on to the centre; a few Germans escaped but twenty-one prisoners were taken. No. 4 Company–No. 2 Squadron Group now took over and was able to reach Hemmelte by dark without further fighting. The whole group spent the night in this area, sending out patrols which discovered enemy positions just to the East and covering a railway track which ran across our line of advance.

No. 2 Company–No. 3 Squadron Group attacked at dawn, but the Germans melted away and eighty-two prisoners were taken before the next village of Warnstedt was reached. Here resistance was keener once more; the leading tank was knocked out by a self-propelled gun and the infantry were held up by machine-gun fire. Some delay was unavoidable and so No. 4 Company–No. 2 Squadron Group swung Northwards by minor roads in the hope of getting through more quickly by this means. In spite of some opposition they reached Sevelten in the early afternoon, where the tanks had a very successful shoot at German transport moving Southwards out of Cloppenburg, which was being attacked by the 43rd Division at the time. From here a rapid advance was made to Cappeln; this was not held and No. 3 Company–No. 1 Squadron Group took over the lead. Two tanks were lost on mines on the way but little other trouble was encountered till Emstek was reached, where heavy and accurate fire from snipers developed. Two troop commanders, Lieutenant J. O'Brien and Lieutenant B. de las Casas, were shot in the turrets of their tanks, the former being killed, and the infantry suffered severely also. The tanks had the means of curing this habit, however, and by the time half the houses were ablaze the sniping ceased. A further advance to Drantum, not much more than a mile short of the final objective, was then made, but by then it was quite dark and a halt was called for the night. The successful day's operations had owed a lot to the leadership of Lieutenant-

Colonel Haslewood, who had only so recently taken over command of the 2nd Bn. Irish Guards.

The Grenadiers had followed uneventfully behind until, when Warnstedt was finally cleared that afternoon, they were told to send a task force along by-roads South of the Irish to Tenstedt, on the chance of getting through to the final objective first. The force consisted of the King's and No. 2 Companies, with No. 2 Squadron, and command of it was taken by Lieutenant-Colonel Lort-Phillips. A column of enemy transport was met about a mile and a half beyond Tenstedt, which was effectively destroyed by the tanks; it turned out to be a small anti-tank group making the usual evening withdrawal after its day's work had been done. But despite this success the state of the roads was such that progress after dark was impossible and they harboured for the night where they were.

The 32nd Guards Brigade followed in its turn and the Coldstream, after passing through Essen, which had by now been evacuated, were held up by a road-block in front of Bevern; this was covered by infantry, but they quickly withdrew and civilians helped to remove it. More serious resistance was found at Lüsche, where there was quite a large number of enemy, and, after setting most of the houses on fire with rockets, an infantry attack was put in while some tanks went round to the South in case of attempts to escape that way. The ruse was successful, as when our men entered the village it was empty, while the tanks were delighted to find harassed Germans retreating into their arms; thirty-seven were captured in this manner. One German officer complained that the use of rockets was "not cricket"; the Scots-Welsh Group later on were almost inclined to agree with him when they arrived to take over Lüsche as their harbour area for the night. Afterwards progress through Hausstette and Vestrup was rapid, though two undefended road-blocks had to be removed. At Schwichtler retreating enemy were found and shot at by the leading tanks, but by this time it was almost dark and the chase had to be called off. Although neither brigade had quite reached its final objective the total number of prisoners taken during the day—eight officers and two hundred and ninety-four men—was a gratifying reward.

The next morning, April 14th, the Irish and Grenadier Groups both advanced swiftly to the road. Not a shot was fired and the only delay was caused by odd groups of Germans who were only too insistent on surrendering.

Conditions had equally softened up on both flanks and the enemy were obviously withdrawing in order to concentrate on the defence of Bremen. The capture of this great port was the immediate intention of XXX Corps, but such an operation would essentially be the concern of infantry. The Guards Armoured Division was therefore told to rest in its present area for a brief spell while the battle rolled steadily onward. Three days were guaranteed and a substantial promise of a week held out.

The rest was not undeserved. For two and a half weeks we had been fighting almost ceaselessly; though this fighting had not been particularly severe, judged by Normandy or Reichswald standards, casualties both in men and in tanks had been serious. Also it had been a very exhausting period mentally in that each day long advances were predicted and hoped for, yet the tale was invariably the same depressing one of road-blocks and craters with the consequent frustrations. The knowledge that other formations who were not having to deal with paratroops were making really spectacular advances did little to make it less trying for us.

But this compels us all the more to place on record our admiration of the handling of the First Parachute Army during a time which must have been positively despairing from the German point of view. Despite appalling losses and their replacement by increasingly lower category men, it still succeeded in fighting a skilful defensive battle. Its resources were simply not adequate to hold us at every point, but the slightest pause, such as at Lingen, was sufficient to enable speedy readjustments to be made so as to impose further delay. The reason lay in the continued existence of the formation and unit staffs, consisting of highly-trained and expert officers, capable of organising and executing competent rearguard actions even with the most unpromising material. Somehow they seemed to contrive the miracle of putting new wine into old bottles and still retaining something of the old quality.

Chapter Thirteen

THE FINAL PHASE

LARGE PROGRAMMES of overhauling and refitting were set in motion, as the vehicles of all units, and particularly those of the armoured battalions, were feeling the strain of continuous movement without time for proper maintenance. But all such hopeful intentions had to be discarded when orders came on April 16th for us to move over to XII Corps on the far side of the River Weser. While VIII Corps, still further to the East, was to invest Hamburg, XII Corps' intention was to clear and dominate the high ground between that port and Bremen, which was in the process of being attacked by XXX Corps. This task and the consequent cutting of communications between the two ports were to fall mainly on our shoulders. Fighting was likely to be hard and progress slow, with opposition from the 15th Panzer Grenadier Division and two marine divisions; it was a disappointing role with no promise of a spectacular break-through or dash across the country.

Early on April 17th the whole division moved, with the 32nd Guards Brigade in the lead. The route lay well behind the front line in a South-Easterly direction, crossing the River Weser at Nienburg and the River Aller at Rethem; altogether it covered nearly a hundred miles. Nightfall found the Scots-Welsh Group in semi-operational positions in the van at Walsrode, with the 5th Guards Brigade still behind the Aller.

Information given us on arrival that the enemy appeared to be reinforcing the area in the path of our projected advance proved to be only too correct when we began to push North towards Visselhövede the following morning. After clearing some woods, which provided a few prisoners, a staged attack by two squadron-company groups was necessary to capture the village of Kettenburg. An attempt to find a way round to the right resulted in the discovery that Ottingen was also strongly held and it was half-past seven before both these places were clear and the main attack on Visselhövede could be launched. Our troops penetrated into the town, but the number of enemy made it obvious that the task could not be completed before nightfall and it was decided to withdraw until the morning.

Meanwhile, in view of the hold-up, the Coldstream Group had been ordered to by-pass Visselhövede altogether to the East and to make directly for Neuenkirchen, further up the centre-line. Some opposition was met with just short of this town, with a road-block and some mines, but the defence was not properly organised and it fell without undue difficulty. Sixty prisoners taken there brought the day's total to one hundred and fifty; almost all were from the 2nd Marine Division and we were able to assess the quality of our new foes. They were nearly all ex-sailors, many of them until lately members of submarine crews. They had had little time for military training and therefore lacked the fighting skill of the paratroops, but their discipline and bravery were exemplary. They were well equipped with bazookas, which they used in particularly daring fashion; their tactics often involved them necessarily in annihilation but their aggressive spirit certainly delayed our progress most effectively.

Next morning, with heavy artillery support, the Scots-Welsh Group attacked Visselhövede from the South while the Coldstream Group sent two companies and a squadron in from the North-East. Fighting was stiff for a short while, but soon the opposition died down and all was quiet. The Coldstream moved out, a squadron-company group of the Scots-Welsh was sent to some high ground to the West, while the remainder consolidated in the town and started to prepare their well-earned dinners. They were however a little premature.

A furious battle arose suddenly without any warning. Two mortar carriers parked in the main street were destroyed by bazookas, while at the same time a bombardment of the houses containing the joint battalion headquarters started. The entire headquarters staff soon found themselves fighting at close quarters for their very lives under the personal direction of Lieutenant-Colonel Windsor-Lewis, who was in his element. The fighting soon spread along both sides of the main street and for the best part of two hours the situation was hopelessly confused. Wireless communication broke down. It was almost impossible to move from house to house with bullets coming from all points of the compass. Gradually the tanks got the upper hand, though most of them ran out of Besa ammunition before the end and were driven to shooting at individual Germans with their guns. By the evening the position was thoroughly restored and altogether the town had yielded nearly four hundred prisoners, including the garrison commander, Colonel Jordan. Five of his staff were taken with him but they were all very security conscious and he himself was shot dead by a sentry while attempting to escape from the cage in a borrowed plain uniform early next morning. Documents and maps captured with him showed conclusively, however, that Visselhövede had been defended by the 5th Marine Regiment, of which he was the commander, while the afternoon episode had, contrary to impressions at the time, been a deliberate counter-attack made by a battalion of the 7th Marine Regiment.

The Coldstream had not been idle during this time. On receipt of news from the Household Cavalry that the main road was strongly held at the approaches to Tewel, the village immediately ahead of Neuenkirchen, orders were given for No. 3 Squadron–No. 4 Company Group to move by cross-country tracks and to attack it from the East; No. 1 Squadron–No. 1 Company Group, starting by the same route, was to make an even wider hook and to attack Deepen, a few miles further up the centre-line. Tewel provided a bit of trouble, but after a bombardment it fell, yielding twenty prisoners; the next village, Söhlingen, was also captured with some prisoners and darkness came as a bridge just beyond was taken intact. Meanwhile the other column had only been delayed by bad roads and marshy ground; they found Deepen undefended and also found an intact bridge duly prepared for demolition with the now familiar five-hundred-pound bombs. During the night two German patrols, led by officers, attempted to retake these bridges; they met with little success. Both officers had served in the *Tirpitz*, and they complained bitterly that they had not yet lost their sea legs.

The next place of importance on our route was Scheessel, a hospital town containing some two thousand German wounded; there was also every reason to think that it was intact and would provide very comfortable billets. The combination inspired the group in Deepen the next morning with the idea of sending a prisoner on ahead, bearing terrible threats of what would happen if the town did not surrender. No sooner was this planned than the surprising discovery was made that the telephone was still working and the burgomaster was promptly rung up. He proved reasonable and only too anxious to safeguard the civilians and hospital patients. The Coldstream were taking no risks and insisted on his proving his good faith by riding on the front of the leading tank, displaying a large white flag. He showed both sincerity and good faith in agreeing willingly to do this and the town was soon in our hands, only a few scattered shots being encountered. For the first time for many a long day the troops concerned slept that night under whole roofs and found such luxuries as drains and water supply intact.

Flushed with this success we made a similar attempt on Rotenburg, a far larger town some five miles to the West and our main immediate objective; it also was an important hospital centre. Unfortunately this time the telephone was well and truly cut and we therefore sent the German medical officer in charge at Scheessel, a jovial bemonocled major, through the lines as emissary. The civilian authorities proved to be enthusiastic at the suggestion of a peaceful transfer and the unit commander was quite willing personally to hand over the town. Unfortunately, however, he did not dare to do so without ringing up his divisional commander, who gave a curt refusal to the project. But we could hardly have expected to be so lucky twice in one day.

As soon as it had been seen that the 32nd Guards Brigade would not be able to achieve a quick passage through on the direct route, owing to the resistance at Visselhövede, the General had ordered the 5th Guards Brigade to move up behind the 7th Armoured Division further to the East; it was subsequently to swing left and attempt to take the enemy defences in the rear. The Grenadier Group was ordered to lead and harboured near Soltau on the night of April 18th. About mid-day the next day specific orders came to follow the tail of the 7th Armoured Division as far as Tostedt, due North of which it had crossed the Bremen–Hamburg autobahn. At Tostedt the Grenadiers were to branch off to the West, cross the autobahn at Sittensen and if possible seize Zeven, a key road-junction some ten miles beyond.

There was a slight delay just South of Tostedt, where a Bailey bridge had only been constructed the previous night and the 7th Armoured Division was not yet clear, but by two o'clock they were able to move on. No. 1 Squadron–No. 4 Company Group was directed along a minor road through the village of Heidenau to the North-West while No. 3 Squadron–No. 2 Company Group led the main body due West along the main road to Sittensen. No enemy were seen until the outskirts of this small town were reached, and even then they barely put up a token resistance and quickly surrendered when two motor platoons deployed and began to work round behind them. They turned out to be a company of a March battalion which was only there by accident, having taken refuge after being shot up by Spitfires on their way to Bremen. No. 1 Squadron–No. 4 Company Group had meanwhile got badly bogged, as their road collapsed and five tanks and two carriers got hopelessly stuck in the mud when they tried to get round through some fields. Nevertheless they managed to get a task force on to the autobahn, which came down to link up with the remainder at Sittensen. It was by now late afternoon but a spirited conversation on the telephone, which was still working, with the postmistress of Gross Meckelsen, the next village after crossing the autobahn, had produced the information that the enemy had withdrawn towards Zeven at our approach. The advance therefore continued without further incident, the postmistress having spoken the truth, until the leading troops were fired on as they approached Weertzen, which was about half-way between Sittensen and Zeven. The resistance was not strong and the village was cleared as well as the fast-gathering dusk would permit. After liberating a French labour camp, the group harboured in a tight perimeter for the night. The Irish meanwhile took over Sittensen and the autobahn crossings, while brigade headquarters harboured near Gross Meckelsen in between.

The position was extremely exposed, with no support on either flank; moreover the bulk of the divisional artillery was with the 32nd Guards Brigade, which rendered any major operation out of the question. Consequently orders for April 20th were to consolidate and broaden the position by making only limited advances. The Grenadiers were ordered to seize Heeslingen and Wiersdorf, three miles North-East and two miles East of Zeven respectively; the Irish were told to occupy Elsdorf, just North of the autobahn and about five miles South-East of Zeven.

No. 2 Squadron–the King's Company Group lost a tank on approaching Heeslingen and Lieutenant P. Prescott was wounded; but resistance was not prolonged and finally an important bridge in the centre of the village was captured intact and seventy-five prisoners in all rounded up. No. 3 Squadron–No. 2 Company Group had a harder time at Wiersdorf, where three tanks and two carriers were destroyed in quick succession by a self-propelled gun and bazookas, and a number of men killed and wounded. A detour to the left was impossible owing to thick woods and so the next troop of tanks and two motor platoons made a wide sweep to the right. Debouching on to the road running North to Heeslingen the leading tank was hit, but the other tanks now succeeded in destroying the offending self-propelled gun in its turn. The following motor platoons then worked in from the North while the third one started again up the main road from the East; gradually the enemy fire slackened until the two forces converged and met. No counter-attacks on either place materialised, though fairly persistent shelling and mortaring made life pretty unpleasant throughout the next three days.

The Irish sent Major M. J. P. O'Cock and Captain C. D. Kennard, D.S.O., with No. 1 Squadron–No. 3 Company Group, to occupy Elsdorf, which they did without incident apart from meeting a few mines which were not covered by fire. Patrols were sent to Wistedt and to Wehldorf, where they cut the Rotenburg–Zeven road; and no sooner were defensive positions organised than they saw to their amazement the head of a German convoy driving straight towards the village up the road from Rotenburg. All guns were brought to bear and the lorries, most of them crammed with troops, were allowed to come on till at a given signal all weapons opened up at them with devastating effect. The lorries seemed to explode with men as the convoy abruptly came to a halt. Dead and wounded littered the road and the others who tried to escape were quickly rounded up by carriers and infantry. Eighty-six prisoners were taken and nearly forty vehicles destroyed or captured. They turned out to belong to an ordnance unit of the 2nd Marine Division; they had been told to set up their shops in Elsdorf and had much valuable equipment with them, some of which we appropriated while the rest was destroyed.

This was not the only loss suffered by the marines at the hands of the Irish Guards that day. Their chief administrative staff officer was also motoring up the main road to Zeven when he fell into the hands of the patrol that had cut it at Wehldorf. He was thoughtful enough to have with him many of those wonderful returns that are peculiar to his branch and which, however long and dull they may be, do after diligent study reveal quite a lot. One interesting fact gleaned from them was that all proposed moves of the division lay North-West, and showed no tendency towards Bremen or Hamburg; this confirmed recent statements by prisoners, which had been doubted at the time because the direction seemed so improbable.

Believing that the Germans must be thoroughly disorganised to make such presents to them, the Irish in Elsdorf began to feel very confident; the war was obviously nearly over and they prepared to receive any further visitors in a fitting manner. Visitors duly arrived early the next morning, but not of the type they were expecting.

During the night a message came, giving orders for a troop-platoon group to occupy Wistedt, which had been reported clear by the previous evening's patrol. This was successfully done an hour before dawn, but no sooner was the position established than a sudden attack came in from the West by a company of infantry supported by two self-propelled guns. One of their first shots set on fire the tank posted to watch the road in that direction. The crew were forced to jump out but Guardsman E. Charlton, the driver, seized the machine-gun and opened up with devastating effect on the advancing Germans. When his left arm was hit and rendered useless he propped the gun up on a gate and continued to load and fire with one hand. He kept it up despite further wounds until finally he collapsed and was overrun. But his action, which was to earn him the Victoria Cross, had just held up the attack long enough to enable his comrades to dispose themselves so as to meet it with most advantage. All the same the village was soon surrounded, a second tank destroyed and the one mounting the seventeen-pounder gun hit in the turret and its commander killed. Guardsman Mendes, the troop-leader's driver, thereupon took over this tank and drove it forward to cover the infantry until eventually it was hit again and set on fire.

Meanwhile the situation in Elsdorf itself had become almost equally critical. The area vacated by the group sent to Wistedt in the Southern outskirts had been occupied almost immediately by an enemy force. This very soon proved to consist of a most determined lot of Germans; worse still, they were supported by several self-propelled guns, mortars and artillery, a combination which proceeded to make life for the defenders exceedingly unpleasant. The first attack was beaten off and a number of casualties inflicted, but one of the self-propelled guns succeeded in infiltrating to within sixty yards of the positions of Lieutenant T. Geraghty's platoon. This pinned the infantry down effectively and a tank which attempted to manœuvre round the right flank was seen and destroyed. Lieutenant Geraghty was killed among numerous other casualties, as were seven more guardsmen by two direct hits on squadron-company headquarters; but somehow the

Germans were held off for what seemed to the defenders an interminable time—it was in fact at least for five hours.

Just as the prospect seemed most hopeless and the possibility of both villages falling had to be faced the voice of Major P. W. B. Pole-Carew announced that he was approaching at the head of No. 3 Squadron–No. 2 Company Group down the autobahn. Repeated reports of the seriousness of the situation and the need for help to battalion headquarters had been unacknowledged for hours and the sudden announcement was therefore all the more welcome. Hardly had he spoken when his tank was hit by a bazooka, which luckily did not explode. The subsequent rather embittered conversation revealed that he was quite unaware of the true facts and had intended merely to pay his respects on his way to occupy the village of Gyhum. He was quickly told that this was probably the present enemy base of operations and that he would on the whole be better employed in helping to clear up Elsdorf first.

From that moment things improved. The rapidly dwindling force in Wistedt was told to attempt to break out, now that the defence of Elsdorf could be ensured, and another troop under Lieutenant J. B. P. Quinan was sent to cover them. The latter lost a tank but succeeded in helping the small band of survivors to get out by a roundabout route, though in the end these only amounted to the platoon commander, Lieutenant C. W. D. Harvey-Kelly, with four men and one tank complete with its crew. Their escape was largely due to further prowess on the part of Guardsman Mendes, this time on foot with a borrowed Bren gun; he was awarded the Distinguished Conduct Medal for his actions this day. Elsdorf was quite clear soon after mid-day but heavy shelling and mortaring continued, with a virulent bombing attack in the evening to add variety. During the bombing Verey lights were observed and it was thought that another attack might be impending; but nothing of the kind materialised, though the Leicestershire Yeomanry had to fire seven separate shoots during the night in order to break up suspected enemy concentrations.

The Germans suffered severely, leaving over fifty prisoners in our hands in addition to losing a large number in dead and wounded. As soon as identifications began to come in it was seen that we were dealing with the 15th Panzer Grenadier Division. This was a surprise, since it had been fully identified at Delmenhorst, West of Bremen, only three days before. Prisoners told us that it had moved from there on April 19th and was then sent East to defend and to keep open the Bremen–Hamburg autobahn; it had failed to arrive in time to give effect to these orders and so had made an attempt to recapture it. The 104th Panzer Grenadier Regiment had been engaged against the Irish while the 115th Panzer Grenadier Regiment was at Zeven. The division had always had a very high reputation and now took great pride in being about the only organised one left fighting. They were pleased to have come up against troops whom they considered to be as good as themselves, a statement that could be taken seriously in that it was not made by a prisoner but to some of our men who were themselves captured when the Germans were temporarily victorious at Wistedt.

To return to the 32nd Guards Brigade's operations against Rotenburg, the Scots-Welsh group could not leave Visselhövede till the afternoon of April 20th; they were ordered to wait till a battalion of the 71st Brigade could take over the town, in order to safeguard our lines of communication. As soon as this was done, they moved through Neuenkirchen on the Coldstream route as far as Hemslingen; there they turned off West on the direct road to Rotenburg. There had already been a bit of trouble from shelling and mortaring on this road junction earlier in the day, and the appearance of this large column brought on a great deal more. Before long the leading troops were held up by a road-block and crater. The mortars had by now become most unpleasantly active and appeared to be sited quite close by; so a company-squadron group hastily led off down a small track towards the village of Bothel. Considerable execution was done, including the destruction of four anti-tank guns, but, though effectively silenced, the mortars were nowhere to be found;

subsequent interrogation of prisoners showed that they had withdrawn in the nick of time.

The ground was such that it was impossible for the column to by-pass the main road; as bridging operations at the spot where it was cratered necessarily took several hours, progress could only be resumed next morning. The enemy had withdrawn during the night and the tanks quickly reached a railway-crossing half-way to Rotenburg, but much sniping was encountered in two villages on the way; there were a large number of Germans about and the mopping-up was a laborious process for the infantry. No sooner was this complete and the advance resumed than exactly similar conditions were met with a mile further on at Hemsbünde.

The Coldstream in the meantime were engaged in the same type of fighting as they pressed down from Scheessel. No. 3 Squadron–No. 3 Company Group under Major P. H. Hunt and Captain I. O. Liddell came up against heavy opposition at a road-block very soon after it started. After stiff fighting this was cleared and our men advanced to the edge of a wood only a mile short of the outskirts of Rotenburg, but they were held up again here by an anti-tank gun. They had now reached their start-line for the attack on the town, but owing to the delays inflicted on the other group this was postponed till the next morning and they were told to consolidate. No. 2 Squadron, under Major A. D. M. Musker, spent a profitable late afternoon clearing two villages to the South where they met little resistance but captured a complete battery of six eighty-eight-millimetre guns and nearly two hundred prisoners. Altogether the brigade total of prisoners for the day exceeded a thousand; it was the first occasion on which this had been achieved during the campaign and made some amends for having to put off the attack on Rotenburg till the morning. During this day's fighting Captain I. O. Liddell was badly wounded and as a result died later in the evening; his award of the Victoria Cross for the capture of the bridge at Lingen was only announced many weeks afterwards.

In view of the postponement it seemed worth while to make one more attempt to have the place surrendered without a fight, in order to save ourselves casualties. Consequently a rain of smoke shells containing propaganda leaflets descended on the town during the late afternoon, followed after dark by more specific messages directed personally to the military commander and to the burgomaster. The wording of these was as follows:

> "The war is lost for Germany and further resistance is useless. It can only result in the unnecessary sacrifice of more lives. British forces are now assembled on three sides of Rotenburg in overwhelming strength. Nothing can prevent us from capturing it the moment we decide to attack.
>
> We know that there are big hospitals in Rotenburg, and we are anxious if possible to save the town and its inhabitants from senseless destruction. In order to effect this you must send representatives to negotiate its surrender to our forces. They should come up the main road to Scheessel not before seven o'clock and not after eight o'clock tomorrow morning, April 22nd, displaying a white flag prominently. They will there meet our forward troops, who have instructions not to fire and will conduct them immediately to a senior officer. In that way only can Rotenburg be spared all further harm.
>
> If no representatives arrive by eight o'clock we shall have no alternative but to fire on the town with all the resources at our disposal. They are so enormous that Rotenburg will be completely destroyed."

Three willing emissaries were discovered. One was a policeman of Rotenburg, who had given himself up to the Scots Guards in Brockel and who volunteered for the task; the other two were prisoners in the hands of the Coldstream, one of them also a native of the town. All three were passed through the lines safely but no answer ever came. Subsequent investigation showed that all three faithfully accomplished their missions and that the policeman was sent back with an answer, though he never turned up. It was a refusal; but in view of an Army Group order just received, a copy of which fell into our hands next day, nothing else could have been expected. This was issued on Himmler's express authority and, after referring to the surrender of certain towns, ended with the sentences: "No German town will be made an open town. Every village and every town will be defended and held by all available means. Every German man who offends against this proper national duty shall lose his honour and his life."

The attack was therefore launched, as planned, at half-past nine the next morning after a heavy barrage which, despite our blood-curdling threats, expressly and effectively avoided the whole hospital area. Both groups went in simultaneously, the Scots-Welsh making for the Southern half of the town and the Coldstream for the Northern. Resistance was light and all was over within two hours, though scattered pockets of Germans held us up occasionally for brief periods. One such group gave the Northumberland Fusiliers' flame-throwers their first real chance of proving how effective they could be. They were called up to help when a tank was hit by a bazooka; one German was indiscreet enough to peer round the corner of a building whereupon he received a jet of flame full in the face and collapsed and died immediately. Subsequent inspection revealed that he had died from shock rather than from the actual result of burning and the effect on his comrades was such that they came out of their hiding-places in shoals, fifteen rushing *en masse* to one carrier to give themselves up to its crew of two; sixty-three surrendered in the course of a few minutes.

In the final phase Lieutenant D. Dick, of the 615th Field Squadron, made a very gallant dash with his reconnaissance party to the main bridge over the railway just North of the town. It was prepared for demolition, with several large bombs lying in the roadway, all obviously connected up; it was also heavily swept by small-arms fire. One sapper was killed and another wounded, but he disconnected all the leads and undoubtedly saved the bridge. He was awarded the Military Cross for this exploit.

Generally the whole operation reflected great credit on the troops concerned, since a town of considerable size was cleared in a very short time at the cost of infinitesimal casualties to themselves. Only one man was killed and about twenty wounded, almost all as the result of shelling from the woods to the North, which continued even after the fall of the town. Enemy losses on the other hand were very severe indeed. The number of prisoners was so great and the stream so continuous that no strictly accurate figure was recorded, but it is certain that the previous day's record of a thousand was completely surpassed. These numbers made it evident that something must have gone very wrong in the arrangements for defence, and indeed prisoners told us that there had been much hesitancy and many changes in orders. Altogether the quality of the resistance, when the garrison was far from small, gives support to the view that our propaganda efforts may not in the end have been entirely without effect.

It transpired that the commandant of Rotenburg, Colonel Schuster, felt that all had not gone as it should. He reached the cage as a prisoner that night. He was so depressed at his all too evident failure to carry out the orders to defend the town to the last man and the last round that, after dictating a statement to another officer, he threw himself out of the railway truck in which he had been placed and broke his neck.

We were relieved of all responsibility for Rotenburg by troops of the 51st Division the very afternoon of its capture and the 32nd Guards Brigade was withdrawn for a rest to the Sittensen area. This lasted a full three days for the majority, but the Coldstream were unlucky and received warning to move under command of the 5th Guards Brigade the following day in order to participate with the Grenadiers in the assault on Zeven on the morning of April 24th. The reason for this was that the Irish were extremely tired and rather depleted after the hard fighting round Elsdorf, where they were still in contact with the enemy and subject to fairly constant shell-fire. They were merely to stage a feint attack from the South-East to try to divert the Germans' attention from the main attacks by the Grenadiers and Coldstream. These were directed from the North-East and East respectively; the Grenadiers were ordered to aim at securing the Northern half of the town and the Coldstream objective was the Southern half.

The troops moved off at eleven o'clock, each group led by two companies supported by tanks, after the usual heavy and encouraging artillery bombardment. Two squadrons of Mitchell bombers were also in attendance, as were the Northumberland Fusiliers with their mortars, machine-guns and flame-throwers. More opposition was met with than at Rotenburg, but by early afternoon all objectives were in our hands. Although our losses in the actual fighting were light, those from shelling, which continued at intervals after the capture of the town, were comparatively heavy. Captain M. R. R. Marriott, of the 2nd Bn. Grenadier Guards, received wounds of which he died a few days later, while the Coldstream headquarters was particularly unfortunate. Captain J. N. Agnew, the adjutant of the 5th Bn. Coldstream Guards, was wounded, together with Major P. H. Hunt and Lieutenant P. A. M. Gell; so were Major J. R. S. Peploe, commander of the 373rd Battery of the West Somerset Yeomanry supporting them, and his entire tank crew. Lieutenant J. G. B. Chester of the 5th Bn. Coldstream Guards won the Military Cross on this day for his gallant leadership of one of his battalion's forward assaulting platoons.

We had expected to be up against the 115th Panzer Grenadier Regiment and to be given a really nasty time, but, as prisoners began to drift in, we discovered that it had been relieved the previous evening and replaced by a battalion of the Grossdeutschland Regiment; this comprised a rather moderate collection of individuals who had been denuded of most of the supporting tanks and had had little time to take stock of their surroundings. Three hundred and ninety were made prisoner and the Coldstream also had two self-propelled guns to their credit; one was a Jagdpanther whose crew scrambled quickly to safety and provided us with the identification, that of the 115th Panzer Battalion.

Nightfall found us in undisputed possession of the whole town, but all roads out of it except those by which we had arrived were obstructed immediately beyond the outskirts. The continued shelling made us suspect at first that a counter-attack might be impending and we heard later that our artillery had broken up an enemy concentration forming up to the South, evidently for the purpose. Gradually during the night all became quiet, though we soon had confirmation from prisoners that the 115th Panzer Grenadier Regiment had not gone far and was disposed in the woods immediately to the West, with the remainder of the Grossdeutschland Regiment extending to the North as far as the road to Bremervörde.

This latter piece of news was particularly disappointing, as we had despatched a mobile force that morning by a circuitous route with the express object of cutting this road. The force, known by the code-name of "Wardforce" after Major E. J. S. Ward, second-in-command of the 2nd Household Cavalry Regiment, who commanded it, consisted of a squadron of armoured cars together with No. 3 Squadron of the 2nd Bn. Grenadier Guards and two troops of No. 2 (Minden) Battery of the 21st Anti-Tank Regiment; the last named were functioning in their new role as motorised infantry. A special bridge was constructed at Kakerbeck, a village far to the North-East just short of Harsefeld, which had just been occupied by the 11th Hussars, the armoured car regiment of the 7th Armoured Division, by friendly arrangement with the burgomaster, and a third troop of No. 2 Battery was left there to act as a firm base. The main body pushed on for some miles against only minor opposition until it approached Anderlingen, the next village before meeting the Bremervörde road, but here sure enough it met mines and heavy fire. Shelling by the tanks and armoured cars produced no effect and so the newly-fledged infantry attacked, supported by carriers in the centre. Although the leading carrier hit a mine the operation went well. The first objective was reached and twenty-one prisoners captured; the second and final objective also, but heavy machine-gun fire was now met with and their own ammunition was running short. Major Ward decided that the job was more than could be tackled with the forces at his disposal and ordered withdrawal into a close harbour for the night. Next morning he found that the enemy had also withdrawn and so he pushed on to Selsingen, on the main road. There was no opposition, but mines and road-blocks were plentiful and the bridges were demolished in the direction of both Zeven and Bremervörde. Our troops engaged themselves in active patrolling to the North and West and during the next night a supply column managed to reach them by the route by which they had come; this was a considerable relief to everybody, as they had been completely isolated, except by wireless, for more than thirty-six hours.

An Irish Guards patrol discovered that the Germans were still in Wistedt on the night of April 24th, after the fall of Zeven, but they had withdrawn by next morning, when it was re-occupied without incident. While doing so the Irish heard fighting on their left and soon heard that the 53rd Division had captured Wehldorf, on the main road running South from Zeven. By evening they had joined forces and this enabled the Irish Group to withdraw its forward troops for a short while to more comfortable billets for a rest.

The advance of the 53rd Division did not however affect the Germans West of Zeven, who were still quite close to the town and very much in evidence all that day. The 32nd Guards Brigade was ordered to break out in that direction the following morning with the object of seizing the only relatively high ground in the neighbourhood; this lay about eight miles away and dominated the rear defences of Bremen, whose fall it was hoped to hasten. There was also a secondary objective of importance; this was a camp at Westertimke, which lay just to the South of the high ground and was known to contain a large number of British prisoners of war.

The Scots-Welsh Group carried out the attack at first light. After a mile an obstruction was encountered at a road-junction, well covered by Germans in the woods at either side. Infantry proceeded to clear these, while a squadron-company group looped left to Oldendorf; there were enemy here too, but by half-past nine it was clear, while the main force had got through the woods and was fighting in the outskirts of Badenstedt. This village necessitated a small-scale attack, as it was held quite strongly and entry was denied by another road-block; by mid-day it was in our hands, but the bridges on both roads leading out to the West over a stream were found to be destroyed and covered. Any attempt to by-pass to the right would have required a major attack, as our troops were in close contact with the enemy at another road-block there and the general area behind was by this time known to be strongly held. A good road however also existed to the left and a squadron-company group was consequently directed this way; but after capturing Brümmerhof with quite a few prisoners the bridge immediately beyond blew up as they approached.

Meanwhile a railway bridge just South of Badenstedt had been left intact. A troop of tanks under Lieutenant S. R. Armitage found that they could get across it and, with the help of some infantry, cleared the Germans covering the destroyed bridges. A whole squadron was thereupon sent across with accompanying infantry and captured Ostertimke, the next village. Although this was effected without great difficulty, the approaches to the railway bridge had now given way and there was no possibility of getting anything more over the stream until the sappers could repair the road bridge. There were also considerable numbers of Germans about, at least three self-propelled guns had been seen and there were many mines; so the squadron consolidated at Ostertimke, where the remainder of the group joined it as soon as the bridge was ready. This was not long, owing to splendid work on the part of the 615th Field Squadron, and an attempt was made to push on to Kirchtimke towards dusk; but heavy opposition was met and after our two leading tanks had been blown up the decision was made to harbour for the night at Ostertimke, the Coldstream Group having in the meantime moved up and taken over Badenstedt. We had taken two hundred and eighty-seven prisoners during the day and found, as anticipated, that we were directly up against the 15th Panzer Grenadier Division. The troops in the woods, who had taken the initial shock, belonged to a scratch battalion hastily formed out of convalescent men from various units, but those behind in the villages were genuine panzer grenadiers. Their artillery had been unpleasantly active throughout the day, with shelling of the centre-line both continuous and accurate.

Quite unexpectedly two emissaries, in the persons of the commandant and paymaster of Westertimke camp, had presented themselves to our forward troops that afternoon with the following document:

> "The German divisional commander proposes to the divisional commander, Guards Armoured Division, a ten hours' truce in which to remove the prisoners of war at present in the camp at Westertimke (8,000 soldiers of the British Empire) out of the zone of danger and hand them over to your division. The truce to commence on the 26th April, 1945, at 15 hours.
>
> Proposed route of transport: Westertimke, Kirchtimke, Ostertimke, Badenstedt. The prisoners of war to be handed over at the North-Eastern outskirts of Badenstedt on the road to Zeven.
>
> The British divisional commander is requested to allow the German camp commander and the accompanying guards to return to the German lines as soon as the prisoners of war have been handed over."

It was signed by Lieutenant-General Roth, whom we knew to be the commander of the 15th Panzer Grenadier Division, and at first sight it seemed an altruistic gesture; but there was a serious flaw, and for that reason we turned down the project on the spot. An agreement had recently been signed by both the British and German governments by which all prisoners of war must be left in situ, and this must have been as well known to the Germans as to ourselves. General Roth was no fool and it was a transparent attempt on his part to get some extra time for the extraction of his division and incidentally also for the whole of his superior formation, Corps Ems. The extent to which he had succeeded already in carrying out his mining and demolition programme was to show us even more clearly next day how right we were not to listen to his proposals. If further proof were needed it can be found in a diary of one of his staff officers which was subsequently captured and in which under the date April 26th is entered: "This day brings a crisis for the division."

The commandant seemed quite willing to be helpful and co-operative once he recovered from his original chagrin at the failure of his mission. He agreed to return to the camp with the War Office representative as soon as it was effectively liberated. It turned out subsequently that he had always been fair and reasonable in his treatment of the prisoners, unlike many of his kind.

The next morning, April 27th, the advance was resumed. After a patrol had reported that Kirchtimke appeared still to be held in strength, two squadron-company groups attacked, one on either side of the road. Weather conditions were appalling; it had been raining all night and the ground was like a morass. Shell- and mortar-fire became intense as the attack developed, but the greatest difficulty of all arose from the mines. Not only were these laid on the main road, where the headquarters group was soon completely blocked, but also on side roads and on all possible diversions; in addition they were buried deeply and sometimes one above another or with delayed action charges, so that even after a road appeared to have been cleared transport using it later was apt to be blown up. Both company commanders became involved in the headquarters hold-up and were cut off from their companies. They followed them on foot over the fields, to find that the attack had been successfully carried through and consolidated by Lieutenant C. M. Campbell. Three self-propelled guns were destroyed in the process. Eventually the whole group got through by the early afternoon, though not without losing further victims to mines; among them was Guardsman McKean of the carrier platoon of the 2nd Scots Guards, who had survived many similar experiences in Africa and Italy.

G Company and No. 3 Squadron, which had been in reserve, were now told to push on and to attempt to reach Westertimke before dark. They had not gone far when the front tank blew up on a mine. Fortunately there were no casualties this time, nor were further mines met once they had passed Kirchtimke. On the other hand there were plenty of Germans in some thick woods on the rising ground to the right. The company routed them after a fierce battle in which they killed twenty and took about the same number prisoner. At the far end of these woods was the area where we had been told that the S.S. guards lived, while the camp holding the prisoners of war lay across the road on the left. A self-propelled gun was seen to escape towards the end of the battle from a prominently marked hospital in the S.S. area where typically it had installed itself. We were taking no chances and the tanks soon set most of the huts on fire with their guns. It was now pitch dark and the Scots Guards rushed the huts in the lurid glare; but the Germans had gone. Major C. A. la T. Leatham then led his squadron cautiously into the village and found nothing but a few Poles, and during the night contact with the prisoners of war was established by a patrol.

In the anxiety to reach Westertimke the Scots-Welsh Group had of necessity had to ignore the ridge which was our other objective. This lay to the North-West of Kirchtimke and the Coldstream had been ordered to occupy it that morning. Two companies and a squadron set off and unexpectedly found that their chief enemy in the undertaking was mud, though they found a few mines. Meanwhile, in order to consolidate our hold against as resourceful an enemy as General Roth, the Irish Group, which had not been engaged since Elsdorf, had in addition been transferred temporarily to the 32nd Guards Brigade and directed on Ostereistedt, immediately North of the Coldstream objective. This area proved on the other hand still to contain many determined Germans. A road-block was met and a village had to be cleared within a bare mile of Badenstedt, and as Ostereistedt was approached resistance became very strong, with mines of the same unpleasant variety found at Kirchtimke laid along all the roads and tracks; there were also some self-propelled guns in evidence. Lieutenant-Colonel FitzGerald and Lieutenant-Colonel Haslewood decided to cut the approaches to the village from each side and so to dominate it before making a direct attack. No. 4 Company was sent to the left and No. 2 Company to the right, each supported by tanks. They made slow progress, largely owing to the mines with which the whole place was littered, but eventually the main road was cut both to the East and West. Lieutenant J. A. R. Pollock's troop dealt summarily with one self-propelled gun that had been causing a lot of trouble and Lieutenant A. Samuelson disposed of another by bringing his troop along a railway-line where, however, he lost one of his own tanks on a mine. Altogether the Irish lost four tanks that day but, when the final attack on the village went in, after a bombardment by medium artillery, the opposition collapsed and two officers came out of their headquarters. One was the commander of the company to which the defence had been entrusted and he explained that his orders had been to hold on to the last man unless definite permission to withdraw was received. It was not, but he had been unable to induce his men to see eye-to-eye with the order. He had therefore told them to withdraw North but he and the other officer had stayed behind, as they would have been summarily shot if they had accompanied their troops. They proved not to belong to the 15th Panzer Grenadier Division, but to the Grossdeutschland Regiment.

That evening we heard that Bremen had finally fallen the previous day. The burgomaster handed over the city on behalf of the civilian authorities and, though the military commander, General Becker, refused to agree and carried on fighting for a while in the dock area, all resistance was at an end within a matter of hours. So long as the Germans held on to Bremen and to the high ground just West of Zeven, which we had just occupied, they could afford to withdraw gradually. The 15th Panzer Grenadier Division had been given the task of holding us off while the slower and less well-equipped divisions made good their escape; this was the reason for the desperate nature of the resistance. To a large extent success had been achieved, despite the failure of the ruse about the prisoners at Westertimke. But now it was imperative for them to retire with all possible speed to the eminently defensible line of the Hamme–Oste canal, and this they did. By next morning the 32nd Guards Brigade was out of contact and the Irish Group returned to the 5th Guards Brigade.

Westertimke Camp proved still to contain over eight thousand inhabitants, despite reports that most of them had been evacuated; half of them were men of the Merchant Navy, but representatives of all branches of the forces, and of most nationalities, were included among the remainder. The most colourful personage met with was a Russian Orthodox priest, complete with robes and beard. Most gratifying for us was the discovery of forty-two guardsmen; the majority were members of the division who had only been captured since the crossing of the Rhine; but two had been in enemy hands since Boulogne in 1940. One of these had been in Lieutenant-Colonel Windsor-Lewis's company at that time, and the reunion gave them both equal pleasure.

The Grenadiers had occupied Brauel, due North of Zeven, without opposition on April 25th. But the bridge over the River Oste was destroyed and they could only establish contact with Wardforce by shouting across the water. Altogether it was two days before the advance could be continued in force in this direction, but the Grenadier Group was then ordered to move on the morning of April 28th with the dual object of breaking through to Bremervörde and of liberating Sandbostel Camp. This was a much larger camp than Westertimke and we had received first-hand information about conditions there from an officer of the Special Air Service, who had reached the 5th Guards Brigade Headquarters after escaping on April 22nd. It contained only about three hundred British prisoners, but the total number was about twenty-two thousand, of whom about half were civilians, largely French and Russian; these latter had only arrived within the last month.

Junction was quickly made with Wardforce at Selsingen, who had a great deal of valuable information to give. But one item was very depressing; the Germans had blown eleven enormous craters in the road leading to Bremervörde the previous night. There was nothing for it but to try to find a way round and No. 2

Company with a troop of tanks were sent off to the East with the object of capturing the important bridge over the Bever at Bevern, three miles South of Bremervörde. The route lay along muddy tracks already reconnoitred by the Household Cavalry and across the river by a wooden bridge at Malstedt, thus attacking Bevern from the rear. The bridge was quickly reached and the company and one tank got across. The other tanks got hopelessly bogged, but the force was quite big enough to deal with the four unsuspecting Germans who were guarding the Bevern bridge. It was prepared for demolition, but the fuses were quickly cut and the position consolidated. Later in the day, after the approach to the wooden bridge had been improved, the other tanks got up and the force spent a quiet night.

The King's Company–No. 2 Squadron Group had meanwhile moved West to Sandbostel. Despite a few mines the column passed quickly through two intervening villages but, as it approached Sandbostel, it came under heavy mortar-fire and the leading tank was knocked out by a self-propelled gun. The village lay on a forward slope East of the Oste canal; on the far side lay the camp, on commanding ground, and all bridges were destroyed. An assault crossing was impracticable in daylight, even had the boats been available; so Major G. Thorne and Major the Hon. G. N. C. Wigram left a platoon and a troop to watch the situation and withdrew the remainder of their force about half a mile to plan for a night assault. The sappers duly produced assault boats and a bridging party, the leader of which, Lieutenant J. Campbell, made a very bold reconnaissance in daylight which was instrumental in earning him a Military Cross. Three platoons of the King's Company then crossed the river unobserved at this point towards midnight; they formed a close bridgehead and the bridging party started work, but the ground was very boggy and it was soon realised that the bridge could not possibly be completed before daylight. As dawn came the Germans saw what was going on and heavily mortared the site, effectively preventing any further work. It became obvious that the bridgehead was untenable and the three platoons were ordered to withdraw. The two nearest the river got back all right in the half-light but the third was caught in enfilade fire; several men were killed and the platoon commander, Lieutenant N. S. Farquharson, and a number of others were wounded; only twelve soaked and frozen men, including Lieutenant Farquharson, all too helpless from exposure to stand, were found when their comrades reached them the next day.

The solitary prisoner taken during the operation told us that a company of S.S. men was defending the camp as well as a considerable number of inferior troops. Altogether it was plain that the task was far too great for one motor company and would require the whole Grenadier Group. The Irish Group, which had returned from the 32nd Guards Brigade the previous day, was therefore told to relieve the force at Bevern and to take over the drive for Bremervörde; this they did during the course of the morning and by the early afternoon the Grenadiers were ready. A strong artillery programme was arranged, avoiding so far as possible the immediate precincts of the camp, and Nos. 2 and 4 Companies crossed the Oste Canal opposite the village of Ober Ochtenhausen, more than a mile South of Sandbostel. They then advanced on the camp from the South, supported by fire from the rest of the group across the river to the East. They were not detected till they neared the camp and, though resistance continued for some time, in the course of which Lieutenant D. B. Ryott and Lieutenant R. V. N. Surtees, among others, were wounded in a sharp skirmish with some S.S. guards, the operation went smoothly to the accompaniment of a thin background of cheers from the prisoners. By the end of the day all was over, the bridge was completed and tanks moved across.

Early next morning the relief column organised by the Assistant Director of Medical Services, Lieutenant-Colonel T. W. Davidson, moved in. Brigadier Gwatkin and Lieutenant-Colonel Moore toured the camp, in order to see for themselves what was necessary in the way of additional assistance. As a result General Horrocks (for we had reverted to XXX Corps after the fall of Bremen) had three hundred German prisoners and two hundred and fifty German nurses sent to clear up the filth and to care for the wretched diseased inmates of the concentration part. Typhus was raging in addition to other horrors; there was little enough that could be done for many of them and indeed more than half died after the relief. The whole camp area was placed out of bounds to all troops except those of the relief column, who had to be dusted each time before they left. The chief problem for the Grenadiers was to keep the more active prisoners, most of whom were Russian, from breaking out to spread disease and to pillage the countryside.

It had been no easy job to deal with the craters on the Bremervörde road. Each one of the eleven was a full sixty feet across and forty deep and some mystery centred for a time on what could have caused them. The solution was provided by a prisoner who was one of the layers of these atrocities; they were sea-mines and could only be laid by specially trained men. As soon as Lieutenant-Colonel Thomas saw the craters he called up all the bulldozers we ourselves had and then promptly asked corps headquarters for more, together with as many tippers as possible. The 14th Field Squadron was set to work and within twenty-four hours the job was complete, a very great achievement. The first eight craters were ramped through and surfaced with rubble from Selsingen and the last three bridged with equipment dragged round the sandy deviation originally taken by the Grenadiers.

At mid-day on April 29th the Irish led off towards Bremervörde. They were accompanied by a naval task force especially sent to take over a secret German naval experimental station at Hesedorf the moment it was captured. By four o'clock this place was reached without serious incident. The secret installations were gladly handed over to our naval colleagues but a plan of the locality, showing where and how more sea-mines were to be detonated, was of direct interest to ourselves. Lieutenant B. A. McGrath rushed to the spot where they were controlled and found a German just about to set them off; he cut all the wires so that further danger on that score was at an end. Attempts to move on towards Bremervörde, however, encountered heavy fire. Prisoners taken at Hesedorf told us that the canal bridge at Bremervörde was defended by a whole battalion of the 351st Marine Division and a plan was made to attempt to take it by stealth during the night; No. 4 Company–No. 2 Squadron Group was first to seize a road and railway crossing half-way, after which No. 2 Company –No. 3 Squadron Group was to make for the bridge.

The first operation succeeded admirably. The marines defending the area were taken completely by surprise and we were installed in their own company headquarters before most of them knew anything about it. Documents found there enabled us to round up the whole company and gave us the dispositions of the remainder of the battalion. But the second part did not go so well. More craters were met with and, though the Irish succeeded eventually in finding a way round, the Germans had now been warned and shortly before they reached the bridge a loud explosion told them that it was gone.

An assault crossing of the Hamme–Oste Canal would now be necessary. As it was a major obstacle this was a job for an infantry division and next morning the 5th Guards Brigade was told that the 51st Division would take over its sector during the afternoon with this end in view. No. 3 Company–No. 1 Squadron Group set to work meanwhile, however, to clear the Eastern bank of the canal and to obtain information about the state of the approaches for the Highlanders who were to carry out the assault. This they succeeded in doing, but Lieutenant S. Hogg was killed and three guardsmen wounded by snipers, whom the enemy had posted for this very purpose.

After a day's rest the 32nd Guards Brigade had been ordered to advance due North and to capture the large town of Stade, with a view to dominating the estuary of the Elbe. A great deal of information about the prospects was provided by the 1st Household Cavalry Regiment, which had joined the division as an extra armoured car regiment on April 27th; while the regiment had spent the war in the Middle East its new commander, Lieutenant-Colonel W. M. Sale, was widely known through his long and valuable service at divisional headquarters. We were quickly shown that it was as adept at its role as its sister regiment, than which no higher praise can be given. We got the encouraging news that, though the main roads were all impassable, practicable alternative routes existed at least as far as Bargstedt and Harsefeld, half-way to our destination. In addition resistance gave the impression of being distinctly light, with only small and isolated groups of enemy involved, who seemed unable to achieve much even against armoured cars.

After an approach march to Ahrenswolde in the evening of April 29th the Coldstream took the lead the next morning. Demolitions were met and caused delays, and occasional small pockets of enemy were encountered; but it proved always possible to find a way round the former, while the latter usually gave themselves up with very little ado. They got within five miles of Stade before they were seriously held up, this time by a blown-up bridge which left a fifty-foot gap, covered by more determined Germans than usual. An alternative bridge was soon found further West, but only to have an armoured car and scout-car blown completely to pieces together with the road at a point about a mile short of the bridge and after a whole troop had already passed over the spot. However, the armoured cars refused to be discouraged and discovered a cross-country track, good enough for the tanks to follow. This enabled us to dislodge the enemy on the main road and we occupied the village of Schwinge, to avoid any chance of their returning to interfere with our bridging operations during the night. A tank of No. 2 Squadron was blown up during this operation under similar circumstances to those under which the armoured car met its fate earlier in the day. It disintegrated completely and the gun was later found buried five feet in the ground a hundred and fifty yards away. The sappers discovered subsequently that these ghastly objects were magnetic sea-mines, which could be connected with a control-box above ground, set to go off after a particular number of vehicles had passed.

That night came news of the deaths of Hitler and Goebbels, so our troops set forth for Stade in high spirits the next morning.

They found blown-up bridges and craters in an arc about a mile distant from the town, but an armoured car patrol managed to find a way round by an unmarked route. It was very bad indeed, but a Coldstream squadron-company group just managed to get through, and that was enough. As soon as entry had been gained the town surrendered. This was not unexpected, as all prisoners taken during the previous two days had said that they believed it would not be defended; it is true that the commandant had refused to agree when we spoke to him on the telephone the day before, but that was no doubt because he was aware of the pleasant fate that would have awaited his wife and children at the hands of the Gestapo, had he come to terms with us before we were actually in the town. It was found to be quite undamaged and with all services running quite normally; it gave the impression almost of being like a liberated town in Belgium or Holland and, though the people did not actually cheer, they looked as if they might do so at the slightest provocation. Many of them were shopping contentedly as our column drove in and their composure was both amazing and annoying to our men. They were soon confined to their houses for twenty-four hours to impress upon them that their town had been occupied. No doubt the relief of the German authorities at witnessing a peaceful occupation was accentuated by the presence of five hospitals containing altogether well over a thousand German wounded. Only four British wounded were found, but three of them were men of the division who had been made prisoner at Elsdorf.

Among the many hundreds of prisoners of no interest who passed through our hands at the time, one of considerable distinction turned up the evening before the fall of Stade. He was Lieutenant-General Wuhlisch, and he was captured at his own home in Schwinge; although discharged ten days before, he had until recently been Chief of Staff to the Twenty-Fifth German Army in Holland. He probably knew as much about the defence schemes there as any living man and seemed in a mood to be helpful about them, as his opening gambit was a statement that he considered the continuation of the war at this juncture no less than "criminal". He also made an interesting point in amplification of General Dittmar's recently stated opinion that once Hitler was dead German resistance would collapse immediately; he suggested as an additional reason for this belief that regular officers would then be released from their oath of allegiance to the Führer.

The war seemed at last to be petering out and for the first time, at any rate in our experience since the fighting in Germany began, the enemy were largely lacking in any determination to fight. The Irish moved North to occupy Elm and Oldendorf, almost without opposition and taking quite a number of prisoners. The Grenadiers launched an ambitious operation against Minstedt only to discover in the nick of time that the Derbyshire Yeomanry was entering it from another side in its reconnaissance role for the 51st Division; thereafter they concentrated in reserve behind the Irish at Mulsum; meanwhile Bremervörde capitulated quite unexpectedly before the assault was launched. Nevertheless attempts to push Westwards from Stade along the main road to Cuxhaven were still opposed. Our armoured cars found Himmelpforten and the woods surrounding it firmly held on May 2nd, with some field guns in support. They withdrew, and the area was given a good shelling during the night, to have the same comedy re-enacted the next morning; Himmelpforten was empty, but the road beyond was cratered and covered by the enemy. An attempt to push North resulted in a similar discovery, and in both cases there was no alternative route by which the Oste could be reached.

Early that afternoon, however, came the welcome news that Hamburg had just surrendered through the direct action of the German military authorities. At the same time the General heard from General Horrocks that the Germans on our front had also offered to surrender unconditionally; no further advance was to be made unless orders to that effect were received. As he subsequently told us, he was determined not to waste precious lives now that the end was so near. So when the burgomaster of Burweg, the village immediately before the Oste crossing on the

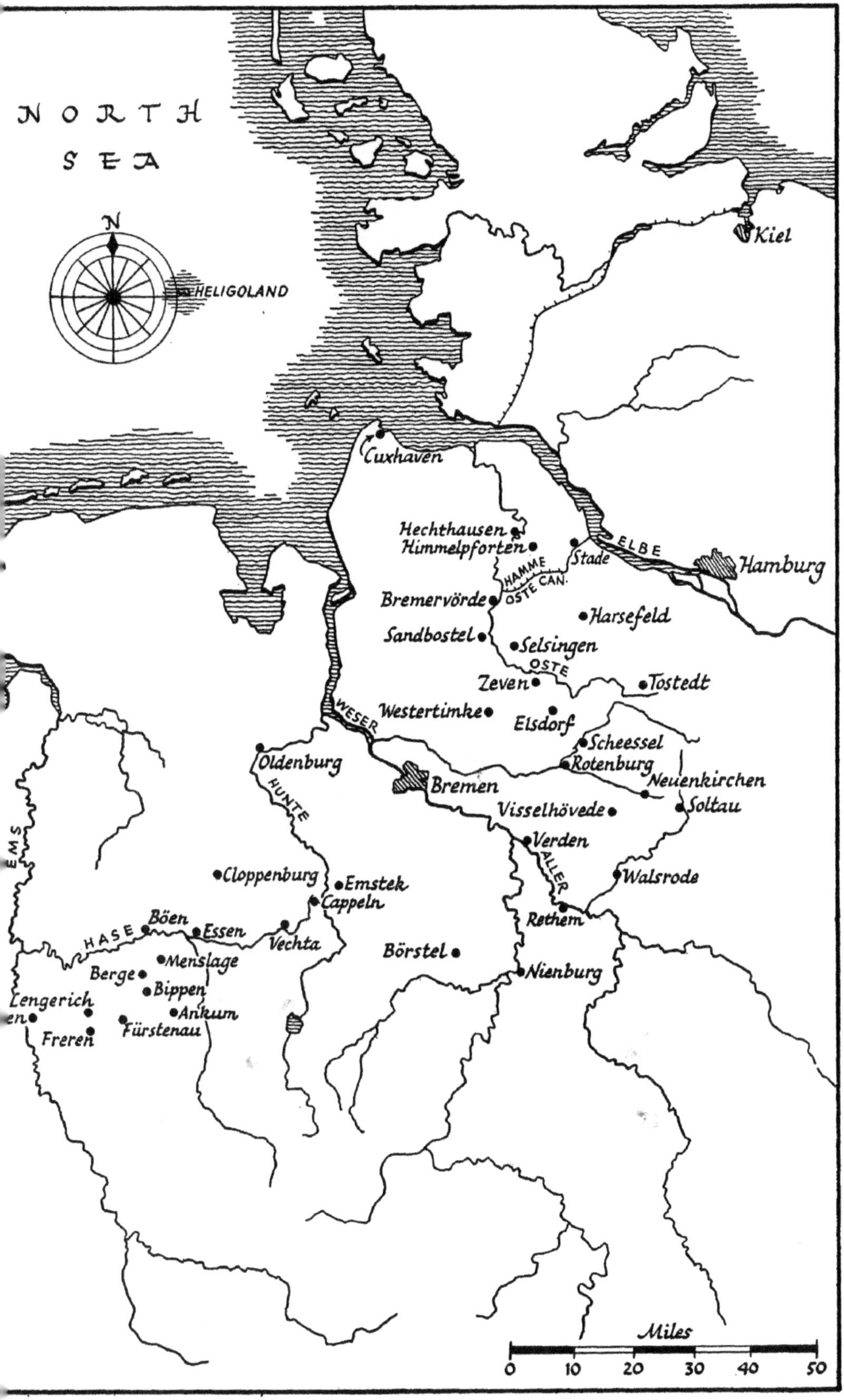
NORTH SEA
N
HELIGOLAND
Kiel
Cuxhaven
Hechthausen
Himmelpforten
Stade
ELBE
Hamburg
HAMME OSTE CAN.
Bremervörde
Harsefeld
Sandbostel
Selsingen
OSTE
Zeven
Tostedt
Westertimke
Elsdorf
WESER
Scheessel
Oldenburg
Rotenburg
Neuenkirchen
HUNTE
Bremen
Soltau
Visselhövede
Verden
EMS
ALLER
Cloppenburg
Emstek
Walsrode
Cappeln
Rethem
Böen
HASE
Essen
Vechta
Börstel
Menslage
Berge
Bippen
Nienburg
Lengerich
Ankum
Fürstenau
Freren
Miles
0 10 20 30 40 50

main road, came to tell us in the evening that the German troops had left and that the civilians would like us to take over, we merely sent a small force to investigate. It found that he was speaking the truth but we left it at that.

Various other straws showed the way the wind was blowing. One was the arrival in our lines at Stade of two officer emissaries from the artillery commander at Drochtersen, to the North by the Elbe. They had walked ten miles from that town, which was under no immediate threat from us, and wanted a three days' armistice, by which time they understood that general terms of "honourable" surrender would be arranged. We agreed to accept any of them at our cage who cared to walk the distance but told them that that was the limit of our interest in them. We also received an appeal from the town of Bützfleth to take it over as the civilians were being murdered by the local Hitler Youth. We declined to accept responsibility for the fate of parents who had so lamentably failed in the upbringing of their offspring.

Most indicative of all was the capture almost intact on the morning of May 4th of the bridge over the Oste beyond Burweg by the 1st Household Cavalry Regiment. The charges for its demolition were in position and forty prisoners were taken at the site, but no attempt was made to set them off nor did we experience any opposition when we proceeded to occupy the village of Hechthausen on the far side. One last tragedy, however, occurred just short of the bridge, when the tank carrying Captain R. P. Wheaton, forward observation officer of the West Somerset Yeomanry, was blown up on another sea-mine. The whole crew were instantly killed. In this case a whole armoured car squadron and five other tanks had already driven over the spot. The 615th Field Squadron filled the crater and made a minute search of the road and its embankments before traffic was allowed to move again. One more mine was duly discovered very cunningly concealed under the road.

That evening we learned that hostilities would officially cease at eight o'clock the next morning, May 5th. We had been waiting for this moment for so long that most of us took the announcement pretty calmly. The strain and fatigue of the months of ceaseless fighting had been such that the end seemed almost an anti-climax when it came.

The occasion did not, however, pass entirely unnoticed. Our gunners decided that it provided an excuse for giving themselves a last treat. They chose from the map an area of desolate marsh-land—"the kind of area", as one of their commanders, Lieutenant-Colonel J. S. Atkins, rather bitterly remarked, "that we are usually given for our gun lines"—and at ten minutes to eight they fired a *feu de joie* entitled "Fire Plan Grand Finale". First they poured into the area metal from all guns of all calibres that were in range. After the metal came a positive Neapolitan ice of every type of smoke shell, pink, orange, olive and petunia, for which not even the most enterprising Staff College graduate had yet been able to find a use. Alas, we were never able to discover whether the effect was thought pretty at the receiving end.

So the war ended for the Guards Armoured Division.

Chapter Fourteen

EPILOGUE

SHORTLY AFTER the official end of hostilities, on the morning of May 5th, General Goltzsch arrived by previous arrangement at divisional headquarters in order to discuss with the General the detailed terms of surrender in our area. General Goltzsch was the commander of Corps Ems, the formation controlling the remaining German troops in the Cuxhaven peninsula, and it was arranged with him that we should cross the Oste at two o'clock on the afternoon of May 7th and move direct to Cuxhaven, where the naval base and all the ships in the harbour would be handed over, thus completing our last operational task. In view of the trouble we had recently experienced from sea-mines the Germans were required to guarantee that the road would be cleared of all hazards and also to produce six vehicles of their own to precede our column.

This was all quite simple, but matters became somewhat complicated by the discovery next day that II Parachute Corps was in process of transit through the area, on their way to fight the Russians East of the Elbe. There seemed to be general agreement, on subsequent questioning, that this was their appointed role and it is interesting in showing how many Germans even in high authority still genuinely thought that there was a reasonable chance of inducing the Western Allies to accept surrender to them, while allowing the war against the Russians to continue. The majority of the paratroops were already in fact across the Elbe, but the larger portion of the 7th Parachute Division, our old enemy of many battles, had not yet had time to get away. No mention of it had been made in the first instance by Corps Ems, which had no control of any kind over it, as it had been expected to be gone before the terms of the surrender became effective. Further difficulty was caused by the fact that General Erdmann had already crossed the Elbe with the 21st Parachute Regiment, leaving the remainder of the division with a staff but with no commander. Corps Ems tried to arrange for General Goltzsch to act as divisional commander, but this suggestion was not well received by the paratroops and in the end Colonel Menzel, as senior remaining officer of the division, assumed command. It was very disappointing to miss catching such an old and distinguished adversary as General Erdmann, but we had the satisfaction of collecting two other familiar figures in Colonel Grassmehl and Colonel Hardegg.

Corps Ems estimated that there were about seven thousand German soldiers in the neighbourhood of Cuxhaven in addition to the paratroops. They were told to direct these into Cuxhaven itself, while the paratroops were to concentrate on the airfield about four miles South of the town. The 32nd Guards Brigade was to deal with the surrender, while the 5th Guards Brigade was to occupy the area between the Oste and the Elbe estuary. Brigadier Johnson ordered the Scots-Welsh Group to lead and occupy Cuxhaven; the Coldstream Group, moving immediately behind them, he told to make straight for the airfield and there to receive the surrender of the 7th Parachute Division.

Promptly at two o'clock Left Flank–No. 3 Squadron Group led off, accompanied by a naval detachment under the command of Captain Lawford, R.N. The whole brigade group moved fully prepared for battle as, although the capitulation had been fully signed and agreed, we thought it just possible that all might not work quite smoothly, both as regards the German sailors and the paratroops, neither of whom would necessarily be over-anxious to abide by arrangements made by Corps Ems, under whose command they had never been. The staff officers of Corps Ems themselves in fact seemed a bit dubious of the paratroops, of whom they were frankly a bit frightened. Actually not a shot was fired nor was any major difficulty encountered, though there were one or two slightly anxious moments, notably one when we found ourselves alongside a flak train that was completely armed and manned from end to end. A battery of the 21st Anti-

Tank Regiment was hastily sent to deal with it, and investigation showed us that the unwillingness of the Germans to leave their guns was due to the presence of a large camp in the vicinity containing Russian forced workers, whose feelings towards German troops they probably had every reason to distrust. Just over halfway we found a German naval officer waiting for us by previous arrangement. After a short conference, at which he assured us that everything was in order, he was placed on the leading tank; he complained bitterly about his loss of dignity, but he stayed there just the same and the column led off again. On entry into Cuxhaven the infantry mounted the tanks and, with the help of guides, made straight for the docks, where they took up positions covering the harbour.

We could not fail to be impressed by the efficiency of the German authorities in carrying out our orders. The streets were empty, guides were ready and both the Admiral and General in command, in addition to the Chief of Police, were waiting outside the principal hotel for the arrival of our commanding officers and Captain Lawford. By the evening everything both in the town and in the harbour was under control. The ships handed over included a destroyer, nine submarines and eleven mine-sweepers in a total of a hundred and one. Particularly welcome was the discovery of the mine-sweepers, as they would appreciably lighten the task of clearing the approaches to the Elbe and Weser for our shipping. In addition five more destroyers arrived from Norway to surrender the following night; so great was their anxiety to give themselves up that they insisted on being taken over in the middle of the night instead of waiting for the morning. It was notable too that there was no tendency to scuttle ships or to attempt sabotage in any way as there was in the German Navy after the 1914–1918 war. We could only hope that this was due to their realisation on this occasion that they were well and truly beaten and that the future of their country depended on the correct observance of all undertakings that were made.

As soon as the Scots-Welsh had deployed in Cuxhaven, the Coldstream moved straight through to the airfield. They reached it at seven o'clock, only to find that all the paratroops had not yet had time to assemble. The confusion was amazing and the situation laughable. German staff cars, filled with resplendent officers, and despatch riders roared up and down our column, presumably dealing with the orders we had given; their horse-drawn transport got mixed up with our tanks as both struggled to reach the same destination. There was nothing we could do but sit back and wait for them to complete their concentration.

By the next morning they were ready and Lieutenant-Colonel Hill ordered them to parade on the airfield at four o'clock. The paratroops assembled in the foreground, while behind, and seen only as a dark mass, stood row upon row of guns, mortars, trucks and carts, all destined never to be used again. The whole was covered by the guns of our tanks, silhouetted on each side against the sky, just in case of accident. The Coldstream felt that the undoubted honour bestowed on them was singularly appropriate in that the 5th Bn. Coldstream Guards had been the first in the division to meet these redoubtable opponents when serving under the 11th Armoured Division at Venray. Subsequently, at Bonninghardt and all the way from the Rhine, they had given all of us some of the toughest battles that we ever experienced. They ranked among the very finest troops in the German Army and had, moreover, refused to surrender to any troops but those of the Guards Armoured Division.

When all was ready the commanding officers, led by Colonel Menzel, went round the division; each unit came to attention as they reached it and they took the salute. The officers were then separated from their men. Over two hundred of them formed up under the guns of the reconnaissance troop and, with the commanding officers at their head, marched to a barracks some six hundred yards from the airfield. The men were then searched and marched off to quarters which had been prepared for them in huts, where they were put under guard. The whole ceremony inspired a curiously moving sense of triumph and achievement in all who witnessed it.

It must be admitted that the troops of the 7th Parachute

Division carried out meticulously all orders transmitted to them, and that our task was made the lighter owing to their co-operation and good discipline; this too despite the attitude of many that they had not been defeated in battle and that they should not therefore be treated as prisoners of war. They were soon disabused of any idea that the surrender had been other than unconditional in all respects and accepted the answer obediently if not with good grace. Their strength both in men and equipment was found to be greater than expected; this once more illustrated the particular genius possessed by General Erdmann for obtaining reinforcements and replacements when other commanders could not. There is no doubt that Colonel Menzel's claim that the division was still a complete and fully disciplined organisation at the close of hostilities was justified, even if it necessarily diverged from normal war establishment in many respects. He never expected it to be entirely broken up and protested vehemently, though he did not go quite so far as General Roth in similar circumstances, who showed that he had not quite learned the lesson we had tried to teach him at Westertimke by suggesting that the 15th Panzer Grenadier Division should be used by us *en bloc* for police duties in occupied Germany.

It seemed that at last the final act was complete. So it was for most of the division, but for a few of us an unusual and somewhat intriguing operation still remained. On May 9th the General was asked to provide infantry to accompany Rear-Admiral Muirhead-Gould, R.N., on an expedition two days later to accept the surrender of Heligoland and to make a survey of that island's defences. Right Flank of the 2nd Bn. Scots Guards was the fortunate company selected, accompanied by a detachment of sappers from the 615th Field Squadron.

There was a distinct atmosphere of excitement as the party embarked early in the morning of a perfect summer's day. Each platoon was carried in a separate minesweeper, with a fourth for company headquarters and the few other members of the division who had managed to be included as spectators. As far as nautical matters were concerned, they were at first entirely in the hands of their late enemies for, with the exception of a bearded naval officer who had asked to come as a sightseer, there were no British sailors in the ships. The intricacies of the minesweepers, the island of Neuwerk, with its cluster of houses perched on the mudflats, and the bells and buoys that bob on the brown muddy waters of the Elbe estuary occupied our men's attention fully until, out of sight of land, the ships started circling slowly to await the arrival of the Admiral, who was coming from Bremerhaven to this rendezvous. As soon as he appeared out of the haze the convoy moved off again, and very soon the high sandstone cliffs of Heligoland came in sight. A few German ships could be seen at anchor, each dotted with soldiers in their grey-green uniforms, and as it entered the harbour, dominated by the massive submarine pen, a thousand hostile faces turned to stare.

The naval party, together with the more important military representatives, disembarked immediately to conduct the formalities of surrender, while Right Flank moved more slowly. Blankets, cookers and all the paraphernalia of a company on the move had to be carried up and down gangways and on to the bombed remains of the quay. It was a very warm day and very warm work; a good deal of clothing was taken off, to the horror of an official photographer, who did not consider that this was at all the proper way for guardsmen to arrive at Heligoland. Company-Sergeant-Major Lindsay was drawn aside and, as soon as the last of the kit was ashore, five chosen men returned to the ship. Then, with caps straight and heads held high, and with Piper Crabbe in the lead, the landing of the Scots Guards was recorded for posterity. The whole expedition meanwhile established itself in the much damaged barracks at the foot of the cliff, where the dilapidated state of the barrack-rooms was compensated for by the magnificence of the cookhouse.

The policy to be enforced was two-fold. While the Navy was making the survey, assisted by the German officers lately in charge of the defences, all Germans, both civilians and military, were to be evacuated. The Germans themselves were responsible for the evacuation, and even as our party landed several ships, those that they had noted, were leaving the harbour with cargoes of soldiers bound for Cuxhaven and captivity. At the time of surrender there were some seven thousand people in all on the island, including two thousand civilians, of whom the majority were Todt workers engaged on the fortifications, and during the next few days all except two hundred essential men were evacuated. Guards had to be found at certain points to control the evacuation and numerous men were also needed to remove the stores of many kinds which were worth removing to the mainland.

Heligoland consists of a high sandstone plateau, on which the guns were sited and the old town built, with the harbour area at its base; the latter is wholly artificial and was designed to contain just sufficient space for two basins, the big submarine pen, the barracks and other military buildings. The two are connected by a stairway, which spirals two hundred feet up the cliff, and by a large lift which was no longer working. The island had been subjected to countless bombings, the last one quite recently on a gigantic scale, and the devastation was as complete as any that we had seen. There were craters every fifty yards, all the houses were mere heaps of rubble, guns had been flung from their mountings in all directions, red powdery dust smothered everything, and even when one looked from the edge of the cliffs into the shallow waters of the sea the bottom was seen to be cratered like the surface of the moon. One particular battery of twelve-inch guns became a showpiece for all visitors, of whom there were many during the ensuing days; these monstrous weapons, solidly mounted in steel and concrete and weighing many tons, had been hurled bodily from their moorings and turned upside down. So pitted was the island that, for the purpose of moving stores from the harbour to the barracks, a distance of not more than a thousand yards, it was found quicker to load them into a motor-boat and carry them by sea than to try to push them in trolleys along the remains of what had once been a road. The only buildings not damaged beyond repair were the barracks and the submarine pen; the latter had been heavily bombed and its roof hit in more than a dozen places, though no bomb had been of sufficient weight to penetrate the great thickness of concrete to the workshops and submarines below. It was hard to understand how the garrison had withstood so much with so few casualties until we discovered the other Heligoland which lies below ground. Cut deep in the rock runs a fascinating and highly complicated system of passages, all linked together, though the levels of some may differ by as much as two hundred feet. Offices, power stations, torpedo rooms, food and wine stores, hospitals were to be found there and a great deal more besides; so vast is the system that the whole garrison had been able to live there in complete safety and even in comparative comfort.

Right Flank remained on Heligoland for six days. By May 17th the evacuation was complete and the company re-embarked for Cuxhaven.

The division had in the meantime been engaged in carrying out the first phase of Operation "Eclipse". This was designed to embrace the complete destruction of the German war potential and the initial stage consisted of herding the troops into compounds, where they were disarmed and the sheep separated from the goats. The latter, the Nazi and S.S. thugs, were sent at once to prisoners-of-war camps, in our case to Westertimke, while the others were concentrated under the titular command of their own officers before being released to work on the farms or in other occupations of a peaceful nature essential to keep the German community alive. Headquarters of Corps Ems, which was temporarily kept in existence for this purpose, moved to Stade on May 15th, and on the following day the vanguard of the defeated German army followed. They crossed the Oste by a bridge built for that very purpose by our sappers, who noted with pride and satisfaction that the fiftieth bridge constructed by them since the Rhine crossing was required for such a use. They moved slowly, in creaking farm-carts and on foot, through Stade on their way to dispersal areas further South. Within a couple of days all German troops had left the Cuxhaven peninsula and the division's task there was altogether complete. We were told to prepare to move South to an area which had been left empty of troops by the advance and which was in urgent need of control.

On May 19th the 32nd Guards Brigade moved to an area centred on Rotenburg and extending South-West as far as the Weser. The next day the 5th Guards Brigade followed to the stretch of country on the further side of the Weser and due South of Bremen. Divisional Headquarters placed itself midway between them, near Verden.

The life of the division was now nearing its close and the police duties which became the background of its existence at this time need not concern us here. As soon as the war had ended it became generally known that sooner or later we would lose our tanks and on reaching the new areas we learned that it was to be sooner and that the date would be June 9th. Infantry is always the essential need of an army of occupation, and apart from that the whole history of the Brigade of Guards is founded on an infantry tradition. We learned furthermore that the 6th Guards Brigade would surrender its tanks at the same time and that it would amalgamate once more with us to form the Guards Division; as such the whole body would move to an occupation area in the Rhineland before the end of June.

During the last days of May therefore the armoured battalions set to work to maintain and paint their tanks in readiness for the farewell parade. To many people a tank may seem just a noisy, smelly, soulless conglomeration of metal, but to the vast majority of those who had nursed them, lived with them and fought with them, their relationship had taken on an almost human aspect. Sensitive to this, the General had decided that a great ceremonial parade should take place to commemorate both the historic and the sentimental aspects of the event. "Farewell to Armour" he christened it, after the Commander-in-Chief had kindly consented to take the Salute.

Rotenburg airfield was the site chosen for the parade. Apart from considerations of material convenience the town had lain on the original axis of advance of the division and had been captured in the operation involved in cutting the German communications between Bremen and Hamburg. Unfortunately it was too far for the Churchills of the 6th Guards Brigade to come to participate, since they were by now at Kiel, more than a hundred miles away, but a token detachment was to make the journey.

The sappers undertook to turn the bomb-scarred airfield into a worthy parade-ground and were given a large number of German prisoners to carry out the menial tasks; these consisted chiefly of scraping up the remains of the many German aircraft that still littered the field and of filling in the numerous craters made by our air force. Then, as the first days of June arrived, small parties of men and tanks from the battalions began to arrive. As we had ended the war at Cuxhaven a large supply of high-quality naval paint was available of which full use was made. The main portion of the tanks was painted shiny battleship grey, with white hatches, black knobs, red tow-ropes and gaily striped aerials. "Peace has fair come on us with a vengeance," said a paint-smeared guardsman to Major Hennessy, as a party from divisional headquarters came round to make sure that all was in order the day before the parade was due to take place.

Came the dawn of June 9th, ushering in a heavenly summer's day. The tanks had been driven to their positions the previous afternoon, two battalions on each side of the ground. At the eastern end lay the saluting base, flanked by the infantry battalions, formed up together with representative detachments from the services. Around and behind the saluting base was the enclosure for spectators; these included not only members of neighbouring divisions but also airmen, sailors, Russian and other displaced persons, even German prisoners who had come to admire the result of their handiwork. In the brilliant sunlight it was a truly splendid sight. On either side stretched the tanks as far as a slight ridge half a mile distant, resplendent in their new paint and with their guns glistening after days of polish. In the centre and at the back, drawn up on the near slope of the ridge, were the vehicles of the other mobile regiments of the division, to which they must also say farewell. These were the armoured cars of the Household

Cavalry, the self-propelled guns of the Leicestershire Yeomanry and of the 21st Anti-Tank Regiment, and the Bofors guns of the 94th Light Anti-Aircraft Regiment. In front of them and directly between the serried rows of Shermans and Cromwells were the massed bands of the Scots and Welsh Guards.

The parade was due to start at half-past eleven and an hour before that time the little airstrip which had been cut on the far end of the damaged airfield was already very busy; at one time fourteen Austers were all circling round waiting to land. Thirty-six aircraft, all bearing distinguished senior officers, had already landed by the time that Lieutenant-General Sir Miles Dempsey, the Army Commander, arrived at a quarter-past eleven. Punctually, a bare ten minutes later, Field-Marshal Sir Bernard Montgomery himself landed. Escorted by a troop of the Household Cavalry, he was driven to the saluting base. As he arrived there the General, standing centrally in the arena, called the division to attention for the General Salute.

The inspection then started, the party moving in four half-tracks escorted by four armoured cars. In the leading vehicle the General took the Commander-in-Chief and the Major-General, who had flown out from England the previous evening. The Army Commander and the Commanders of I and XXX Corps travelled in the second vehicle, and in the third and fourth a distinguished gathering from all three Services.

The inspection completed, the massed bands moved to a flank as the party once more took up its position on the dais for the "salute of the armour". "Crews mount," ordered Brigadier Gwatkin, followed by "start up", at which the air was rent by a great roar of two hundred and fifty engines. As each tank commander was ready he held up his hand and then, slowly and with great dignity, four columns from the four armoured battalions came out from the flanks and counter-marched across the parade-ground. Every commander, as his tank passed the Commander-in-Chief, traversed his gun and himself saluted, afterwards turning to drive back over the ridge. When the moment came for the last files to cross each other the central block at the back began to draw away, the diesel engines of the self-propelled anti-tank guns leaving their usual pall of blue smoke, which added greatly to the effect. As the turrets of the tanks slowly disappeared over the horizon and the roar of engines changed to a distant rumble the massed bands took up the strains of "Auld Lang Syne" until the last chorus faded out to complete silence.

The infantry, who had stood respectfully to attention during the salute, now turned inwards towards the dais and stood at ease, while the massed bands wheeled into the centre of the arena and marched away up the ridge to the crest where the 2nd Household Cavalry Regiment, now the divisional reconnaissance regiment, alone had remained in position, as the artillery regiments were destined to leave us altogether. At this moment the heads and shoulders of marching infantry began to appear over the horizon. There was a momentary pause on the line of the armoured cars, then came the command, "Brigades, by the centre, quick march." Columns of "armoured infantry" from the 2nd Bn. Grenadier Guards, the 1st Bn. Coldstream Guards, the 2nd Bn. Irish Guards and the 2nd Bn. Welsh Guards, with a composite column from the 6th Guards Brigade in the centre, swung down the centre of the arena while the massed bands played each regimental march in turn.

Can it be that the cramped living conditions of a tank crew prompt them to stretch and exert their limbs the more vigorously when let loose? At all events these former tank men came forward in such style that not even the deep ruts, cut a few minutes earlier by their own tanks as a last protest against their banishment, could throw them out. On reaching the saluting base they halted, when the scene presented eleven columns of infantry in sixes, with the massed bands immediately behind them, and in the rear, strung out in a single line, a squadron of the 2nd Household Cavalry Regiment.

For the first time the General called the Guards Division to attention. "God save the King" was played, and the ceremony was over.

Field-Marshal Montgomery then called on the assembled company to gather round and delivered an address. He began by saying that, now that the war with Germany was over, it was interesting to consider how it was that we had won, when in 1940 and 1941 such an ending had seemed impossible. There were many reasons for this, but he considered that two were basically the cause of the Germans' defeat. The first lay in their own mistakes, the greatest of which were the deliberate attacks on Russia and the United States, thus bringing those two great nations in on our side. The second lay in the good fighting qualities of the Allied soldiers, among whom the fighting man of the British Empire could stand comparison with any.

He then proceeded to speak in less general terms:

"I want to say something now about your division. When this war began the Guards were infantry, but at a time of great material danger in 1941 they turned their attention to armour. Subsequently, Guards Armoured Division and the 6th Guards Armoured Brigade have fought throughout this historic campaign in Western Europe.

"I do not suppose that there is any officer who can speak with such weight of experience as myself about the relative standards of battle efficiency of this or that formation or unit; from Alamein to the Baltic, I have had many formations and units under my command. I want to say, here and now, that in the sphere of armoured warfare you have set a standard that it will be difficult for those that come after to reach. In modern war it is the co-operation of all arms, armoured and unarmoured, that wins the battle, and in this respect you have achieved great results. In fact, the Guards have shown that whatever they are asked to do, whatever they take on, they do well; they maintain always the highest standards and give a lead to all others. You will long be remembered for your prowess in armoured war.

"Now you are to return to your traditional role of infantry. Some of you may wonder why this is so. Firstly, the King wishes it. Secondly, the Brigade of Guards as a whole is anxious that this should be done. Thirdly, I myself, an infantry soldier of many years' service, would say to you that you are needed as infantry. The infantry arm has come right to the fore in this war; it is the most versatile of all the arms; nothing can be done without infantry and there is never enough for the tasks that have to be done. It is vital that the infantry should be a firm and strong rock on which to build the post-war British army; it is the central core of the fighting machine, on which all else depends. We need you in the infantry; we need your high standards, your great efficiency in all matters and your old traditions of duty and service; all these are needed to help weld the infantry arm into a truly solid basis on which to build.

"So I welcome you back into the infantry. You can look back with pride on your excursion into the realms of armoured warfare, and the experience there gained will always be valuable to you.

"I do not know whether the officers and men of the Guards Armoured Division, now the Guards Division, realise how much they owe to General Allan Adair. From my position as Commander-in-Chief I do and can tell you why. He trained the division for battle in England; he took it across the Channel to Normandy and commanded it in the great battles there; he then led it through France, through Belgium, through Holland and into Germany. He commanded it till the war ended and throughout all this time he never failed me and he never failed you; he gave of his best that the division might do well in battle and he has reaped his full reward. You owe to him more than you can ever repay and I will go further; I would say that the Brigade of Guards was lucky to have ready such an officer to handle this armoured warfare for them, as few could have done it so well. In front of you all I wish to congratulate him on having brought the matter to such a successful conclusion."

The obvious sincerity of this truly generous tribute was tremendously appreciated by all members of the division, who felt doubly grateful to the Commander-in-Chief for expressing in his own words the views that we had held all along about our General.

With the conclusion of the ceremony the final chapter had been written and, as we dispersed, the universal sentiment was:

The Division is dead, long live the Division!

Epilogue to the New Edition by Richard Doherty

In spring 1941 the Commander-in-Chief Home Forces, General Sir Alan Brooke, concerned that the Army lacked sufficient armour to counter a possible German invasion, ordered the creation of two new armoured divisions. One was formed by re-rolling 42nd (East Lancashire) Division; the other was formed from the Brigade of Guards who had yet to form a full division as in the First World War.

On 17 June 1941 the Guards Armoured Division came into being with Major General Sir Oliver Leese Bt, Coldstream Guards, as GOC. Initially it included two armoured brigades, a support group and various ancillary units. By the end of 1942 the new standard order of battle, an armoured brigade and an infantry brigade, was adopted with 5 Guards Armoured and 32 Guards Infantry Brigades and 2nd Household Cavalry Regiment as divisional reconnaissance unit.

Training was intensive and, as expected of the Guards, standards high. In September 1942 Leese, promoted to command a corps, was succeeded by Major General Sir Allan Adair, a Grenadier. Within his brigades there were already battalions of Grenadier, Coldstream, Irish and Welsh Guards. However, as Scots Guards battalion was transferred out of 32 Brigade it was not until the closing months of the war that the Scots were again represented in the Division.

Although Guards Armoured was the last armoured division to deploy to France in late June 1944, it took part in Operation GOODWOOD, Montgomery's attempt to break through the German defences before Caen. While there were some gains, the operation did not achieve all its objectives. Importantly, it held the bulk of the German armour on the eastern flank, preventing the panzers opposing the planned American breakout, Operation COBRA, on the western flank.

An immediate lesson from GOODWOOD led to a change in the structure of Guards and 11th Armoured Divisions. They adopted the system already used by 7th Armoured: closely-wedded groups of armour and infantry, even down to troops and platoons. In Guards Armoured the initial marriages matched units laagered close together when the change was implemented but this soon changed to 'family' groups: Grenadier, Coldstream, Irish and Welsh.

One remarkable incident during GOODWOOD involved an Irish Guards' Sherman knocking out the first King Tiger encountered in Normandy. Lieutenant John Gorman, on his first day in action, immobilized the King Tiger by ramming it after his Sherman's gun had misfired and earned the Military Cross. Casualties in 2nd Welsh Guards included Lieutenant Rex Whistler, the renowned artist, the first of the battalion killed in Normandy.

Guards Armoured participated in the desperate attempts to break out of the bridgehead, including Operation BLUECOAT and the Canadian Operation SPRING. Once clear of Normandy, Second Army moved quickly through France and Belgium. Guards Armoured led the way to Brussels, which was liberated by Adair's men on 3 September, the fifth anniversary of the outbreak of war. En route the Division had captured the German commander of HQ Somme Corps who was preparing to hold the British along that river. He had been taken completely by surprise. On their way to Brussels some 2nd Welsh Guards' Cromwell tanks (the other units had Shermans) are said to have touched 60mph on the main road. In the event, the Shermans of the Grenadiers arrived in the city at the same time. Hordes of Belgian civilians greeted them, 'careering madly about in such a frenzy of joy that movement was almost impossible'.

In typical British fashion this advance was referred to as the 'great swan'. In reality, it was a British blitzkrieg that provided a master class in mobile warfare to the Germans whose attempts at opposition were overcome by skilful use of mobility and firepower. During this advance the British armour, principally Guards and 11th Armoured Divisions, had broken the cohesion of the German command structure and taken thousands of prisoners. It was 'a classic example of exploitation by armour'.

As the Germans regained their equilibrium opposition hardened. However, advancing from Brussels the Grenadier Group made for Louvain, a squadron of Household Cavalry seizing bridges along their route. The Division then advanced eastward to secure crossings over the Albert Canal, with 5 Brigade led by the Grenadier Group and 32 Brigade by the Welsh Group. Tough fighting followed, but the Coldstream Group pushed on to Bourg Leopold, the Belgian Aldershot. The close-knit groups, from armoured battalion/infantry battalion down to troop/platoon, proved their value as all four continued the battle.

On the evening of 10 September, 3rd Irish Guards, under Lieutenant Colonel J.O.E. Vandeleur, captured the bridge over the Meuse-Escaut canal outside Neerpelt while the Welsh Group engaged German forces in the vicinity. The bridge was taken intact and held against several German counter-attacks. Immediately dubbed 'Joe's Bridge', it was to be used in Operation MARKET GARDEN, the attempt to take the bridges over the Lower Rhine by airborne coup de main followed by the speedy arrival of XX Corps, which included Guards Armoured Division.

The Division provided the spearhead of XXX Corps with the Grenadier Group and US 82nd Airborne Division taking the Nijmegen Bridge. In spite of the gallant efforts of Guards Armoured Division, the infantry of XXX Corps and 8 Armoured Brigade, it proved impossible to break through to the final bridge at Arnhem, which the British 1st Airborne Division and Polish Independent Parachute Brigade had tried to capture. Since the only route to Arnhem for armour was along a road raised above the saturated ground leading north from Eindhoven the tanks were vulnerable to enemy anti-tank fire. Lacking air support and with the artillery out of range the tanks of the Irish Guards, leading the Division, became easy targets for anti-tank guns. Of the first eighteen tanks to move off, nine were knocked out by 88mm anti-tank guns. In the end the operation failed and 1st Airborne Division was lost, although many soldiers were evacuated from the bridgehead. The success of that evacuation, Operation BERLIN, was partly due to the work of a patrol of Household Cavalry which had found a way into Arnhem using by roads and lanes. That route was used for the evacuation.

During the winter elements of the Division were deployed to counter the German Ardennes offensive and 32 Guards Brigade Group held part of the line until relieved by 5 Parachute Brigade. Then came Operation VERITABLE in February 1945, described by Lieutenant General Sir Brian Horrocks as 'the biggest operation I ever handled in war'. This included a thrust through the Reichswald by XXX Corps, then 200,000 strong. Initially only the Division's infantry was involved but the armour deployed on 21 February. In very difficult terrain and adverse weather Guards Armoured gave such a good account of themselves that a German parachute battalion commander expressed his satisfaction with being made prisoner by 'First Guards Panzer Division'; he described this as an honour. As the operation came to a close the Division had broken General Schlemm's lateral near Menzelen after a very stiff fight. Schlemm was commanding First Parachute Army.

Guards Armoured crossed the Rhine on 28 March in Operation PLUNDER, spearheading XXX Corps yet again. On 3 April the Coldstream Group was leading when a patrol of 2 HCR reported that a bridge across the Ems river near Altenlingen was still intact but defended by a force of infantry, with three 88mm anti-tank guns, and prepared for demolition. The Coldstream were ordered to seize it but this seemed impossible before the bridge was blown. However, Captain Ian Liddell, commanding a company of 5th Coldstream, deployed his two forward platoons to the near bank before sprinting towards the bridge. Scaling a 10-foot-high roadblock he neutralized the charges under heavy enemy fire. Not only did he do this on the deck of the bridge, but he also did so with charges underneath the structure. He then climbed onto the roadblock to signal his leading platoon to advance. For this 'magnificently planned, perfectly timed and bravely executed action' Liddell was awarded the Victoria Cross. Tragically he was killed in action on 21 April without knowing of the award.

On the day that Captain Liddell was killed another Victoria Cross was earned by Guards Armoured Division. This was awarded posthumously to Guardsman Edward Charlton, Irish Guards. As the Grenadier and Irish Groups were advancing from Elsdorf, an Irish troop/platoon post at Wistedt was attacked by a German company supported by two SPGs. Charlton was the driver of a Sherman which was hit by the first German round and caught fire. The crew baled out but Charlton saw enemy infantry racing towards his position and scrambled back onto the Sherman, removed its Browning machine gun from the turret and engaged the enemy. Although wounded, he continued firing, propping the weapon on a gate after receiving a wound to his left arm. He fired and reloaded with one hand until a burst of fire hit him in the right side and he collapsed. Subsequently a German officer PoW told his captors of Charlton's courage and he was recommended for the Victoria Cross. His was the last VC of the European war.

In the dying days of the war Guards Armoured Division continued to prove its effectiveness. Its soldiers also witnessed the horror of the concentration camps, especially that at Sandbostel. There was still fighting to be done, often against small but determined groups of German soldiers or marines en route to Bremervörde. By this time a Scots Guards battalion had joined, replacing a Welsh Guards battalion that had suffered heavy losses. The Division also had a second HCR unit as an armoured car regiment and 1st Household Cavalry Regiment 'proved itself as good as its sister regiment in the reconnaissance role while leading the Division north to Stade to dominate the Elbe estuary'. The capture of Stade was the Division's last engagement.

On 9 June 1945 Guards Armoured Division surrendered its tanks and reverted to the infantry role. In its four years of existence, and eleven months of hard fighting, it had served and fought with élan as the guardsmen's predecessors had done over centuries and demonstrated that the Guards regiments are flexible, highly adaptable and always professional in whatever they do. Brooke's decision to form an armoured division using Household troops had been fully vindicated while the leadership of Major General Sir Allan Adair proved inspirational and effective. He led with the touch of a commander who knew his men and understood how to get the best from them. Never a showman, he was nonetheless popular because his soldiers knew he cared for them. With an excellent staff around him and highly competent brigade and battalion commanders, his Division proved itself to be one of the finest fighting formations that Britain has ever put in the field.

Appendix 1

ORDER OF BATTLE—JULY 1ST, 1942

General Officer Commanding

Major-General Sir Oliver Leese, Bart., C.B., C.B.E., D.S.O.

G.S.O. I.—Lt.-Col. D. S. Schreiber, M.V.O., 11th Hussars.
A.A. & Q.M.G.—Lt.-Col. R. G. Feilden, Coldstream Guards.

2nd Household Cavalry Regiment
Commanding Officer—Lt.-Col. H. Abel Smith.

5th Guards Armoured Brigade
Commander—Brigadier W. A. F. L. Fox-Pitt, D.S.O., M.V.O., M.C.
Brigade Major—Major Lord Tryon, Grenadier Guards.
1st (Motor) Battalion Grenadier Guards
Commanding Officer—Lt.-Col. E. H. Goulburn.
2nd (Armoured) Battalion Grenadier Guards
Commanding Officer—Lt.-Col. C. M. Dillwyn-Venables-Llewellyn.
1st (Armoured) Battalion Coldstream Guards
Commanding Officer—Lt.-Col. R. Myddelton, M.V.O.
2nd (Armoured) Battalion Irish Guards
Commanding Officer—Lt.-Col. C. K. Finlay.

6th Guards Armoured Brigade
Commander—Brigadier A. H. S. Adair, D.S.O., M.C.
Brigade Major—Major the Earl of Lewes.
4th (Motor) Battalion Coldstream Guards
Commanding Officer—Lt.-Col. N. W. Gwatkin, M.V.O.
4th (Armoured) Battalion Grenadier Guards
Commanding Officer—Lt.-Col. O. W. D. Smith.
3rd (Armoured) Battalion Scots Guards
Commanding Officer—Lt.-Col. the Hon. H. K. M. Kindersley, M.B.E., M.C.
2nd (Armoured) Battalion Welsh Guards
Commanding Officer—Lt.-Col. W. D. C. Greenacre, M.V.O.

32nd Guards Brigade
Commander—Brigadier G. L. Verney, M.V.O.
Brigade Major—Major W. A. G. Burns, M.C., Coldstream Guards.

5th Battalion Coldstream Guards
Commanding Officer—Lt.-Col. Lord Stratheden.
4th Battalion Scots Guards
Commanding Officer—Lt.-Col. A. V. C. Douglas.
1st Battalion Welsh Guards
Commanding Officer—Lt.-Col. G. St. V. J. Vigor.

Royal Artillery
Commander Royal Artillery—Brigadier L. C. Manners-Smith.
Brigade Major Royal Artillery—Major F. A. Bibra.
55th Field Regiment
Commanding Officer—Lt.-Col. R. D. Bolton.
153rd Field Regiment
Commanding Officer—Lt.-Col. D. C. W. Sanders, O.B.E.
21st Anti-Tank Regiment
Commanding Officer—Lt.-Col. G. K. Bourne.
94th Light Anti-Aircraft Regiment
Commanding Officer—Lt.-Col. A. L. Matthews, M.C.

Royal Engineers
Commander Royal Engineers—Lt.-Col. A. Dove, M.B.E.

Royal Signals
Commander Royal Signals—Lt.-Col. D. M. Smith, M.B.E.

Royal Army Service Corps
Commander Royal Army Service Corps—Lt.-Col. F. C. J. Goodyer Pain.

Royal Army Medical Corps
Assistant Director of Medical Services—Colonel H. L. Glyn Hughes, D.S.O., M.C.
19th Light Field Ambulance
Commanding Officer—Lt.-Col. T. M. H. Ahern.
128th Field Ambulance
Commanding Officer—Lt.-Col. A. L. Crockford, M.C., T.D.
225th Light Field Ambulance
Commanding Officer—Lt.-Col. J. B. Forsyth.

Royal Army Ordnance Corps
Assistant Director of Ordnance Services—Lt.-Col. F. B. H. Villiers.

Royal Electrical and Mechanical Engineers
Commander, Royal Electrical and Mechanical Engineers—Lt.-Col. F. A. Hibberd, C.B.E.

Appendix 2

ORDER OF BATTLE—JUNE 6TH, 1944

GENERAL OFFICER COMMANDING

Major-General A. H. S. Adair, D.S.O., M.C.

G.S.O. I.—Lt.-Col. P. R. C. Hobart, M.C., Royal Tank Regiment.
A.A. & Q.M.G.—Lt.-Col. W. M. Sale, Royal Horse Guards.

2nd Armoured Reconnaissance Battalion Welsh Guards

Commanding Officer—Lt.-Col. J. C. Windsor-Lewis, D.S.O., M.C.

5th Guards Armoured Brigade

Commander—Brigadier N. W. Gwatkin, M.V.O.
Brigade Major—Major the Hon. M. F. Fitzalan Howard, M.C., Grenadier Guards.
D.A.A. & Q. M.G.— Major T. F. C. Winnington, Grenadier Guards.

1st (Motor) Battalion Grenadier Guards

Commanding Officer—Lt.-Col. E. H. Goulburn.

2nd (Armoured) Battalion Grenadier Guards

Commanding Officer—Lt.-Col. J. N. R. Moore.

1st (Armoured) Battalion Coldstream Guards

Commanding Officer—Lt.-Col. R. Myddelton, M.V.O.

2nd (Armoured) Battalion Irish Guards

Commanding Officer—Lt.-Col. C. K. Finlay.

32nd Guards Brigade

Commander—Brigadier G. F. Johnson.
Brigade Major—Major J. D. Hornung, M.C., Irish Guards.
D.A.A. & Q.M.G.—Major T. C. Dundas, Scots Guards.

5th Battalion Coldstream Guards

Commanding Officer—Lt.-Col. Lord Stratheden.

3rd Battalion Irish Guards

Commanding Officer—Lt.-Col. J. O. E. Vandeleur.

1st Battalion Welsh Guards

Commanding Officer—Lt.-Col. G. W. Browning.

No. 1 Independent Machine Gun Company, The Royal Northumberland Fusiliers

Commander—Major R. M. Pratt.

Royal Artillery

Commander Royal Artillery—Brigadier H. C. Phipps.
Brigade Major Royal Artillery—Major G. E. Maitland.

55th Field Regiment

Commanding Officer—Lt.-Col. W. L. Newell, D.S.O.

153rd Field Regiment

Commanding Officer—Lt.-Col. J. S. Atkins, T.D.

21st Anti-Tank Regiment

Commanding Officer—Lt.-Col. R. C. Hulbert.

94th Light Anti-Aircraft Regiment

Commanding Officer—Lt.-Col. E. I. E. Strong.

Royal Engineers

Commander Royal Engineers—Lt.-Col. C. P. Jones, M.C.

Royal Signals

Commander Royal Signals—Lt.-Col. W. D. Tucker.

Royal Army Service Corps

Commander Royal Army Service Corps—Lt.-Col. A. K. Woods.

Royal Army Medical Corps

Assistant Director of Medical Services—Colonel B. J. Daunt.

19th Light Field Ambulance

Commanding Officer—Lt.-Col. B. M. Nicol.

128th Field Ambulance

Commanding Officer—Lt.-Col. J. M. Scott.

Royal Army Ordnance Corps

Assistant Director of Ordnance Services—Lt.-Col. F. B. H. Villiers.

Royal Electrical and Mechanical Engineers

Commander, Royal Electrical and Mechanical Engineers—Lt.-Col. L. H. Atkinson.

Appendix 3

ORDER OF BATTLE—SEPTEMBER 3RD, 1944

GENERAL OFFICER COMMANDING

Major-General A. H. S. Adair, D.S.O., M.C.

G.S.O. I.—Lt.-Col. J. D. Hornung, M.C., Irish Guards.

A.A. & Q.M.G.—Lt.-Col. W. M. Sale, Royal Horse Guards.

2nd Armoured Reconnaissance Battalion Welsh Guards

Commanding Officer—Lt.-Col. J. C. Windsor-Lewis, D.S.O., M.C.

5th Guards Armoured Brigade

Commander—Brigadier N. W. Gwatkin, M.V.O.

Brigade Major—Major the Hon. M. F. Fitzalan Howard, M.C., Grenadier Guards.

D.A.A. & Q.M.G.—Major T. F. Winnington, Grenadier Guards.

1st (Motor) Battalion Grenadier Guards
Commanding Officer—Lt.-Col. E. H. Goulburn.
2nd (Armoured) Battalion Grenadier Guards
Commanding Officer—Lt.-Col. J. N. R. Moore.
1st (Armoured) Battalion Coldstream Guards
Commanding Officer—Lt.-Col. R. F. S. Gooch, M.C.
2nd (Armoured) Battalion Irish Guards
Commanding Officer—Lt.-Col. G. A. M. Vandeleur.

32nd Guards Brigade
Commander—Brigadier G. F. Johnson.
Brigade Major—Major the Hon. M. Fitzalan Howard, M.C., Scots Guards.
D.A.A. & Q.M.G.—Major T. C. Dundas, Scots Guards.
5th Battalion Coldstream Guards
Commanding Officer—Lt.-Col. E. R. Hill.
3rd Battalion Irish Guards
Commanding Officer—Lt.-Col. J. O. E. Vandeleur.
1st Battalion Welsh Guards
Commanding Officer—Lt.-Col. J. F. Gresham.
No. 1 Independent Machine Gun Company, The Royal Northumberland Fusiliers
Commander—Major R. M. Pratt.

Royal Artillery
Commander Royal Artillery—Brigadier H. C. Phipps.
Brigade Major Royal Artillery—Major G. E. Maitland.
55th Field Regiment
Commanding Officer—Lt.-Col. B. Wilson.
153rd Field Regiment
Commanding Officer—Lt.-Col. J. S. Atkins, T.D.
21st Anti-Tank Regiment
Commanding Officer—Lt.-Col. R. C. Hulbert.
94th Light Anti-Aircraft Regiment
Commanding Officer—Lt.-Col. E. I. E. Strong.

Royal Engineers
Commander Royal Engineers—Lt.-Col. C. P. Jones, M.C.

Royal Signals
Commander Royal Signals—Lt.-Col. W. D. Tucker, O.B.E.

Royal Army Service Corps
Commander Royal Army Service Corps—Lt.-Col. A. K. Woods, O.B.E.

Appendix 3

Royal Army Medical Corps

Assistant Director of Medical Services—Colonel B. J. Daunt, O.B.E.

19th Light Field Ambulance

Commanding Officer—Lt.-Col. B. M. Nicol, O.B.E.

128th Field Ambulance

Commanding Officer—Lt.-Col. J. M. Scott.

Royal Army Ordnance Corps

Assistant Director of Ordnance Services—Lt.-Col. F. B. H. Villiers, O.B.E.

Royal Electrical and Mechanical Engineers

Commander, Royal Electrical and Mechanical Engineers—Lt.-Col. L. H. Atkinson, O.B.E.

Appendix 4

ORDER OF BATTLE—MAY 5TH, 1945

GENERAL OFFICER COMMANDING

Major-General A. H. S. Adair, C.B., D.S.O., M.C.

G.S.O. I.—Lt.-Col. J. D. Hornung, M.C., Irish Guards

A.A. & Q.M.G.—Lt.-Col. H. P. T. Prideaux, 3rd Carabiniers.

2nd Armoured Reconnaissance Battalion Welsh Guards

Commanding Officer—Lt.-Col. J. C. Windsor-Lewis, D.S.O., M.C.

5th Guards Armoured Brigade

Commander—Brigadier N. W. Gwatkin, D.S.O., M.V.O.

Brigade Major—Major T. F. Blackwell, Coldstream Guards.

D.A.A. & Q.M.G.—Major R. S. A. Hardy, Grenadier Guards.

1st (Motor) Battalion Grenadier Guards

Commanding Officer—Lt.-Col. P. H. Lort-Phillips, D.S.O.

2nd (Armoured) Battalion Grenadier Guards

Commanding Officer—Lt.-Col. J. N. R. Moore, D.S.O.

1st (Armoured) Battalion Coldstream Guards

Commanding Officer—Lt.-Col. R. F. S. Gooch, D.S.O., M.C.

2nd (Armoured) Battalion Irish Guards

Commanding Officer—Lt.-Col. J. S. O. Haslewood.

32nd Guards Brigade

Commander—Brigadier G. F. Johnson, D.S.O.

Brigade Major—Major the Hon. M. Fitzalan Howard, M.C., Scots Guards.

D.A.A. & Q.M.G.—Major T. C. Dundas, Scots Guards.

5th Battalion Coldstream Guards
Commanding Officer—Lt.-Col. E. R. Hill, D.S.O.
2nd Battalion Scots Guards
Commanding Officer—Lt.-Col. H. N. Clowes, D.S.O.
3rd Battalion Irish Guards
Commanding Officer—Lt.-Col. D. H. FitzGerald, D.S.O.
No. 1 Independent Machine Gun Company, The Royal Northumberland Fusiliers
Commander—Major H. B. van der Gucht.

Royal Artillery
Commander Royal Artillery—Brigadier H. C. Phipps, D.S.O.
Brigade Major Royal Artillery—Major G. E. Maitland.
55th Field Regiment
Commanding Officer—Lt.-Col. B. Wilson, D.S.O.
153rd Field Regiment
Commanding Officer—Lt.-Col. J. S. Atkins, D.S.O., T.D.
21st Anti-Tank Regiment
Commanding Officer—Lt.-Col. R. C. Hulbert.
94th Light Anti-Aircraft Regiment
Commanding Officer—Lt.-Col. J. M. Northern, M.B.E.

Royal Engineers
Commander Royal Engineers—Lt.-Col. J. N. Thomas, D.S.O., M.C.

Royal Signals
Commander Royal Signals—Lt.-Col. W. D. Tucker, O.B.E.

Royal Army Service Corps
Commander Royal Army Service Corps—Lt.-Col. A. R. Purches.

Royal Army Medical Corps
Assistant Director of Medical Services—Colonel T. W. Davidson.
19th Light Field Ambulance
Commanding Officer—Lt.-Col. P. L. E. Wood, D.S.O., M.B.E.
128th Field Ambulance
Commanding Officer—Lt.-Col. J. M. Scott, O.B.E.

Royal Army Ordnance Corps
Assistant Director of Ordnance Services—Lt.-Col. F. B. H. Villiers, O.B.E.

Royal Electrical and Mechanical Engineers
Commander, Royal Electrical and Mechanical Engineers—Lt.-Col. L. H. Atkinson, O.B.E.

Appendix 5

THE ADMINISTRATIVE SYSTEM

THE SYSTEM adopted by the Guards Armoured Division differed somewhat from that in force in other divisions in that there was no Rear Headquarters, and all the services were grouped into the Administrative Group which was virtually a brigade of its own with its Commander, Staff, Signals and Provost. All Q Staff Officers were at Main Divisional Headquarters.

This group contained all administrative units except such units, or elements of them, that required to be further forward owing to their functions, such as Petrol Points, Ammunition Points, Advanced Dressing Stations, etc.

The group was organised on a service basis and comprised:

Headquarters
Brigade Companies, R.A.S.C.
Brigade B Echelons
R.E.M.E. and R.A.O.C. areas with the two Brigade Workshops and their Ordnance Stores Sections
One company of a Field Ambulance (if in reserve), the Field Hygiene Section and Field Dressing Station (if not deployed)
Tank Delivery Squadron
Tank Transporter Company (if allotted)
Infantry reinforcements

MOVEMENT

The group contained about 800 vehicles and over 3,000 men. It sometimes moved as one body, but often was dribbled forward in small blocks. Like other Units, it had to ensure that its route was clear of mines, and patrols were often sent out to ensure that the route was also clear of enemy. On more than one occasion the Administrative Group cleared the centre-line of appreciable German forces with their own resources.

UNIT TRANSPORT

First-line transport was divided into three echelons, F2, A and B.

F2 was a fighting echelon which accompanied troops into action; it was very small.

A was an echelon required under battle conditions to supplement F, and was normally controlled by brigades. It was kept as far forward and as small as possible, and was always at short notice. It was the chief link between units and second-line transport.

B was an echelon whose services were not required during battle and at such period it remained within the Divisional Administrative area.

SUPPLY OF COMMODITIES

Petrol and supplies were normally sent forward daily, by second-line transport to A echelons.

R.A.S.C. convoys were organised on a commodity basis; that is to say, one company dealt with supplies, one with petrol and one with ammunition. A Supply and Petrol Point was laid down by Divisional Headquarters. It was possible to have separate Supply and Petrol Points, but whenever possible they were located in the same place, from which A echelons drew at the time ordered.

Mail, ordnance stores and replacement vehicles were also delivered at Supply Points, but tanks and scout-cars were sent direct to units by the Forward Delivery Squadron. Reinforcements, other than armoured personnel, were also sent up to Supply Points.

SUPPLY OF AMMUNITION

Here the system was different. Second-line ammunition was divided into three echelons, the most forward being the Ammunition Point, or A.P. This was supplemented by the Forward Ammunition Column, or F.A.C., which in turn was supplemented by the remainder of the Ammunition Company R.A.S.C.

The A.P. consisted of about 20 vehicles located just behind Divisional Headquarters and carried only the minimum of ammunition for which there was a rapid turn-over, chiefly 25-pounder and mortar ammunition. The F.A.C. was a larger column located further back and carrying a greater variety of ammunition.

When the Royal Artillery required ammunition they sent back a guide to the A.P. and he took forward a lorry; other units sent their own lorries to load. When a lorry at the A.P. was emptied a wireless message was sent back and a similar lorry was sent up from the F.A.C. and this in turn was replaced by the Ammunition Company.

MEDICAL

One Field Ambulance was normally allotted to each brigade. The Field Dressing Station was generally kept in the Divisional Administrative Area and looked after the sick and lightly wounded, thus preventing them from being sent further back and being delayed on their return by having to pass through the lengthy reinforcement channels.

Appendix 5

PRISONERS OF WAR

These were sent back to Supply Points whence they were taken back in second-line transport to the Administrative area. From there they went to the corps cage.

PROVOST

The six sections were allotted to Divisional Headquarters and prisoner-of-war duties; to the Administrative area; to Supply, Petrol and Ammunition Points; for marking and patrolling centre-lines (two sections); and reserve.

R.E.M.E.

Light aid detachments travelled in the rear of their own units.

An Advanced Workshop detachment travelled behind each brigade and was used chiefly for recovery and for clearing the route. Damaged vehicles were towed back to Brigade Workshops in the Administrative area.

ORDNANCE

Normal stores were delivered at Supply Points. An Advanced Ordnance detachment travelled well forward with brigades, carrying mechanical transport and other spare parts most likely to be required.

PLANNING FOR D-DAY

Brigadier W. M. Sale, C.V.O., O.B.E., has supplied this personal account of the problems that had to be faced by those responsible in the division for planning the landing in Normandy.

> "At the close of Exercise Blackcock in the wolds in the autumn of 1943, the Divisional Commander was informed of the role of the division in the Invasion, and planning began immediately under the 8th Corps.
>
> As the division was to be a 'follow-up' division, there was no 'G' planning to be done. A small planning staff was set up, consisting of Lieutenant-Colonel Sale, Majors J. Harvey and the Viscount Errington and Captains A. Pryce-Jones and Lord Lloyd. Planning started in Yorkshire and when the division moved to Sussex it continued in the new Headquarters at Heathfield in the attics of the house. The windows were surrounded with barbed wire, and the rooms were guarded day and night, nobody but the Divisional Commander, the G.I. and the members of the team being allowed in. Three devoted clerks did an immense amount of typing.

Orders said that one thousand vehicles would be left behind and would not rejoin until the division had been ashore for two or three weeks. The first problem was, therefore, to decide which vehicles should remain in England when the division sailed. Obviously as many fighting vehicles as possible would have to go in the first flight, and the administrative services would have to provide the lion's share of those being left.

For purposes of calculation, two motor-cycles counted as a jeep, and two jeeps as a lorry or tank, which were the basic vehicles for calculation. By tying all motor-cycles on lorries or tanks, a great many more vehicle-spaces were made available.

The next problem was how to split the vehicles up between ports; some were to sail from Tilbury, others from Portsmouth. All the armour had to go from the latter as it was the Tank Landing Ships' port, but other types of vehicles were also carried in L.S.T.s, and a great deal of juggling had to be done to get the maximum left at each port.

All this required very detailed staff tables, in which every man, vehicle and weapon had to be shown, giving the port from which they were to sail, and whether they belonged to the first flight or were 'shut out'. Frequently, no sooner were the tables completed than a change would be made in the Order of Battle, or in the proportions to sail from one port.

All sorts of devices were resorted to in order to carry as much ammunition and stores as possible. Every wheeled vehicle down to staff cars and jeeps had to carry so many rounds of 25-pounder ammunition; every tank was festooned with motor-cycles, oil drums or other paraphernalia. This led to indignant protests from Battalion Commanders who did not know that they were to 'follow-up' and were expecting to have to fight their way ashore.

Arrangements also had to be made to re-assemble the division in Normandy, for it would disintegrate into small fragments when the order came to move from England, and for this purpose lectures were given on models to all those concerned. There were also a mass of other administrative matters such as pay, postal arrangements, burials, and so on.

When the great day came, Advance Parties left first, and then the remainder of the division dribbled off in bits and pieces, to be assembled again in Normandy some days later. The last of the 'left-behind' vehicles joined up on the eve of the division's first battle at Caen."

Index

Index